P9-BZY-367

VOICES OF TRAGEDY
IN THE WAKE OF A MADMAN

THE KILLER: "The only way society will be safe from people like me is when it starts using the death penalty." —Charles Hatcher

THE LAWYER: "Have you ever heard . . . a false confession? It's easy . . . We have the police saying: You can get hurt. You're going to go to jail. I can help you. It's going to be bad. Come on, just tell us."
—Closing arguments of Lee Nation,
Melvin Reynolds' defense attorney

THE INVESTIGATOR: "I was naive to think that everybody would work just as hard to get an innocent man out as they would to put a guilty one in." —Joe Holtslag, FBI

THE MOTHER: "I would want him to go to the gas chamber if there was a possibility that he could ever kill again . . . The system let Hatcher go how many times? You cannot live in fear."
—Mother of Hatcher's last victim

INNOCENT BLOOD

"Disturbing . . . Justice is shown to triumph —ultimately—in this engaging, instructive true-crime study."
—*Publishers Weekly*

INNOCENT BLOOD

BLOOD

A True Story of Terror and Justice

(published in hardcover as
St. Joseph's Children)

Terry Ganey

ST. MARTIN'S PAPERBACKS

Innocent Blood was published in hardcover under the title *St. Joseph's Children.*

Published by arrangement with Carol Communications, Inc.

INNOCENT BLOOD

Copyright © 1989 by Terry J. Ganey.

Cover photograph of Eric Christgen courtesy *St. Joseph News-Press/Gazette;* cover photograph of Charles Hatcher courtesy San Francisco Police Department.

Library of Congress Catalog Card Number: 89-22291

ISBN: 0-312-92269-8

Printed in the United States of America

Lyle Stuart edition published 1989
St. Martin's Paperbacks edition/July 1990

10 9 8 7 6 5 4 3 2 1

"The innocent and the just you shall not put to death, nor shall you acquit the guilty."
—EXODUS 23:7

INTRODUCTION

THIS IS A TRUE STORY OF SERIAL MURDER AND ELU-
sive justice. It is based partly on information that is
confidential by rule and custom. Research for this
book included dozens of interviews with police officers, psychiatrists, prosecutors, judges, defense
lawyers, prison officials and crime victims.

In addition to the standard forms of research in
official accounts, police reports, court documents
and prison files, I found opportunities to tap resources usually cloaked in secrecy. Thousands of
pages of confidential psychiatric reports enabled
me to probe, as deeply as possible, the mind of a
homicidal psychopath. A videotaped recording of a
murderer who was interrogated while under the
influence of a truth scrum enabled me to recreate
the scene of a murder from his mind.

Other confidential documents, such as the transcript of a closed grand jury hearing and FBI reports obtained under the Freedom of Information
Act, provided many of the facts of this true story.

All of the characters in the book are real, and the
dates, times and places of the events described are
as historically accurate as possible. Some of the
brief dialogue is recreated based on the recollec-

tions of those taking part in the conversations. I have also included the thoughts and feelings of various individuals, based on recollections that they shared with me. Longer discussions or interrogations are taken from transcripts or tape recordings of the actual events.

To spare them embarrassment, the names of survivors of violent sexual attacks and of one prison inmate have been changed.

To aid the reader, a chronology of events has been included at the end of the book which lists Charles Hatcher's various crimes and periods of incarceration.

This book would not have been possible without the help of friends and family. Research, encouragement and advice were provided by Kathryn Kranhold, Thomas J. Ganey Jr., Jim Mosley, Brenda Tanner, Georganne Wheeler Nixon, Bob Popp, Tim Fairclough and Harriet Frazier. The editors of the *St. Louis Post-Dispatch*, particularly Richard K. Weil, were responsible for getting me started on this project. The editors of the *Columbia Daily Tribune* and the *St. Joseph News-Press/Gazette* provided valuable resource material and photographs. I would also like to thank Hillel Black, President of Birch Lane Press, and Liza Wachter, Editor at Birch Lane Press, who sharpened the original manuscript. Thanks are also owed to my wife Judy, who did without a husband, and David, Tim and Colleen, who did without a father, until this book was completed.

Finally, there are the people of St. Joseph, Missouri, who provided hospitality and information in equally copious quantities.

—TERRY GANEY
March 18, 1989

National law enforcement authorities believe that at any one time at least 35 serial killers who murder at random are roaming the country. Charles Hatcher was one of them.

CHAPTER ONE

"He was the happiest kid I've ever seen in my life."

      —Edwin Christgen describing his son Eric

"ERIC! . . . ERIC!"

Karen Carter's frantic cries mixed with the bustling sounds of business as usual. Unanswered, they bounced off the brick and concrete walls of downtown shop and office buildings hunched along Felix Street. Shoppers, posted like pickets in front of the stores, stopped to stare and then looked away.

The little boy's babysitter ran from shop to shop, stopping at each to peek through stenciled signs on the plate glass windows, hoping to spot the missing youngster. Duling Optical . . . Einbenders' . . . The Little Children's Shop . . . A.J. August's.

How far can a little boy go in five minutes? she wondered.

Once or twice, Karen would step quickly inside, expecting to see his blond head. At each store, she distracted the employees and their customers with questions.

"Is there a little boy here?"

"Have you seen a little boy?"

Each negative response fed her panic. Back in the street, she searched once more around the small play area and the slide, where she had left Eric only minutes earlier. It was deserted.

From Mannschreck's, an office supply store, she placed a desperate telephone call to police.

"Communications," answered Marilyn Griffith, dispatcher for the St. Joseph Police Department.

"Yes, I'd like to speak to somebody about helping me find a little boy," Karen said, her voice cracking.

"Okay. Is your little boy lost?"

"Yeah."

"Okay. What is your address?"

"Uh, I'm at the mall."

"Oh, downtown mall?"

"Yeah."

"Okay. Whereabouts on the mall are you?"

"Mannschreck's."

"By Mannschreck's. Okay. Could you give me a description of your boy?"

"Okay. He has a red and blue shirt on, blue jeans, blond hair and he's about . . ."

"Wait a second. Red and blue shirt, blue jeans, blond hair?"

"Yeah."

"Okay. And he's a white male?"

"Yeah."

"How old."

"Four."

"Beg pardon."

"Pardon me."

"How old is he?"

"Four."

"Four. Okay. And his height?"

"Ummm."

"Approximately, or if you don't know that . . ."

"Three and a half foot."

"All right. And his weight?"

"He's thin. I don't know."

"That's okay. What's your name please?"

"Karen Carter."

"Karen Carter. Okay. We'll get somebody down there, Karen."

"Okay. Thank you."

As she waited anxiously for the police to arrive, Karen wondered if something had happened to make Eric want to run away. That Friday, May 26, 1978, had begun like many others for Eric Scott Christgen and Karen Ann Carter. They met bright and early at the Walnut Products Co., a business owned by the Christgen family and managed by Eric's father, Edwin B. Christgen.

Karen was a wood inspector, but sometimes she cleaned Ed Christgen's office. Once or twice a week, Ed would bring "the happiest kid I've ever seen in my life" to work with him, and Karen would do what she could to occupy the energetic boy.

On that cloudless spring day, Ed had given his son lunch money, and Karen and a co-worker, Kathy Roth, had taken Eric to eat at Long John Silver's, where he collected precious plunder—a plastic coin and a cardboard pirate ship. He hadn't been very hungry. It had been a day of animal crackers, strawberry pop, cough drops and candy.

That afternoon, he talked to his mother, Vicki, on the telephone. She asked him if he wanted to come home.

"No, I'm having too much fun," he said.

Later, Karen took Eric in his dad's white Cadillac on a series of errands around the city. First, she hauled home a desk she planned to refinish. Then, she stopped off at a store to buy supplies. And finally, she headed for Mannschreck's on a patriotic mission. The Memorial Day weekend was approaching, and Ed Christgen had asked her to buy an American flag to display.

It was after she parked the car and they were walking toward Mannschreck's that Eric spotted the slide, and he tugged at Karen's hand and pestered her to stay outside to play on it. Walking toward the store, Karen gave in to Eric's pleadings and let go of his hand. As she entered, she saw Eric sprint to the slide and climb the ladder like a midshipman scrambling up a yardarm. Karen went to the back of the store where the flags were located. She selected one and paid for it. When she emerged from the store a few minutes later, Eric had vanished.

As she anxiously mulled over the day's events, Karen reassured herself that nothing unusual had happened. Eric had seemed content. Nothing had come between him and his babysitter to make him want to run away. Although he was only four years old, Karen knew Eric was not a child who would thoughtlessly wander far beyond her reach. At that very moment, she thought, Eric was probably bawling his head off in the arms of some passerby. For a moment, that thought cheered her. But then, she also remembered that he was a very outgoing little boy who was not afraid of strangers. And that brought her to the sickening suspicion that someone had taken Eric from the mall.

Waiting for the police to arrive, Karen searched once more around the wood and metal playground equipment that the merchants had placed in the mall in an effort to make downtown as cheery and clean as the shopping centers on the city's fringes. The mall was created by closing the streets in the city's core to vehicles. Trees replaced parking meters. Benches squatted where cars had once competed for space. The Chamber of Commerce proclaimed the new downtown mall a bright and convenient shopping area and a valuable asset to the city. But some St. Joseph shoppers considered it to be an inner city area where the unemployed and the homeless congregated.

According to a study of some 8,000 calls, the average response time of the St. Joseph Police Department to an emergency is 4.3 minutes. So, it did not take long for officers to arrive at the downtown mall to interview the distraught babysitter.

"I had the little boy with me. I parked the car and got out and went into the mall at Mannschreck's," Karen told them. "The boy wanted to play outside, so I went in and I got the flag. It took me about five minutes. When I came out, he was gone." Karen believed she had entered Mannschreck's at about 2:50 P.M. She estimated she had spent seven or eight minutes searching for Eric. Her telephone call to the police department had been electronically logged and tape recorded at 3:01 P.M.

To the police, this was not just another lost child. They recognized immediately that the missing boy was the son of a wealthy and well-known St. Joseph family. Walnut Products was one of St. Joseph's best-known companies. One of Eric's uncles had held elected office in county government. "Christgen," pronounced "Christian," was to the city of St. Joseph what Hearst, Busch and DuPont were to other bigger cities.

The officers again asked Karen to describe the boy, and she quickly repeated what she had told the dispatcher. She did not have the chance to tell them how the blue in Eric's eyes seemed to match the sky of a clear spring day. There was no time to relate how Eric's eyes competed with his smile to show how happy he was. And yes, his hair was blond, but it was like fine golden strands of thread that would dance with the slightest breeze.

There were other things that could be said about the boy. About how his laugh seemed to jingle. How when he spoke, he sometimes substituted an "F" for the "S" sound. But she could not tell them about all that now. The police were moving quickly; four officers immediately began searching the mall and the surrounding office buildings.

When the police told Edwin Christgen the terrifying news that his son was missing, he mobilized the considerable resources of his family and company. His two brothers, Kenneth and Dennis, and their father, Kenneth Christgen Sr., came downtown to help look for the boy, and a short time later, his wife's father, John Warner, was there too. While they hunted on the ground, the company plane circled low over downtown.

When the police department's second shift came on at 4:00 P.M., the day shift officers remained on duty and continued the search. Detectives joined uniformed officers, and the reserves were called in. Soon, there were not enough police cars to accommodate all the men on duty, so they used their own. In the tangled woods and empty lots between downtown and the Missouri River, two men rode on horseback and a third used a motorcycle. Along the riverfront, searchers checked inside the vacant warehouses and abandoned shells of buildings that had become brick monuments to a more prosperous time in St. Joseph. Boat owners joined in, cruising slowly in the swift, brown current like trolling fishermen. Two city workers were ordered down into the sewer system to see if Eric was there.

Detective Robert Eaton joined the case at 4:00 P.M. and he was disgusted to find that no officer had taken charge and organized the search. He was 27 years old, but he had already logged eight years with the department—six as a patrolman and two as a detective. During that time, he had applied a professional approach to the police work that he loved, and he was often frustrated by the department's lack of organization.

Eaton began to methodically direct the search efforts, although there were more senior and experienced men on duty at the time. He established a command post in front of Mannschreck's. With a map, he plotted areas for the police and volunteers to cover, and he dispatched them two at a time. When they searched an area and reported back to him, Eaton colored in the area on his map. As the hours went by, Eaton slowly filled the city map from the center outward, and still there was no sign of Eric.

The city of St. Joseph sits on a landing below limestone bluffs on the eastern bank of the Missouri River. Upriver and below, the cliffs climb 200 feet above the swirling muddy water, and from them, millions of fertile gold and green Kansas acres can be seen to the west. Before the white man arrived to open a trading post, the Fox, Sac and Iowa tribes shared the wide trough of land that sloped gently from the hills down to the river's edge. It was sacred ground to the natives, who believed that gods had once dwelt there. They called the area the Blacksnake Hills, and they told the white newcomers that it was wah-wah-lanawa, "the holiest place on earth."

As the day of Eric's disappearance turned to night, the police and volunteer searchers frantically continued their search. When darkness fell, the command post for the search was moved to police headquarters, where Eaton continued to man the telephones and radios. Members of the Christgen family stayed in the same room with him, and they hung anxiously on each call with the hope that the boy would be found.

At midnight, Eaton took a new tack. He split the searchers in half, and directed one group to begin from downtown and work its way south to Walnut Products, where Ed Christgen's office was located. He told the other group to begin at the wood company and work its way north. Eaton believed that perhaps Eric had decided to walk to his father's office and had become lost. He thought that before the two groups of searchers met, Eric would be found. But at 3:00 A.M. there was still no trace of the boy, and the search was called off. They agreed to meet again at 7:00 A.M. in the parking lot of City Hall.

In the absence of a ransom demand, 24 hours must elapse before the FBI will enter a case on the presumption that a kidnapping has taken place. But Joe Holtslag, the St. Joseph FBI agent, was flexible, open-minded and willing to gamble that his help would be needed. So as police and volunteer searchers combed city streets, Holtslag summoned a squad of six agents from Kansas City to begin preliminary work on the boy's disappearance. They brought along a mobile command post, a cramped van packed with electronic gear, and parked it in front of the spacious Christgen home. They used it to monitor developments in the search and were prepared to record and trace the ransom demand in the event the kidnapper telephoned.

Holtslag risked embarrassment, especially from his inconvenienced fellow agents, should Eric turn up in a lost and found department somewhere. But to be poised for action, he was willing to take the chance. The "cover your ass" concept did not guide

Holtslag's work, and he was willing to let his imagination and intuition lead him. Sometimes, his unique style got him in trouble. But ultimately, it was this willingness to take risks which uniquely qualified him to bring the Eric Christgen case to its conclusion.

On the day of Eric's disappearance, the agent bounded up the steps leading to the front door of the Christgen home. His movements were smooth and fluid, and no one would suspect that he had brought a leg injury back from Vietnam. In a business suit, his 190 pounds on a six-foot-two frame had the look of an executive who had once been an athlete. Some people thought he resembled Clint Eastwood. Women—like Millie Humphreys, the wife of his former FBI partner—thought he was handsome.

As he waited for someone to answer his knock, Holtslag pondered what little he knew of the boy's disappearance. He was anxious to learn more as quickly as possible. He sensed that he was stepping into a major case, but at that point, Holtslag had no idea of its dimensions. He had no way of knowing that he was on the threshold of a crime that would dominate his entire law enforcement career.

It was not just because of the circumstances of the crime. In the dozen years that he had chased lawbreakers—nearly all of them in northwest Missouri—Holtslag had dealt with an interesting mix of evil. He liked the variety that kept the daily routine interesting. The area he covered was a remote province in the Justice Department cosmos, and agents in larger cities had a better chance of encountering that one, big, well-publicized, notorious case that could cap a career. But when Eric's abductor was finally brought to justice, the facts turned out to be so bizarre, the perpetrator so evil, and the irony so grotesque that it was far beyond what any policeman would ever expect to encounter.

St. Joseph police officers accepted and respected Holtslag as a quiet and friendly federal lawman who helped them out and who sometimes needed their help. His early involvement in the Christgen disappearance was welcomed and reassuring. The local police opened up to him, furnished him with all available information and allowed him immediate access to the few witnesses in the case. This openness was in sharp contrast to what would happen years later, when St. Joseph finally discovered what really happened to Eric. By the time Holtslag had investigated the way the police had handled the case, and the chief of police had threatened to go to the FBI headquarters in Washington to stop him, Holtslag's friendship with local lawmen had been severely eroded by suspicion, distrust and counteraction.

The St. Joseph police suspected initially that Eric had been kidnapped. Although no demand for money had been made, Edwin Christgen had broadcast an announcement on television that night that he would pay $10,000 for information leading to the safe return of his son. While the search for Eric was still underway, agents had begun collecting information concerning Karen Carter by interviewing her neighbors. Attention had focused on her based on the theory that the kidnapping had been set up, with the babysitter providing inside information to the kidnappers relating to the best time and location for the abduction. Just hours after Eric disappeared, Karen underwent a lie detector test administered by Lieutenant Terry Boyer at the St. Joseph Police Department.

Kidnapping and a brutal child killing were no strangers to St. Joseph, the city named for the Protector of the Child Jesus. Twenty-five years earlier, the city had been the scene of Missouri's most shocking kidnapping and murder. Bonnie Brown Heady lived in St. Joseph, and on September 28, 1953, she traveled 50 miles south to Kansas City. Posing as his aunt, she snatched from an exclusive private school six-year-old Bobby Greenlease, the son of a Kansas City millionaire. She and her boyfriend, ex-convict Carl Austin Hall, collected $600,000 in ransom from Robert Cosgrove Greenlease Sr., who was willing to pay anything for the safe return of his son. It was the largest ransom payment in U.S. history. The day Bobby was abducted, long before the money was turned over, he was killed with a single shot to the head from a .38-caliber revolver. The kidnappers were arrested in St. Louis eight days later. The backyard of Heady's home in St. Joseph yielded Bobby's body.

Less than two months after the kidnapping, Heady and Hall were executed together at the Missouri State Penitentiary in Jefferson City. When Hall was arrested with Heady in St. Louis, he had $592,000 of the ransom in three suitcases. But after he had been processed by St. Louis police detectives, only half of the $600,000 ransom was recovered. Many believe the police stole the money from the kidnappers. The details of the Bobby Greenlease murder still stained the memories of many of St. Joseph's 77,000 residents. But the death of Bobby Greenlease was about to be eclipsed by new and more horrible crimes.

The disappearance of one of its little children hit St. Joseph like a natural disaster. At 7:00 A.M. Saturday, 200 searchers assembled in the City Hall parking lot to help look for the boy, and dozens more volunteered to serve them coffee and food. Reports of sightings were processed. Several people reported that they had seen a little boy with a Buster Brown haircut walking with a man downtown Friday afternoon.

The most promising lead came from Jeff Davey, a plumber, who said he had seen a blond boy and an older man at about 3:30 P.M. Friday, walking along the railroad tracks between MacArthur Drive and the Missouri River in the northwest corner of the city.

"This guy has seen him," said Charles Robinson, the St. Joseph police officer who debriefed Davey. "This is for real."

Robinson gave the information to Eaton, who was still directing the search with just three hours sleep. After lunch, Eaton ordered the volunteers to march "fingertip to fingertip" northward between the Burlington Northern railroad tracks and the river. Their orders were to go from 2nd and Jules Streets, where MacArthur Drive begins, all the way up to the waterworks, nearly two miles away. It was the roughest area the searchers were asked to cover because a dense forest had taken command of the desolate tracts between the city and the river. The weather had changed too, and rain fell from an ash-colored sky. Water, dripping from shoulder-high scrub cottonwoods and sycamores, soaked the searchers' clothes as they sliced through the thicket. Their wet pantlegs were weighted with mud, and, wary of water moccasins, they moved slowly through the weedy undergrowth. Often they stumbled over upriver debris that had been washed ashore. Whiskey bottles, broken furniture, and other stray items lay imbedded in the wet, black soil like fossils for the future. The muddy riverbank sucked at their heavy boots, and they slipped on the steep slopes of the railroad track bed along MacArthur Drive.

Just as they reached the waterworks, it began to rain heavily, and workers opened the water plant so that searchers could take shelter among the pumps until the shower passed. Eaton then directed them to cross MacArthur Drive and to work their way back toward the city's center along the base of the steep cliffs that flanked the road on the east. The rain had turned the asphalt road a shiny black and the woods around it a gleaming emerald. From the search plane overhead the scene resembled ants crawling over the unmoving body of a black snake in deep green grass.

Charles Jones was working his way through the dense undergrowth. He was a member of the Citizens Band radio club, one of the groups that had volunteered for the search. Jones had spent most of the day covering the difficult terrain.

"Everything is overgrown," he had advised other searchers. "It's real dangerous, like a jungle. There are no paths and you've got to make one yourself."

For hours, Jones had slogged along MacArthur Drive, the railroad tracks and the lush riverbank. Searching with him were his brother-in-law and sister-in-law, George and Karen Goldizen.

At dusk, as squadrons of mosquitoes swarmed to harass, Jones scrambled along the base of the steep bluffs that the river had carved through the centuries. As another sunset approached, sometime between 6:30 and 7:00 P.M., Jones came across something he had not seen all day—a path. It was not well traveled, but the weeds were trampled just enough to show that a person or large animal had cut through the area recently. A few steps down the vague trail, he found Eric in the underbrush. In the fading twilight, he first saw the boy's red and blue striped shirt, then, the lifeless body, lying on a stone ledge. Just beside him, like a toy that slips from the hands of a sleepy child, rested a bird's nest. It was filled with eggs as blue as Eric's eyes. Karen Goldizen left to notify the police.

Jones had stumbled upon the body by hiking south along the base of the bluffline. It was more difficult to get to the area from MacArthur Drive. Eaton was one of the first to arrive at the scene, and to get there, he had to scramble up a steep ravine and then get down on his hands and knees to crawl under fallen logs and branches. When he arrived, he made mental notes on the position of Eric's body and the condition of the surrounding foliage. Eric was lying on his back on top of what appeared to be an altar of broken branches. It was as if Eric had been the victim of some pagan sacrifice. The body was 60 feet to the east of MacArthur Drive, about one quarter mile north of Jules Street in a weedy ravine some 20 feet above the level of the roadway. It was a 20-minute walk from the slide where Eric had been playing. As Eaton examined the grass above the body, he saw a group of people walking through the woods from the road. Police Chief Glenn E. Thomas was leading them and at the rear were reporters and photographers from the *St. Joseph News-Press*. Eaton tried to stop them, but in minutes, the crime scene was contaminated, and any hopes of extracting clues from it were lost.

"Damn," Eaton said to himself. "I had hoped we'd do something right for once."

Holtslag was manning the mobile command post at the Christgen home when word arrived that Eric had been found dead near the river. It was unclear from the first report whether the body was found in Missouri or on the Kansas side, and for several confusing minutes, authorities did not know whether to label the crime as a local murder or a federal case.

One of the FBI agents assigned from Kansas City telephoned the Christgen home from a spot near the crime scene. He confirmed for Holtslag the fact that the body was found in Missouri.

"Well, we are out of it, at least officially," Holtslag said.

"Joe, you ought to be down here."

"Why?"

"Joe, they are screwin' up this crime scene something terrible. We've got press up here walking all over the place, taking pictures. They haven't put up a police line. The body's still lying up there. They are trampling any footprints that are still there."

"Back off and forget it," Holtslag said. "It's not our case. We're not going to get into telling them how to run a crime scene."

Holtslag hung up and ordered the agents to pack up the special truck and return to Kansas City. For now, the case that would one day haunt him belonged to other jurisdictions. He now had to tell Edwin and Vicki Christgen that the searchers had found their son. And it had to be done quickly. The report of the grim discovery was racing through the city rapidly, and often incorrectly. At the Hoof and Horn Restaurant near the old stockyards, murmured conversations and the tinkling of dinnerware halted when the owner interrupted the dinners of more than 150 people, including Buchanan County prosecutor Michael Insco. There was applause when the restaurant owner announced that Eric had been found alive. A few minutes later, the owner's wife apologized in a strained voice and said that the first announcement had not been correct. "Eric is dead," she said. The room became as quiet as a church.

Nothing is chiseled so deeply in a memory as that horrible moment when one is informed of the death of a loved one. Telling the Christgen couple that their son was dead was the toughest thing Holtslag had ever done in his life. He used his warm brown eyes and a soft voice to break, as gently as he could, the news that devastated Eric's parents.

Statistics collected by the National Center for Missing and Exploited Children show that when a child is abducted in something other than a parental custody fight, the chances are only one in 10 that he or she will be found alive. Many are never found, and those who are—about 2,500 per year— are found murdered. The Christgens had spent a sleepless night worried that a parent's most feared nightmare might visit them. When the news of Eric's death finally arrived, it brought successive waves of grief, anger and frustration. The information as to how Eric died made it an even deeper hurt, and forced Eric's parents to wonder about what kind of person could kill a little boy that way. Later, they experienced the numbing realization that they faced a lifetime of loss.

Between his birth and death certificates, the only documents that bore witness to the existence of Eric Christgen were crayon-streaked coloring books and pages of scrawled attempts at printing. When Eric was alive, his parents often traded anecdotes about the funny things he had said and done. But after his death, they closed the door of his room, the room that contained the little stories, because they couldn't bear the pain of resurrecting and repeating them.

* * *

When darkness enveloped the site where searchers had found Eric's body, the Fire Department set up gasoline-powered generators with lights that produced a ghostly glow in the woods beside MacArthur Drive. Lieutenant Loren "Buck" Powell, a 24-year veteran of the St. Joseph Police Department, supervised the attendants, who put Eric's body on a board and loaded it into an ambulance that threaded its way between the spectators' cars parked along the road. Holtslag accompanied Ed and Vicki Christgen to St. Joseph Hospital, where they observed the body. Vicki longed to reach out one more time to hug Eric, but police told her not to touch the body.

Later that night, Gary Howell, director of the regional crime laboratory in Kansas City, examined Eric, took samples from his body and placed them in plastic evidence bags. He believed a forensic pathologist was needed, and shortly after midnight, Dr. James Bridgens, from Shawnee Mission, Kansas, arrived to perform the autopsy. He concluded that Eric had been sexually abused and asphyxiated. Although the precise method of murder was not made public, Bridgens told investigators that Eric had not been strangled but had died as the result of an act of oral sodomy. Bridgens said the child simply could not obtain oxygen, could not breathe.

"He would lose consciousness in three minutes and there would be irreversible brain damage in five to seven minutes," Bridgens said. "And I'm sure this kid put up a significant fight. Even small babies put up a tremendous struggle when something occludes their airways."

Other pathologists might have been more professionally cautious, leaving themselves some room by offering other possible causes of the asphyxiation. But Bridgens was emphatic about his conclusion. He said there was no other alternative, judging from the results of the examination of Eric's body. His was an antiseptic description of the most hideous crime in St. Joseph history. And it was explored the next day in the pages of the *News-Press*. A front page picture of Eric's body, his pants unbuttoned, startled subscribers between breakfast and church services. Readers wondered what sewer the murderer was hiding in, and others, enraged by the newspaper's use of the picture, wrote letters to the editor complaining that the photograph was in poor taste. Within hours of Bridgens' gruesome findings, a special police unit was forming to find the murderer.

The squad had been organized just two months earlier to handle major cases just like this one. The Northwest Missouri Major Investigations Squad (NOMIS), which had yet to handle an investigation, would be baptized with the Eric Christgen murder case. Officers from the city, the Buchanan County Sheriff's Office and the Missouri Highway Patrol filled its ranks. The squad's lead investigator was Sergeant Robert Anderson, a 21-year veteran of the state patrol. Anderson had been part of the investigating team since he had grimly observed Bridgens perform the autopsy. Eaton was on the team too, and at 7:00 A.M., after only four hours sleep, he was back at the crime scene digging for evidence.

Although it was not a federal case, Holtslag's supervisor told the FBI agent to stick with the investigation for a week. He instructed Holtslag to act as a liaison with NOMIS, providing it with any assistance it requested. Anderson and Holtslag were respected as a team. Just a few months earlier, the two men had cracked one of the more bizarre bank robberies in northwest Missouri. The key to the solution had been Anderson's ability to extract information from a suspect. Holtslag believed that Anderson was the best interrogator he had ever seen. Holtslag and Anderson were friends. They regularly played poker together.

NOMIS established a separate headquarters in donated space in the old American National Bank Building in downtown St. Joseph. A special line was installed to handle incoming calls, and the telephone rang constantly. Police had little evidence other than the few physical clues that had been silently yielded by Eric's body. A public appeal was made for information on the killer or killers, and valuable leads were filed among useless tips, gossip and rumors. All information was filed on index cards which were passed into the officers' nicotine-stained fingers during morning meetings. The investigators, running on cigarettes, coffee and adrenaline, worked round-the-clock shifts, sorting and checking the cards. They worked until fatigued, rested for a few hours, and then resumed their work.

On Monday, day two in the life of NOMIS, the police set up roadblocks on the routes from the downtown mall to the spot where Eric's body had been found. They stopped afternoon motorists whose regular habits may have placed them on the route taken by Eric and his abductor on the day the boy was killed. They questioned anyone who might have seen the youngster and sifted through reports which indicated that a little boy had been spotted several times that afternoon with an old man.

Carl Simpson, who lived just over the river in Elwood, Kansas, gave police a description of the man and the boy. Simpson worked at the Wire Rope Co., and told the police that he had seen a boy and a man as he was leaving the cable company parking lot a little after 3:00 P.M. The location was about eight blocks from the point where Karen Carter had last seen the boy and about halfway from where the body was found. Simpson said a gray baseball cap shadowed most of the man's features, but he described a man with a light complexion and a thick, broad nose. He said the man appeared to be 50 to 55 years old, five-feet-ten and 200 pounds.

The police talked again to Jeffrey Davey, whose initial report had helped lead to the discovery of Eric's body. On the day of Eric's disappearance, Davey, a plumber, had driven to MacArthur Drive to remove dirt from the clay cliffs there. He needed the dirt to fill an excavated site he had used in a plumbing job.

To help unlock the secrets of Davey's memory, the police brought in Maynard Brazeal. Sheriff Jack Fleck had asked Brazeal, an instructor at the Kansas Law Enforcement Training Center in Hutchison, to help out in the investigation. A former Kansas City police lieutenant, Brazeal was the Midwest's trailblazer in "investigative hypnotism," preferring to call the technique "focus concentration." The courts have since all but put an end to the use of hypnotism in criminal cases. But in 1978, hypnosis was just one of several new investigative techniques the police used, hoping to crack the Christgen case.

On Tuesday, Holtslag sat in on the session with Davey and Brazeal. An artist, supplied by the Kansas City police department, was there too, to sketch any descriptions that might emerge from the interview. As Brazeal hypnotized him, Davey was not asleep, but in a deep state of relaxation. He was cognizant of the world around him. He heard voices, including his own, although he did not believe it was his. His vocal chords were relaxed, and his words came out in a deep slow monotone.

Davey responded well to the hypnosis and was able to recount intricate details of his experiences of Friday, May 26. Davey described how he had been at MacArthur Drive and Jules Street at about 2:55 P.M. He was in his truck, waiting at a blocked railroad crossing.

"Is there a car in your rear view mirror?"

"Yes."

"What kind is it?"

"A Toyota."

"What color is it?"

"Yellow."

"Is there anything in front of you?"

"Yes."

"What do you see?"

"A truck."

"Is there anything special about it?"

"It's carrying fireworks."

"Can you see the license number?"

Davey paused.

"Jeff, there is a black shroud that is blocking this information," Brazeal said. "Now I want you to pull away the black shroud and read that number to me."

Davey read off a string of numbers.

Holtslag was amazed at the precision of Davey's responses and irritated that Brazeal had not lined up his questions better.

"You act like you're fishing," Holtslag had told Brazeal after an earlier 90-minute session with another witness. "You haven't even prepared your questions."

"That's right," Brazeal said. "I want to come into this thing cold. I don't want it to be structured. I don't want anything I have been told or read to get in the way."

Brazeal had purposely avoided studying the police reports or reading newspaper accounts of the murder. He did not want to know, for example, what clothes Eric was wearing when they found his body. He did not want to taint the session with suggestions. Instead, he allowed Davey to tell him what he had seen.

Davey's answers were not elaborate and the information came slowly. He related that after the train passed, he drove a short distance up the road and stopped at a remote and lonely section along MacArthur Drive. There, he stepped out and began digging and loading dirt into his truck. After about 15 minutes, Davey walked to the front of his truck to slap on some suntan oil. As he stood squinting in the afternoon sun, he saw a man and young boy walking north along the Burlington Northern Railroad tracks, the rail line that snakes between the river on the west and MacArthur Drive on the east. They were only about 35 yards away. Davey's voice slowly droned on, while the anxious detectives devoured every word.

"What does this man look like?"

"He has thick shoulders and a medium waist."

"How old would you say he is?"

"He appears to be in his 60s."

"What color is his hair?"

"He has grayish-black hairy arms, with gray hair on the side of his head. It is dark and streaky on the top."

"What color are his clothes?"

"He is wearing a gray print shirt with short

sleeves. The sleeves end just above the elbow. His trousers are dark."

"What else do you see?"

"The man's right arm looks like it is slightly turned out. Like it has been broken before."

"Is he alone?"

"There is a little boy with him."

"What are they doing?"

"Walking."

"Where are they going?"

"He is holding the boy's right arm with his left hand. They are not talking, but it appears the boy is going with him willingly."

"What does the boy look like?"

"The boy is very young with long, brownish-blond hair."

"What is he wearing?"

"A shirt with horizontal stripes and blue jeans."

"Anything else?"

"The boy's hair looks like it had been cut with a bowl on his head."

Davey did not watch to see where the two were going, and he left at about 3:30.

As Holtslag listened to Davey's droning voice, the agent's brown eyes seemed to glaze over as if he too were in a trance. It was a trait Holtslag's friends had noticed in him before; he sometimes seemed to become distant and removed in the middle of conversation as if he were thinking about something else. Sometimes conversations with him were punctuated with uncomfortable periods of silence. People meeting him for the first time thought Holtslag was not listening. Those who knew him better had learned that in this way he filed away important information in his memory; his mind carefully recorded and categorized the data while his eyes seemed to stare into space. The description of Eric's killer sank deep into Holtslag's brain, and would remain there several years before blossoming.

CHAPTER TWO

"There is no reason to think that this man will not repeat this crime again."
—From FBI agent Roy Hazelwood's profile of Eric's killer

AS JEFFREY DAVEY WAS HYPNOTIZED, ERIC WAS BURied in the Memorial Park Cemetery, which was still covered with flowers from Memorial Day. More than 500 mourners filled the Wyatt Park Christian Church for the services. The funeral procession, the longest in memory, blocked traffic for 20 minutes, and motorists blinked back tears as the procession moved past.

The same day, a grieving father reached out to the community in an open letter printed in the morning edition of the *St. Joseph Gazette.*

This past weekend, Vicki and I suffered the most tragic event of our lives. The loss of our four-year-old son Eric is something that we had not even been able to contemplate until now. Things like this do not happen in St. Joseph, but rather in faraway places like New York or Chicago. But indeed, it did happen here.

Now, we are trying to live with the realization that Eric is gone, and we have a gigantic feeling of emptiness. But, through the despair, we see what a truly warm and wonderful city we live in. The thousands of people that assisted the authorities in trying to locate our son exemplifies the true soul of St. Joseph. Our police department worked around the clock directing the efforts while the officers and men could not have been more kind and considerate to our family.

Vicki and I are suffering a grief more overpowering than any force I thought possible while trying to answer the question, Why? But through the grief, the knowing and feeling of the love of our family and friends for us and the knowledge of the type of city we live in and the warmth and concern of the people here give us a great deal of strength.

Even though Eric could live only 4½ years, I thank God he was able to live in St. Joseph.

Ed Christgen

Worried parents throughout the city used Eric's death to remind their children about dangerous strangers. There were programs in St. Joseph that were designed to encourage youngsters to protect themselves. Eric's father had taken him to one.

"We went to Safetytown a year before, and in that program they talked about not going with strangers," Ed Christgen said. "That was the summer before he went away. I don't know what else could have been done. He had been taught to like everybody, but not to go off with anybody. He was very outgoing."

The *St. Joseph News-Press*, one of two city papers owned by the family of David Bradley Sr., voiced community reaction in a front page editorial: "The horror and sadness which comes from the tot being found dead hang over this community in a cloud of disbelief. The child was slain by someone whose derangements are a continuing threat to children as long as the person is loose among us.

Until that person is identified, jailed and put someplace where he or she will never again commit such horror, no family is safe. No child is safe."

Edwin Christgen's letter had put into words the nagging thought that had gripped St. Joseph since the day Eric had been found. How could St. Joseph have harbored such a person without him coming to the attention of police? The murderer had to be a stranger. Some thought that only an emissary of the devil, some creature on an extended weekend furlough from hell, would be capable of such a crime.

Mayor Gordon Wiser summed it up: "What bothers me is that there is that type of person in town. Not in New York or somewhere else, but right here. It's scary."

St. Joseph's citizens for years had consoled themselves that with all its drawbacks, the city was a safe place to live. Culturally, socially, and economically, St. Joe lived in the shadow of Kansas City and its people accepted that. St. Joseph had a rich, historical tradition. It was the place the Pony Express began and Jesse James ended. Its residents could reminisce that once St. Joseph was bigger than Kansas City, 50 miles to the south. In 1978, St. Joseph was too far from Kansas City to be considered a suburb but too close to be considered a completely independent metropolitan area. If you wanted to shop, be entertained or enlightened, Kansas City was just an hour away.

The prevailing attitude in the community was that the city fathers had been asleep since the turn of the century and that the city was in a time warp. While other communities had grown, St. Joe had remained the same. Its climate didn't help. Summers were long, hot and humid, and in the winter, superchilled winds came down from Nebraska and whipped the city with an icy sting. But the people were willing to live there reassured by the security the city provided. Unlike the situation in bigger cities, there was no crime problem in St. Joseph. If you asked citizens why they lived there, they would reply that it was a great place to raise a family.

On the day after Eric's funeral, the police took a 39-year-old man into custody. He was a maintenance man and a former mental patient at the St. Joseph State Hospital. They questioned him several times, but finally released him. Twice, information was received that sent an investigator out of state, but both leads turned cold on closer examination. As the days dragged on and there were no breaks in the case, police began to feel as though they were searching for a phantom. During morning meetings when the frustrated detectives discussed their leads, Eaton kept returning to the description Davey had given them and hammering away at it.

"When we find that guy, we have to try to prove to ourselves that he didn't do it," Eaton told the other officers. "If we can't prove that, we've got our man."

Police were told that a man matching the description of the suspect was living at the St. Charles, a cheap downtown hotel. A detective was posted in the hotel for a day, but he did not see the look-alike.

In addition to the physical description obtained, the police received a profile that included the psychological background and likely living habits of the killer. The FBI's Behavioral Science Unit, based in Quantico, developed the profile in an attempt to narrow the search. It was based on reports from the crime scene, witness accounts, the autopsy results and years of studying and talking with hundreds of murderers. Roy Hazelwood, an FBI agent, analyzed the Eric Christgen case and provided the killer's profile. He was not interested in trying to answer the "why" of the crime.

"What we're interested in is that he DOES it and that he does it in a way that leads us to him," Hazelwood said.

In providing psychological profiles, the agency warns local policemen not to take any profile too literally and not to limit investigations to people who exhibit the characteristics in the sketch. The profile is supposed to describe a general type of person, not point to a certain individual. The FBI also cautions that a profile can be dead wrong. In fact, one drawn up by Hazelwood in a Georgia case turned out to be the most inaccurate in the agency's history. But, although investigators would not realize it for a long time, Hazelwood's picture of the killer in the Christgen case was uncannily accurate:

Based on the information and the pictures we have available to us, we feel that this was a crime of opportunity as opposed to some type of planned situation. We feel it is simply a set of circumstances which placed Eric and the perpetrator at the same place at the same time, and he took advantage of the situation.

We feel that you are probably looking for a pedophile, a lover of children, white. Statistically such people will range between 35 and 45 years, perhaps a little older in some cases, and in this case, perhaps between 45 and 50. We feel that he probably is living alone, is unmarried and is from a lower income background with a poor education and, if he is employed, is employed in a menial type of occupation. The time of the occurrence or at least the abduction would tend to indicate that he probably was not employed at least that day or was employed in some type of shift work.

Statistically, the pedophiliac is a repeating type of offender and as such we feel there is a record of this individual for some form of child molestation or homosexual activity either locally or in departments in the surrounding one or two hundred miles. We also feel that he has committed offenses at least where he would attempt to abduct a child or have relations with a younger boy on numerous occasions in the past. We do not feel he is a driver or drives an automobile at least on a continuing basis. He may well have a drivers license or some such thing. But we do not feel he is a normal driver in the sense that the average person drives to work and so forth. This is an interesting characteristic which is often seen in pederasts and is something to be considered in this area.

We also don't feel the murder itself was premeditated. We feel rather that it occurred in connection with the attempts of the individual to satisfy his sexual appetite and was in a sense an accidental outcome. The method of the attack and the extent of the attack leaves us with the opinion that he may well have a homosexual orientation with obviously a preference for young boys. However, he may have been dealing with older boys in the past, and over the years has been unable to attract the older homosexual child and has had to resort to the younger boy.

He probably lives or works in the general vicinity of where that boy was taken. The time of day, the fact that there aren't really too many children on those malls at that time of day, would tend to indicate that he had some other reason for being in that location other than simply waiting for a child to appear. This could have a lot of meanings whether he was passing through or getting off work or going to work or coming or going to a bar. There is no way of knowing, however. There has to be some reason that he was in that particular area at that time of day.

In about 80 percent of the cases of this form of child molestation, the individual has been drinking, and so the approach and information that is obtainable from bars is always pertinent to such cases, and in many cases the bartenders and so forth can offer some direction, hopefully. But they often are drinkers and unskilled and previous offenders from lower income brackets. One would suspect wine and beer as opposed to the more exotic drinks.

Of importance is the fact that this is or most of these people are repeat offenders. There is no reason to think that this man will not repeat this crime again. Whether he kills the next one or not is debatable, but we have been discussing this and we would offer a prediction that he would repeat again by October or November of this year, since they usually will repeat within six months of the previous occurrence. The fact that this death may well have been accidental would indicate the possibility that he has of course attacked children in the past and not killed them, and that they are around with the knowledge of his face and description.

Hopefully, previous cases can be located and descriptions can be obtained from them. We have cases where these individuals have been employed in such occupations as body and fender men and painters, plumber helpers, building construction trades, maintenance men, janitors, various types of day labor, invariably unskilled and semi-skilled jobs.

Very often these people will be seen around places where children congregate. This will be reported as a man acting strange or a man who doesn't seem to have any place to go watching kids or trying to give candy to kids or some such thing. Most of these individuals, particularly in this age group, tend to be something in the way of a loner as far as their job is concerned. They are not a gregarious group. They are not big talkers, and while there have been salesmen who fell into this category, it is uncommon for them to be often in the company of other men. The very fact that they are using children as sexual objects indicates that they feel inadequate to the idea of approaching a mature woman, or if homosexual, a mature man, and so in their inadequacy, approach a boy, a child.

There is little likelihood that the perpetrator would leave town as a result of the killing itself. He may leave town for purposes of occupation or merely because there is another place to go to. But it is unusual for this type of person to run from one town to another as a result of the crimes. He would tend to have considerable guilt feelings over what happened, and if interviewed, would confess if approached from an understanding, considerate, type of an approach. The particular type of approach in interviewing is not all that easy to do, and interviewers should prepare well when they feel that they have a good suspect of this type and prepare to do a certain amount of acting.

Specific attention, as previously mentioned, should be given to records of child molesters and homosexuals who are interested in younger partners going back five to seven years past, and in all the surrounding towns. These examinations of the records should not be limited strictly to homosexuality. However, I think it would be fair to limit them to attacks against younger individuals or at least attempts to abduct or con younger individuals to go with them whether they are successful or not.

The fact that the individual would appear to have gone up an embankment with the victim and the fact that he laid the victim out part way up another bank would tend to indicate that he is physically fairly adequate and probably rather muscular. He didn't seem, at least there isn't any evidence, that he had trouble getting up the embankment. A less muscular individual probably wouldn't have bothered to go up the embankment at all, but would have made the attack at the foot of the first embankment. Also the fact that he was willing at least to pick up the child in such a way as to place him partially up an embankment would indicate the person is quite capable of lifting reasonably heavy material with his arms and that both arms are at least functional.

The psychological profile was one of many investigative tools the St. Joseph police department had at its disposal, but few officers were trained to apply it. Rather than using the profile to narrow the range of suspects, NOMIS used a shotgun approach, hoping to net the killer who officers were convinced was still in town. As part of the police investigation, detectives rounded up 150 of the "usual suspects."

"We've interviewed every known pervert in town," was the way one officer described it. Flashers, fondlers, peeping toms and "known police characters" were brought in for questioning. NOMIS received a report that a child was seen in the company of an elevator operator at the Corby Building, a 14-story office building which sits on the corner just west of the spot where Eric was abducted. This report led them to Harry Fox.

The secretaries and lawyers who worked in the Corby Building called him "Foxy" but he was about as agile as a walrus. Fox matched some of the findings in Hazelwood's profile, but physically Fox was quite unlike the man that witness Jeffrey Davey had described. He weighed more than 200 pounds which he moved with great difficulty between his home and job. When he talked, his drooling mouth had trouble forming the words. On the day that the police found Eric's body, Harry Fox quietly celebrated his 64th—and last—birthday. For 23 years, he had been a janitor and elevator operator in the building, working the 3:00 to 11:00 P.M. shift. Often he arrived early for work. He lived an uncomplicated life of polished banisters, swept floors, classical music and sports books. Fox had never married. He lived alone and kept to himself in a tiny apartment. He had no close friends, only a brother, Ray.

"Fox was a peach of a guy," said William Rosenthal, a lawyer with an office in the Corby Building. "We all liked him. He was the kind of guy who was very quiet. The kids all liked him."

Detectives knew that Fox liked kids, too, and the Corby Building was very close to the scene of the abduction. Two detectives went to the building and questioned Margaret Hoehn, manager and secretary-treasurer of the building. They told her Fox was a suspect, and something in their attitude frightened her.

"They talked in a cold, arrogant and vindictive way," she said. "And I told them Mr. Fox was here from 1:00 to 4:00 P.M. the day the Christgen boy was kidnapped. I never dreamed the officers would question him. If I had thought they planned to question him, I would have talked with some of the attorneys in this building and would have asked them to be with him while the officers talked to him. I told them I knew what type of man he was, that he was a Christian man, could hurt no one and was loved by all. The officers looked at me like I was a nitwit. I knew if they ever talked with Mr. Fox with that cold, vindictive look, they would frighten him."

They questioned him twice. The first time was just a quick pass, with detectives watching for a flicker of guilt in his eyes as they asked him routine questions about his whereabouts on Friday, May 26. After the first interrogation, Eaton and another detective tailed Fox for a day. Riding in a car, they had trouble going slowly enough without attracting attention. Fox shuffled his feet, laboriously scooting one in front of the other as if his shoes were filled with lead. Eaton knew Fox could not be their man. Eaton had climbed to the tangled terrain where Eric's body was found and believed that Fox would be physically incapable of reaching that spot. Eaton became convinced when Fox came to the 10th Street hill, where the grade leading to his home rises at a 45-degree angle. There Fox turned around and walked up the hill backwards. He could not climb the hill facing forwards because he could not raise his toes off the ground. Going backwards was the only way he could get to the top.

"There's no way this guy could have done it," Eaton reported back to the other detectives. "He had to climb that whole block backwards. It would have taken him two days to get out of MacArthur Drive, and he would have never been able to get up that ravine with the boy."

But on Monday night, June 5, detectives brought Fox in for questioning. When Eaton saw him, Fox was pale, wide-eyed and slobbering. When they led him into the interrogation room, Fox quickly searched the surrounding furniture and walls like a trapped animal looking for a way out.

"I don't understand why I'm here," he said. "I didn't do anything wrong."

Two members of the St. Joseph Police Department began interrogating Fox at 8:17 P.M. Eaton was not one of them. Instead, he went home wondering about Fox and how upset he was. Shortly after Eaton had arrived at his home, he received a telephone call from another officer.

"Foxy is in trouble," Eaton was told.

Fox had been questioned for about 30 minutes when he went into convulsions. The two officers were questioning Fox, when he asked for a drink. After he was given a drink, Fox leaned over in his chair, with his arms on his knees. He began to change colors. He coughed and wheezed, vomited and collapsed onto the floor. The police attempted to resuscitate him and called an ambulance that took him to the hospital where Eric's body had been taken. Fox was pronounced dead at 10:19 P.M. Dr. J.H. Ryan signed the death certificate which indicated that Fox died of a heart attack. Sheriff Fleck, the head of NOMIS, told reporters a few days later that Fox had died "of an explosion of the heart."

"It was a sad event for all of us, but something which I guess couldn't be helped," Fleck said. "We are all sorry it happened. On the other hand, we are charged with conducting a kidnap-murder investigation and must question everyone we think might have seen something on the mall when the Christgen boy was kidnapped. If we failed to question someone, we would be derelict in our duty."

Fleck talked about Fox's death as if Fox had been

considered a witness rather than a suspect. But the detectives had brought him in as a suspect. He had denied that he killed Eric. If Fox was the boy's murderer, he had taken the information to his grave. If he was not, then Eric's murderer had claimed another victim.

After Fox died, Margaret Hoehn sat in a beauty shop and overheard two women talking about him. The women believed that Fox died because he was guilty and could not stand the interrogation. Ms. Hoehn asked the two women how they knew this, and they replied that it was "all over town."

Hoehn was so upset by the rumors that she wrote a letter to the newspaper defending Fox. "I want to state emphatically that I knew Mr. Fox real well," she wrote. "He was a man of high intelligence, but couldn't talk very well. He was a student of history and a lover of music. It was inhuman for those officers to talk with him after I told them all about him. He was a kind, lovable person and everyone liked him. He was a fine man and I want everybody to know it. A great injustice has been done to a good and kindly man."

In addition to the story that Fox was guilty, another rumor that moved through St. Joseph after he died was that police interrogators had terrorized him with a boa constrictor on a chain. The police used many exotic tactics to crack the Christgen case, but terrorizing Harry Fox with a snake was not one of them. There were other stories sweeping the city, mostly about how Eric died. Two weeks after Eric's disappearance, the *St. Joseph Gazette* began demanding answers from NOMIS:

"The result of its ineptness has been confusion and the proliferation of unfounded rumors. This case is NOMIS's first, and what an investigation for the newly-formed squad, composed of area law enforcement officers. The murder of the little boy generated a public emotional intensity that few of us have seen before in this community. The pressure is on the squad to get results. The people of St. Joseph, and indeed the entire region, are vitally interested in seeing the slayer of little Eric Christgen apprehended and brought to trial. The massive public involvement in the search for him is evidence of our concern. The public has the right to better and more complete information about the investigation than it has been getting."

Fox's death was a blow to the NOMIS investigation, and 11 days later, on day 21 of its existence, the special squad was disbanded. Its officers had pursued 231 leads and questioned 450 people at least once. A third of them were questioned a second time. Twelve thousand manhours were spent on the case. Twenty-one persons underwent hypnosis and 12 took polygraph tests. After officers felt they had gone over every lead, they had studied them again.

"In looking back, I will admit that NOMIS did make some mistakes," Sheriff Fleck said. "But this was our initial case and we have learned some things the hard way. I feel sure that this case will most probably be solved. But that still may be some time down the road. I, like most of the men on the NOMIS team, believe we could have wrapped the case up if we had just been able to receive that one very important tip. But the right person never came forward."

CHAPTER THREE

"Did you kill the boy?"
"No. But I'll say so if you want me to."
—From a conversation between Police
Lieutenant Terry Boyer and Melvin Reynolds

FOR THE TIME BEING, FBI AGENT HOLTSLAG DRIFTED
away from the case. NOMIS closed its office, and
its files and the responsibility for investigating Eric's murder reverted to the St. Joseph Police Department. Among the smudged index cards in the
gray metal filing box was "follow-up lead number
25, Melvin Lee Reynolds." When police swept the
city, there was little doubt that the skinny, unemployed cook would be questioned. Melvin could
feel it coming. He had known it from that stomach-
churning moment, three days after the killing,
when he read in the newspaper how police believed Eric had died.

"No one but a homosexual would kill a kid and
do what he did," Melvin said to himself. He
thought about leaving town, but realized that
would only add to the suspicion that would inevitably surround him.

Because of his background, the police would
have questioned Melvin eventually. And his background contributed later to the officers' dogged belief in his guilt. But the focus sharpened early on
him because someone had tipped NOMIS that Melvin might be involved. On June 2, a week after Er-

ic's abduction, an anonymous caller told the police that Melvin was observed on the mall the afternoon the child disappeared. The day the call came in, two officers went to Melvin's house and questioned him for 15 minutes. The wide-eyed young man denied being on the mall, but something in his attitude prompted officers to bring him in the next day for more questions.

By age 25, Melvin Reynolds had made all the familiar stops of a tattered life: childhood disease, disrupted family life, poor education and finally, trouble with the law. A childhood attack of rheumatic fever had left him a frail wisp of a boy. To his father, who rode a rodeo circuit, he was not what a son should be. The family that included Melvin and his two sisters moved at one point from a farm to St. Joseph, where Melvin's dad drove a bus. When Melvin was six, he saw his father beating Wanda, his mother, on the front porch. Divorce soon followed, and Melvin's troubles really began.

"There was an old lady up the street," he said. "She didn't like my family, so I stuck a hot dog in my zipper and went up there and asked her if she'd ever seen one. She called the police."

It was the first of many times Wanda would have to answer for the boy. Melvin was enrolled in St. Mary's, a Roman Catholic school, where one day he tried to impress the nuns during show-and-tell with a matched set of gag male and female hot dish holders. The nuns did not get the joke and expelled him. He ran away from home twice, and once "just to be mean," he set fire to his closet.

Melvin would later recall to a reporter: "When I was that young, I liked to do things like that. Mom couldn't take it no longer, so she made an appointment with one of the judges and had me put in the

Boys Home." Melvin was 10, and his sexual initiation at the home came when an older, stronger boy gave him a choice—sex or a dunk in the toilet. "I was the youngest and the littlest one in there. I don't think I was, you know, turned out that way when I went down there, until the guys started forcing me. I couldn't say anything 'cause that'd be a snitch, so I just kept on doing it. A lot of times there was more than one guy. One would do it and the others'd be waiting in line. One would quit and the other'd get on."

Two years later, Melvin's mother married a man named William O'Meara. Melvin kept his name, which first and last, was identical to his father's. He returned home a slow learning, sexually confused, tousle-haired youngster of 12. At Lafayette School, Melvin was teased about his effeminate manner and his enrollment in special education classes. In the first semester of 1969, when he turned 16 and was in the ninth grade, Melvin dropped out of school. He spent his days watching soap operas.

Melvin told the reporter: "If you really sit down and watch it and think about it, soap operas are a lot like people's lives; a lot like mine—screwed up."

He attempted to develop a career through the Job Corps and traveled to South Dakota to learn to cook. His employer sent him home because of his sexual activity with others in the program. The longest period of time that he held a job was three months. His dirty mouth repeatedly caused his termination. Each time he was fired, he was able to find a new job. Once, through a temporary employment service, he landed a job sweeping the parking lot and stacking lumber for Ed Christgen's company. He held other jobs as well: he cooked in a nursing home, pressed clothes at a dry cleaners, tested and packaged wire at a cable company, poured cement for a grain elevator, boxed hats at the Stetson factory and took blood tests for a veterinarian.

Between jobs, he chose friends who were just as troubled as he was, and shoplifting kept the club together. He was picked up a dozen times for either "borrowing" the car from a lady up the street or for petty theft. Often he stole for others—to gain their acceptance. For instance, he took the automobile from his neighbor so that he could give rides to his friends. The police came to know him by the dresses he wore. He liked to wear them, and they gave him a place to hide goods. The officers chuckled about the young man who would reach into his purse to pull out a pork chop, or up his dress to turn over stolen lunchmeat. A story circulated in the community that Melvin had molested his three-year-old nephew. Melvin and his family, including the little boy's mother, denied the story. But the rumor persisted, and the police heard the story.

The year before the Christgen murder, Melvin had been diagnosed at the St. Joseph State Mental Hospital as exhibiting signs of "mental retardation" and "antisocial behavior." Melvin's description was more terse: "I was a brat." A hospital psychologist began working with Melvin, encouraging him to develop relationships with women. One night while in a gay bar with a friend in drag, Melvin met Rita Anderson, a nurse's aide at Methodist Hospital. Rita knew from the beginning about Melvin's sexual double life, but this did not hamper their relationship. "If you love one another, you should be able to trust one another," she said. Melvin and Rita became a couple. Wanda, Melvin's mother, was glad to see him bring a woman home for a change. They became engaged and planned to be married on October 6, Wanda's birthday. Melvin wanted a son.

Melvin's face in profile was balanced by two features: a strong chin and an evenly defined nose in proper proportion to the rest of his face. His thin lips parted easily and often in nervous smiles, and disclosed two even rows of teeth. His eyes, which peered from behind the curly brown hair that hung down over his forehead, always transmitted his true feelings precisely. They always seemed to reflect sadness or desperation.

At 25, he was half the age of the man Jeff Davey and Carl Simpson said they had seen with the boy. His youth was not the only physical aspect that seemed to rule him out as a suspect. His build seemed to exclude him too. Melvin was five foot eight inches tall, and weighed 145 pounds. The man Davey and Simpson had described was heavier set.

Sergeant John Muehlenbacher, one of the officers who had questioned Fox, was waiting for Melvin at police headquarters. Muehlenbacher interrogated Melvin for two hours. Melvin Reynolds was terrified by his tone and shocked by the photographs of the Christgen boy's body. At the end of the session, he was tired and shaken. Muehlenbacher asked him if he would be willing to take a polygraph, and Melvin agreed. When Lieutenant Terry Boyer arrived to administer the lie detector test, he found Melvin a nervous wreck. Before he connected the agitated young man to the machine, Boyer tried to calm him down.

After Melvin seemed to relax somewhat, Boyer attached two tubes around Melvin's body. One stretched like a fat rubber band around his hairless, narrow chest and the other wrapped around his abdomen. Boyer clipped a small spoon to a finger of each of Melvin's hands, and then he slipped a blood pressure cuff around Melvin's meager bicep. Boyer's lie detector tests usually lasted about two hours. But Melvin's test lasted twice that long. Boyer asked Melvin hundreds of questions—about his sex life, his friends and family, his schooling, his working habits, and his involvement in the Christgen murder. Melvin thought he would never stop. The entire time, Boyer stared intently at the twitching needles that inked peaks and valleys of Reynolds' reactions on rolls of polygraph paper.

"Melvin, were you on the mall that day?"

"No."

"Did you kill the boy?"

"No." Melvin paused. He looked up at Boyer appeasingly, like a dog with his ears pressed back against his head. "But I'll say so if you want me to."

Terry Boyer searched for signs of truth or deception among the squiggly lines of Melvin's polygraph test. He found sharp reactions to questions about Melvin's sexual practices. But there was no fluctuation when asked about whether he killed the boy. He concluded that Reynolds was telling some lies, including whether he was on the mall. But Boyer also believed Reynolds was telling the truth when he said that he did not kill Eric Christgen. It was this finding that Boyer delivered to Chief Glenn Thomas.

"Show him the door," the chief said. He confided to his wife that there were "too many indications that Reynolds did not do it."

"And he'll say anything to please anybody." Thomas kept thinking about the psychological profile. He thought whoever murdered Eric was not a local, but a transient who just happened to be passing through. He thought he was probably quite adept at luring children, and that he had probably killed before. To Thomas, the killer was like some visiting plague of the Middle Ages which swept through a village and picked victims at random, or in ancient times, a pagan god demanding a sacrifice from the villagers. The offering had been a beautiful son of a prominent family.

Perhaps he'll never be caught, Chief Thomas thought.

After NOMIS was disbanded, responsibility for solving the case had fallen on Thomas, who had been with the department for 45 years, 11 of them as chief. The Christgen murder occurred just four months before he was scheduled to retire. As the police were continuing a murder investigation that always seemed to lead to a dead end, the city's crime commission was searching for Thomas's successor. There were suggestions that the commission should look outside the city to bring new blood into the department. The suggestions came from people who were not lifelong St. Joe residents. What St. Joseph needed, they said, were fresh ideas and new approaches. The police department was inbred, they said.

Despite these sentiments, the commission selected James Robert Hayes, an experienced St. Joseph police officer and a criminal justice instructor at the local college.

On paper, Hayes, 53, had a lot of experience. He had attended the FBI training academy. He had been in charge of campus security at Missouri Western State College in St. Joseph. At the same time, he had earned an associate degree in criminal justice and then a bachelor of science degree in political science. He had earned a master's degree in criminal justice administration from Central Missouri State University in Warrensburg, and was certified to operate a polygraph. He had taught various criminal justice courses at Missouri Western for five years when members of the St. Joseph crime commission approached him regarding the possibility of his becoming chief of police. Hayes had the inside track for the job.

Short, with a full head of closely cropped gray hair, Bob Hayes talked with a deep voice that sounded as though it came from the bottom of a well. He carefully formed his words, as if they were bound for a dictating machine, and this practice led some officers to believe that their conversations with Hayes, in the chief's dimly lit office on the third floor of the police department, were secretly recorded.

Hayes became police chief on July 31, 1978. He announced almost immediately that finding the solution to the Christgen murder case would be his top priority.

"The case won't be closed as long as I'm here. We'll work it as long as there is the smallest lead."

One of his first orders was to appoint two detectives—Charles "Skip" Jones and John Muehlenbacher—to the case fulltime. In August, he issued a public appeal for information on the case. The prime suspects were re-questioned, and Melvin was one of them since the police believed that he had lied when he said that he had not been on the mall the day Eric disappeared.

Holtslag was not on the case at this time, but Sergeant Bob Anderson of the Highway Patrol was back into it. His first involvement had ended with the termination of NOMIS; however, in mid-July, the Highway Patrol loaned him to the St. Joseph Police Department solely to solve the Christgen murder. The three lawmen—Jones, Anderson and Muehlenbacher—had 50 years worth of law enforcement experience among them. When they questioned Melvin again in August, he admitted being in the mall area on May 26. He said he had borrowed a car that afternoon from a neighbor, Frances Pierce, and had washed rugs for her. He said he had driven to the rear of the Corby Building—where Harry Fox had worked—and had walked to the corner near the location of Eric's abduction. He told the officers that he had remained there for 30 to 35 minutes and then had gone to the telephone company building to pay a bill. From there, he had gone to the Methodist Hospital to visit Mrs. Pierce, who was a patient there. Melvin also said that he had gone to the mall that evening and had encountered a friend, Bunny Terry, who told him that she was looking for a little lost boy named Eric Christgen. Melvin said that he then began to look for Eric and spent two or three hours on the search. He said he then walked to a friend's house where he spent the night.

When the police checked Melvin's story with neighbors, some of it fit and some of it did not, and to the investigators, a lying suspect might be a guilty suspect. Each time they questioned him, Melvin divulged a bit more. Over the next few months, the investigators kept returning to him. They questioned him nine times between June 2, 1978 and February 14, 1979. Melvin wondered what he would have to say to make them go away. He clung to his story about borrowing the car, although officers had checked into it and found it to be untrue. Melvin felt himself being sucked into a pit.

"Why did you lie about the car?" asked Anderson, during another session.

"I was scared," Reynolds replied.

On October 3, 1978, Melvin was brought in for a

second polygraph test. Boyer questioned him from 10:00 A.M. until 11:20 A.M. Again Melvin denied killing Eric, but said he would admit it if Boyer wanted him to. October 6th passed, and the plans for the wedding between Melvin and Rita were postponed. In November, the investigators brought Melvin in again and hypnotized him. He stuck to his story, but detectives continued to appear on his doorstep. Their attitude frightened him. His answers no longer seemed sufficient and there were times when he could not remember what he had done on the day Eric was abducted. Two days before Christmas, the police turned to another novel investigative tool. They took Melvin to Methodist Hospital where he was given a dose of sodium amytal—which is also known as a "truth serum." It was during this session that Reynolds gave a statement that convinced Anderson of his guilt.

"I didn't have anything to do with it," Melvin said when the drug took effect. "I saw the boy on the mall. I didn't have anything to do with it." Then Anderson heard what he believed was an involuntary admission: "Before I killed . . . before I went to the unemployment office." It was a remark that convinced Anderson that Melvin was good for the crime.

On Valentine's Day, 1979, Sergeant Muehlenbacher telephoned Melvin and told him that the police wanted to talk to him again. Anxious to please, Melvin was waiting for officers when they arrived. For months, Melvin had cooperated with his inquisitors and had not consulted a lawyer. He had been afraid to tell the police that he was tired of their questions and wanted to be left alone. Submission seemed to be the story of his life. Melvin had come to the conclusion that it was best not to resist the inevitable.

This time, officers took him to Anderson's office at the Highway Patrol headquarters on the edge of the city, rather than the St. Joseph Police Department downtown.

"I'm glad you brought me out to the Highway Patrol. I don't like the police station."

Once they were settled in Anderson's basement office, they turned on a tape recorder and asked Melvin to waive his rights. For Melvin, it was the beginning of a nightmarish, marathon question-and-answer session that lasted from 10:30 A.M. until 1:00 A.M. For Anderson it was the moment of truth in the Christgen case. Anderson knew how to question people. Other officers said he knew how to ride the gray line. He knew how to handle his subjects and how to outsmart them.

"Those things you told us, Melvin, weren't true. Why did you lie to us?"

"I was afraid. I was afraid you was going to pin this on me, and I was scared."

"You did not see anything downtown? Nothing unusual? I don't want to pull it out of you."

"Pull what out of me. If I didn't see anything . . ."

"I don't want to come up there every month and pick you up, Melvin. I don't want to do it, but I'm going to if we're going to have to do it the hard way. There's a multitude of things we can charge you with. I don't want to do it. But I'll bring them up just to show you."

Anderson then accused Melvin of various thefts.

"We're going to keep following what you've been involved in and what you aren't. Now, I want you to get your head on straight. I want the truth. I don't want to slap these charges on you. You don't know what it is to tell the truth."

They took a break every 45 minutes or so, and

then resumed their interrogation. Between the sessions, Melvin would go to the restroom or get a cup of coffee. At 1:30 that afternoon, Jones joined Anderson and Muehlenbacher. Anderson began asking Melvin about his wedding plans.

"You're going to get married," he said, raising his voice. "You've found a girl you've apparently fallen in love with."

"Yes," Melvin said quietly.

"You want to get married. And how in the hell are you going to do all this if you're going to start telling lies and getting involved in these other burglaries and thefts and stealing? How you gonna do it?"

"There's no way," Melvin replied softly.

"There's no way," Anderson agreed. "Unless you get married in jail. Do you think that woman loves you enough to get married in jail or wait for you?"

Melvin said he didn't.

"I don't either, Melvin. Now I'm telling you, we want the truth about this and everything else. Just wipe the slate clean and be done with it. Let's don't come back to your place . . . and pick you up and bring you in. Do you understand?"

Melvin felt his head spinning. He had run out of words. He had run out of answers. He could never marry Rita if he was in jail for burglary. But if he confessed to the Christgen murder, he would be in prison as well and for a lot longer. He was beginning to wonder himself if in fact he had done the crime. How could he have done such a thing? Tears welled in his bloodshot eyes, but he tried not to cry. Melvin lowered his head. When he blinked, teardrops fell to the gray tile floor. After a long moment, it was Melvin's turn to ask a question.

"Do you think that I'll go to the penitentiary?"

"Melvin," Anderson said, "I'm not your judge or

jury. I don't know whether you will or whether you won't. Do you think you need to go to the penitentiary?"

"No, I don't think I do. I think I need help at the state hospital."

"Melvin, are you willing to talk to us, get this off your chest, tell us what really happened?"

Melvin was weary. He had grown tired from concentrating on all the questions. After a total of nearly 40 hours of questions by police over the last nine months, he had had enough. Perhaps if he gave them their answers, they would leave him alone. Maybe he'd end up in the mental hospital, and be out soon enough to marry Rita.

"You know, it's awfully hard to talk about it."

"I can understand that. It was a serious crime."

"Do I have to talk to all three of you?"

Jones stepped in and offered Melvin a deal.

"Melvin, would you let us fill out six questions and furnish them to you? Then you can write the answers. They'd be very short."

He agreed. Jones wrote them out in ink, and handed them to Melvin. The detectives stepped from the room, leaving Melvin to stare at the questions on the yellow paper on the table before him. It was like the tests Melvin had struggled with at school.

"When did the boy die?" With his pencil, Melvin wrote, "Don't remember just what time."

"How did the boy die, accident, on purpose?" Melvin wrote "yes" beside the word, "accident."

"Where did you first meet the boy?" "Mall."

"How did you get to the bluff area, walked or car?" "Walked."

In two of the questions, Melvin was asked whether he had sodomized the boy. He answered yes.

Eight, ten minutes later, Melvin knocked on the door, and handed over what became the first page of his final exam. The three officers studied it.

"Melvin, this is fine," Anderson said. "The only thing is we are going to have to go into a little more detail."

Again they turned on the tape recorder and reminded Melvin that he had waived his rights. The officers and Melvin began discussing how Eric died. Then Anderson wrote out a statement, and asked Melvin to read it and sign it. Melvin agreed and, after explaining that no threats or promises had been made against or to him, delivered a complete confession.

Anderson told Melvin to read the statement and correct it. Melvin did. There were a couple of problems with it. One glaring discrepancy concerned the 35 minutes Melvin said he observed the child after the woman had gone into a store. Karen Carter said Eric had been out of her sight for only five minutes.

The police told Melvin to write the account of the murder in his own words and sign it. Melvin agreed. When he did, Melvin used many of the same words, terms and phrases that Jones and Anderson had used in their questions and narratives.

Melvin finished writing the statement shortly after 5:00 P.M. The police allowed him to walk around the building, while they telephoned Chief Hayes. Hayes went to the patrol headquarters to listen to the tapes and to study the three confessions that had been solicited from Reynolds. Hayes was excited. Finally, after nearly nine months, they were on the brink of solving the Christgen murder. He called Mike Insco, the county prosecutor.

"I need to see you. I want you to come out to the

Highway Patrol headquarters," Hayes said. "I've got something you are going to be interested in."

"What is it?" Insco asked.

"I'll tell you when you get here."

When Insco arrived, he found Hayes and Reynolds together in the interrogation room.

Hayes looked at Reynolds.

"Tell him what you told me," Hayes ordered.

"I killed Eric Christgen," Melvin Reynolds repeated. He then added a few details to his statement. Insco and Hayes stepped from the room, and the police chief suggested to the prosecutor that they immediately call a joint press conference to make an announcement that the Christgen murder had been solved.

"No. I'd like to get another tape recording," Insco said. "We need to get some questions answered. I'm afraid of the fact that he might just be telling us what we want to hear."

At 8:03 P.M., the tape recorder was turned on again. During this interview, which lasted 46 minutes, Melvin Reynolds admitted again seeing Eric Christgen on the mall.

"I watched the boy for a few minutes. About 30 minutes later, I walked up to him and said: 'Want to take a walk?'" Once in the wooded area, Reynolds said he sexually assaulted the boy until he fainted and fell over backward.

"Is there anything you can think of you haven't told us before?"

"I've told the truth so far. Why should I start lying now?"

"Maybe you forgot."

"No."

"Give us more details—what about the expression on the boy's face?"

"It was like he was scared and didn't know what to do. He just had tears in his eyes."

Melvin described the MacArthur Drive location where he left Eric's body, but he was unclear on some other details, such as whether Eric had worn briefs or boxer shorts, or which direction the boy's head was pointing when he left him. Insco was still not convinced, and he told the detectives and the chief that he would not charge Melvin Reynolds until he led them to the scene of the crime.

Melvin had been interrogated for nearly 13 hours. Instead of taking the confessed child killer to jail, the officers returned Melvin to his home with the understanding that they would return at 7:00 A.M. so that Melvin would take them to the place where he had left Eric's body. In the intervening six hours, Melvin could conceivably have been on his way to anywhere. Kansas City International Airport was a 30-minute drive from his home. If Melvin did not have the money for an airplane ticket, he could have driven a car to Omaha by the time officers arrived at his front door that morning.

"Well, I felt like and the other officers felt like, that we knew Melvin," Anderson said later. "He wasn't going to run away. He agreed that night to take us to the crime scene."

When they dropped him off in front of the darkened house, officers told Reynolds that they would pick him up at 7:00 A.M. the next day. Melvin quietly slipped into the house. Everyone was asleep. On a small table, he found a Valentine arrangement his mother had made, as well as a card for her from Melvin and Rita. He took a piece of Valentine candy and went upstairs to his room. He was too frightened to sleep.

Melvin was dutifully waiting on his front porch

the next morning when Anderson and Jones appeared. He was angry because they were late and he had had to wait for them in the chilly winter air. He waited outside so that his mother would not know that the police were coming to pick him up again. He did not want his mother to discover that he had confessed to killing Eric Christgen. When the car came to a stop, he climbed into the back seat next to Jones.

"You tell me where to drive, and I'll drive wherever you say, Melvin," said Anderson. Melvin directed the trooper like a cab driver. As the car crept slowly along the river road, the only sound was the crunch of the tires in the deep snow that covered the ground. Melvin was seated on the right hand side, and stared at the river bluffs as they rolled along. After they had driven about a mile, Melvin told Anderson to turn the car around, because they had gone too far.

"It's somewhere around here," Melvin said.

"Would it help to get out of the car?" Anderson asked. Melvin replied that it would. Anderson stopped the car and Melvin stepped out with Jones. A cold wind whipped off the ice-cluttered river and chilled Melvin through his Navy pea coat. He trudged off into the knee-deep snow heading for the bluffs, with Jones following 30 yards behind. Often they slipped on a snow-covered ravine beside the road, and once both Melvin and Jones were forced to crawl through the snow on their hands and knees to get under a large log that blocked their way.

"Anything look familiar?" asked Jones.

"I think this is the spot," Melvin replied after a few minutes.

"Melvin," Jones said, "can you show me the exact spot for sure where you last saw the boy?"

He took a few more steps. "It's right there."

The spot Melvin pointed to was in the general vicinity, but was not the exact spot where Eric had been found. But for the police, it was close enough. Melvin stood for a minute on a small plateau. He felt himself starting to cry. Eric had been just a kid, he thought. What a horror his parents must have gone through. What would they think of Melvin once his name appeared in the paper?

CHAPTER FOUR

"Melvin Reynolds could not have committed that crime."
— Detective Robert Eaton talking to Chief
James Robert Hayes

AS MELVIN FEARED, HIS NAME WOULD SOON BE IN the newspapers. Insco was still trying to decide whether to charge Reynolds when he started receiving telephone calls from news reporters at rock radio stations inquiring whether he was about to charge a suspect in the Eric Christgen case. The calls were coming from one-man news departments not known for their ability to dig up stories. Somebody was calling them, feeding them the information, suggesting that they call the prosecutor.

"That sonofabitch Hayes," Insco said to himself. "He's calling up these reporters. He's trying to push me into charging Reynolds." Insco knew the tactic. He knew how games could be played with the press. Despite Chief Hayes' enthusiasm, Insco still had misgivings. When police told him where Reynolds said he left the body, Insco knew he had picked the wrong place. The prosecutor theorized that perhaps the body had rolled from the spot identified by Melvin, or perhaps Reynolds had simply forgotten.

In Missouri, a county prosecutor has tremendous discretion regarding whether to charge an individual with a crime. He is uniquely positioned to prejudge every felony criminal case brought to him by the police. The prosecutors weigh many factors before a decision is made to bring charges. The possibility of a conviction, the expense of the trial, the nature of the crime and the likelihood that charges may lead to a plea of guilty are only a few of these factors.

Many cases are concluded by plea bargaining. A defendant who pleads guilty under this type of arrangement will be sentenced less severely than a defendant who actually proceeds to trial and is found guilty of the same offense. Insco had a reputation as a prosecutor who preferred to go to trial rather than plea bargain a defendant down to a lesser offense.

Politics can enter into the equation as well, although few state's attorneys will admit it. Most prosecuting attorneys wish to amass strong records of successful convictions. This type of record can lead directly into private law practice or politics. Many times prosecutors proceed with cases in ways which will garner publicity and notoriety.

Prosecutors always must consider community feeling. At times, cases consisting of little or no evidence must be brought to trial to reassure the public that wrongdoers must answer at the bar.

A prosecutor does not have to be completely convinced of an individual's guilt before he brings a charge. But there are times when a prosecuting attorney may have doubts concerning a case the police department has brought him. When those doubts linger, a prosecutor can seek consolation in a grand jury, a panel of citizens, which decides not a person's guilt or innocence, but whether or not there is a likelihood that the person committed a crime and should be tried. Of course the ultimate assurance for a doubtful prosecutor is the final backup system, the trial court jury, which is designed to sift the guilty from the innocent. In the end, a person is guilty of a crime if 12 people say he is.

Insco decided to seek charges. Someone else in the same position might have done otherwise, but Insco was a policeman's prosecutor. In a sense, he owed his job more to them than to the voters of Buchanan County. The cops had helped him get where he was. He was a law and order man, who believed in harsh punishment for criminals. He was very young, only 27, when Eric was abducted. He was very inexperienced, only three years out of law school, and confronted with the kind of case few lawyers would ever encounter. Before he went to trial, Insco doubted that he could win. And when the man who killed Eric was finally sent to prison, Insco called it "a one-in-a-million kind of case."

Like Hayes, the prosecuting attorney was a product of St. Joseph. Early on, Insco had focused his attention on civil litigation and had planned to become a plaintiff's attorney. Insco's law school classmates believe that the fate of a hardware store owner Insco was close to may have played a role in Insco's later decision to focus on criminal law. The hardware store owner was gunned down in a robbery.

"He hung on as a vegetable for a few weeks, and then died," Insco said. "It was all so senseless. They only got away with a few bucks."

Insco's fellow classmates recalled that Insco had said at the time that nothing would give him more pleasure than prosecuting and convicting the men who had killed his friend. The incident reinforced Insco's notion that there were people in the world who needed to be protected and there were others who needed to be punished.

When he graduated from law school in 1975, he returned home and interviewed with Buchanan County Prosecuting Attorney Richard Heider. There was a vacancy on Heider's staff, and Insco believed this would be a good place to get his practice started. He never thought he would like being a prosecutor, and he viewed the position as a stepping stone to private practice. He came back to St. Joseph for the same reasons others had stayed there—it was comfortable; it was safe.

Once Insco began working in the prosecutor's office, he found that he liked it, and he quickly made a name for himself. He refused to routinely reduce cases to lesser offenses, and the policemen liked and respected him for that. To the merchants' delight, he was aggressive with bad check complaints.

In the summer of 1977, Heider unexpectedly announced he was resigning to take a job with a private law firm, and it was up to Governor Joseph Teasdale to decide who would succeed him. Insco mounted a fierce letter-writing campaign for the position against the early favorite, Cindy Clark, an assistant county prosecutor. The appointment was delayed for months, as Teasdale vacillated over whom to pick. The prosecutor's office became a pressure cooker, since no one knew who was going to become the boss. Then on September 23, 1977, the announcement came: Insco got the job. He planned to change certain things in the office. He believed that the prosecutors in the office should become more involved in the law enforcement community.

The lawyers who worked in the same courtrooms as Insco thought he had his sights on Congress or a judgeship, and that he played to the press. They also described him as the "darling" of Norman Steward, the veteran courthouse reporter for the *News-Press.* Insco's tough approach to crime was trumpeted by the conservative newspapers—the *News-Press* and *Gazette,* and Steward gave Insco all the space and ink he needed. Once, Insco publicly criticized a judge for giving a convicted criminal a sentence the prosecutor thought was too light, and Steward supported the prosecutor's remarks in his own column. Another attorney said that the newspaper had "adopted" Insco and "fed him the heady wine of media adulation."

Insco brought second degree murder charges against Reynolds a few hours after Melvin visited the place along MacArthur Drive where Eric's body had been found. Reynolds was arraigned before Associate Circuit Judge Randall Jackson, who appointed Richard Dahms, the public defender, to represent him. A preliminary hearing, in which evidence would be presented to determine whether Melvin should stand trial was set for February 23.

At 4:30 that afternoon, Chief Hayes held a news conference and announced that he was absolutely certain the police had the right man.

"County prosecutor Mike Insco filed the case and we have 100 percent confidence and agreement with him," Hayes said.

Sheriff Fleck, who had headed the NOMIS investigation, said Reynolds was close enough to the killer's profile.

But Bob Eaton, the man who had led the search for Eric, could not believe it. Eaton had attended school with Reynolds and his sisters and did not think he was capable of such an act. In addition, there was the description of the older, larger man seen leading the boy down the railroad tracks beside MacArthur Drive.

Eaton considered Hayes not only his boss but also a friend of his family. Eaton thought he could talk to him man-to-man about the case, and on the way home from a class at Missouri Western, he stopped by the chief's house to explain why Reynolds could not be Eric's murderer.

"What are you doing here?" Hayes asked when he found Eaton at his front door.

"Chief, there's something I've got to talk to you about. It's very important."

"Tell me about it tomorrow."

"I don't think you've got the right guy in the Christgen case. Melvin Reynolds could not have committed that crime."

"Who in the hell do you think you are coming over and bothering me with this?"

"He doesn't even match the description."

"The prosecutor thinks we have the right guy, and I think we have the right guy. That's good enough."

"Chief, nobody knows more about that case than I do."

"I don't want to talk about it anymore. Goodbye."

The next day, Eaton was called into the chief's office and berated for going to his house off duty to argue about a case.

"Who do you think you are, coming over to my house. Would you have gone to Glenn Thomas' house and told him?"

"Probably. I thought you were a friend."

"What do you mean friend? I don't even know you. Leave it alone. We got the right guy and you don't need to talk about it."

Boyer the polygraph operator also did not think

Reynolds killed Eric. He reminded the chief that his lie detector tests indicated that Melvin was telling the truth. Boyer had even sent copies of his charts to his polygraph instructor in New York, who reviewed them and agreed with the conclusion that Melvin was telling the truth. The chief told Boyer that he would do no more polygraphs for the department. And although Boyer was at the top of the list to be named captain, he did not receive any promotions.

The arrest of Melvin Reynolds also seemed inconsistent to a federal agent in St. Joseph. Since NOMIS was dissolved, Joe Holtslag had lost touch with the Christgen case, and he was surprised to read about Reynolds' confession. The picture of the skinny, bushy-haired young man in the newspaper was not consistent with the description Holtslag recalled hearing from Jeffrey Davey, the hypnotized witness.

"That's not the way I remember it," Holtslag said to himself as he read about Reynolds' confession.

But when he asked Anderson and Jones how the murderer could be Reynolds, Holtslag was given a logical explanation. First, Reynolds had said that he had not seen anyone as he led Eric up MacArthur Drive, so it was possible that no one had seen him. And Holtslag was told that investigators had learned that an elderly man and his grandson frequently hiked along the Missouri River and the railroad tracks that ran beside it. The officers theorized that they were the pair both Davey and Simpson had seen along the river the day Eric was abducted.

"Okay, I'll buy that," Holtslag said.

But there was also Etta Louise Anderson, who was no relation to Rita Anderson, Melvin's girlfriend. Etta and her son would pick up newspapers beside Reynolds' home. Her son delivered them. Mrs. Anderson did not particularly like Melvin. But she came forward and told both the police and the *St. Joseph News-Press* that she had seen and talked to Melvin on the front porch of his home at about 3:25 P.M. the day Eric was abducted. Melvin's home was more than a mile from the scene of the murder. She was sure about the time because she knew when the papers were delivered.

"I wish I didn't remember this, but I do," she said. "I really wouldn't want to be involved in all this. I have to live with myself. If I didn't say what I did, I wouldn't be doing what's right."

Her information conflicted with the possibility that Melvin was with Eric. A newspaper reporter asked Hayes about her story, but Hayes refused to comment.

The day after he was charged, Melvin gave another confession to Kansas authorities about a separate child killing. In response to questions by agents of the Kansas Bureau of Investigation, Reynolds said he had sexually molested four-year-old Christopher Edward Chapin. Chapin was a Rushville, Missouri boy, whose body was found in Atchison, Kansas, on August 26, 1978, three months after Eric's murder. The body of the child was found in an unused swimming pool at the Melrose Motel just outside the Atchison city limits. Reynolds signed the confession, but said, "I hate to say if I killed him or not, that embarrasses me. Will that go harder on me?" The KBI discounted the confession. The Kansas agents said there were too many inconsistencies in what Reynolds said.

While a few people were skeptical about whether Melvin Reynolds had committed the crime, there were plenty in St. Joseph who were convinced that he was guilty. On Sunday, the newspaper ran an in-depth story which profiled Melvin and his back-ground. The story prompted letters to the editor critical of the paper's handling of Reynolds' case.

"Since when has the *News-Press* been appointed judge and jury of homicide cases in St. Joseph?" one reader asked. "You have already convicted this man, Reynolds."

The news of Melvin's arrest deeply affected the home of his mother Wanda O'Meara and her hus-band, William. Late at night, people started throw-ing bricks through the windows of their little frame home. The first brick flew into the living room, and then a rock was hurled through the kitchen window. People began to break windows in the garage. Melvin's family decided to move. They found an old house on a gravel road on the edge of town, and told no one but relatives and close friends where they were.

Instead of presenting evidence against Melvin in an open preliminary hearing, Insco asked that a Buchanan County grand jury consider weighing the charges. Because a grand jury's proceedings are secret, the Christgen family would be spared the ordeal of having to live through the case twice —once at the preliminary hearing and once at trial. At the same time, there would be no public airing of specific evidence against Melvin, and Dahms objected to the procedure.

During this time, Melvin remained behind bars because his bond was set at $50,000. There was no guarantee of his safety in jail, since someone had telephoned the sheriff's office and threatened his life. The guards isolated him from other jail in-mates and later moved him to other lockups in small, nearby towns. After a time, Melvin was re-turned to the Buchanan County Jail. Ever eager to be liked, he began painting the cells with yellow and gray paint the county supplied for him. He used the yellow on the cellblocks and catwalks and the gray to trim the bars. Melvin repeatedly told those around him that he did not kill Eric Christgen. He would add that he only made the statements to the police to make them cease questioning him.

On March 7, the grand jury indicted Melvin on a charge of felony murder in the second degree. The indictment stated that Melvin had caused Eric's death "in the perpetration of the felony of sodomy."

His mother, Wanda, and his stepfather, Bill O'Meara, never doubted his innocence. With their combined salaries, they struggled to raise money to hire a Kansas City defense lawyer, Lee Nation, who had been recommended to them.

Rita also stuck by him, and went to the parking lot nearly every day, on the uphill side of the jail just below his cell, where they could talk through the barred window and plan their future together. Both felt sure that Melvin would be found innocent. Rita sent letters to tourist bureaus around the country and in Canada to find a place where they would live after his release. Later, when his attorney sent Melvin to the Missouri State Hospital in Fulton for psychiatric tests, Rita wrote him long letters every other day. Melvin said they were "mushy," but he read them over and over again.

Reynolds' trial had been set for June 4, 1979, but it was delayed after Lee Nation sought the psychiatric evaluation of his client. Nation, who had been brought into the case March 1, at first thought he would plead Melvin not guilty by reason of mental disease or defect. Between June 25 and August 2, Reynolds underwent a battery of tests and evaluations at the mental hospital to determine whether he was mentally competent to stand trial. One test he took showed he had an I.Q. of 75, the "dull normal" range.

He kept to himself at the hospital. He told a newspaper reporter who was interested in his case that he was told to keep to himself.

"Who told you?" the reporter asked.

"Some of the aides when I first come in. And the doctor."

"Why did they tell you that?"

"Because of what I'm in here for," Melvin replied.

"Have you talked about it with other patients?"

"Yeah. They already know. One of the aides must have told somebody. It's got around. I just tell them the truth. I didn't do it. Why lie about it?"

"How was the kid murdered?" the reporter pressed.

"I don't know much about that. All I know is he was supposed to be suffocated or something."

"Why did the cops think you did it?"

"Because of my background."

"Did you used to get in a lot of trouble?"

"No. That wasn't it. It was being gay. That's why they picked me up because they thought it would have to be a gay person that did it."

"Why is that?" the reporter asked.

"Let's see. Okay. The way I read it in the paper— or the way I heard it, I should say, too—is okay, whoever it was stuck their whatever—I don't want to say it—in his mouth, and did something to him, you know, and then I guess he just left him there because that's the way he was found."

"How did you first hear about the murder?"

"Okay. Wait a minute. On the news."

"What was your reaction when the cops picked you up?"

"Oh. I figured they would because of my past."

"How long after the murder did the cops come after you?"

"About two days—didn't waste no time. They just kept it up and kept it up, and I finally just got tired and said, 'Yes, even though I didn't do it, if you want me to admit to it, I will.' "

"Did you realize that if you said 'yes,' you were headed for a lot of trouble?"

"Yes, but I was scared."

"Of what?"

"They just kept pressuring me and pressuring me where I couldn't take it no more."

"So you'd rather say you murdered somebody?"

"Well, the deal was, see, they was going to take me to jail anyway, so I thought, 'Why not give them something to take me to jail for?' Was kind of stupid, I know."

The reporter asked him about the prosecution.

"Piss on the prosecuting attorney. I don't like him anyway. Everybody calls him the hangman cause he wants everybody hung. And he's after my ass anyway. The night I admitted to it, he came down and listened to the tape. Ever since then, he's been after me. A lot of people can't take much of that stuff."

"When you were a kid, did you think about what you wanted to be when you grew up?"

"At that time, I couldn't care less. I probably should've and I wouldn't be in all this trouble."

"Do you wish you could just start over?"

"Do you mean my whole life or just from a certain point?"

"Well, if you could, from what point would you start over?"

"Ten. Anyway, I'm just hoping when I go to court, the son-of-a-bitch that did it, I just hope his conscience bothers him so bad he can't take it no more and he just confesses to it."

He also told the reporter about his plans to marry Rita.

"We were just getting to know each other real, real good, and now this happens," he said.

The romance with Rita had become a factor in Reynolds' pretrial evaluation. The tests showed only that, if anything, he was mildly retarded. In Reynolds' case, a presumption of mental illness would have to be associated with a desire to molest children, but certainly not with retardation. Rita's involvement in his life seemed to negate the possibility that Melvin had a desire to molest children.

If he were declared insane, Reynolds could be classified as unfit for trial and could be retained indefinitely for treatment as a sex offender. On August 2, Dr. Sadashiv Parwatikar—known locally as "Dr. Sam"—examined Reynolds. It took him only 35 minutes to render a diagnosis that would affect Reynolds for the rest of his life.

"Based on all the evidence," Dr. Sam said, "I felt that at the time of the alleged crime, he knew and appreciated the nature, quality and wrongfulness of the alleged act. Because he was lacking in any serious mental illness at the time, which might need further evaluation or treatment in a hospital setting, I felt he did not need to be in a hospital and should face the charges."

Melvin Reynolds told a reporter that his lawyer sent him to the Missouri State Hospital for the mental tests "because he had some more stuff to be worked on."

"So he was just buying some time?"

"Yeah. He said he had a bunch of stuff for my

side; he said the only thing that needs doing—the reason I'm down here—is so he could find the loopholes or whatever the state's got."

"You feel as though you're competent and responsible?"

"Yeah. I'm not crazy or nothing. The only reason they picked me up was because of my background. My lawyer told me I didn't have anything to worry about. I'm pretty sure I'll get out of it because he's had 33 murder cases and hasn't lost a one."

Reynolds and his family had pinned their hopes on Lee Nation to help extricate Melvin from the trouble he was in. Melvin was proud his family had hired a lawyer instead of relying on Richard Dahms, the Buchanan County public defender.

Melvin paid more than just a $10,000 fee for Nation's expertise. He gave up the chance to be represented by a man who knew the community and was known in it. Dahms may have been an overworked, underpaid, state-hired defense lawyer, but he knew how to navigate the intricacies of the St. Joseph criminal justice system. A former probate judge, Dahms was voted out of office after the St. Joseph newspapers wrote a series of unfavorable stories about him. Dahms believed the stories were written about him because he refused to keep secret the records of an $11 million estate belonging to the father of the man who owned the newspapers.

Dahms knew where the holes were in the prosecution's case against Reynolds. Before Nation was called in, Dahms had done some preliminary work on Reynolds' defense. One key issue he planned to present at the trial was Melvin's dissimilarity to the man witnesses had seen leading the little boy down MacArthur Drive the afternoon Eric was abducted. Dahms planned to call both Carl Simpson and Jeff

Davey, whose description of an older and larger man could put a reasonable doubt in a jury's mind concerning whether Reynolds was guilty.

The notes Dahms made on the Melvin Reynolds case were turned over to Nation, and Dahms said he was ready to give him any help he needed in defending the young man. But Nation never contacted him.

The very act of hiring Nation may have hurt Melvin. By turning to a big city lawyer, he may have appeared to be guilty; his case seemed so desperate that he was forced to hire a high-priced, out of town lawyer. In a close case, such a subtle notion in a single juror's mind can tip the scales of justice.

Nation was known for his eccentricities. His hair was long and wavy and he would only shave when he felt like it. His attire included a pair of cowboy boots, which might be considered stylish in Kansas City but not in the courtroom. When not in court, he wore navy blue coveralls in the winter and cutoff army fatigues in the summer. He was best known around the courthouse for the festive Christmas parties he hosted.

Nation and Insco had gone to law school together. A fellow student had found both likable but very ambitious in different ways. She said Nation was "witty and intelligent" and that Insco was "decent and honorable." Nation was younger than most of the other students. Insco said he was "a kid," and Nation thought Insco was "a wimp."

In addition to the $10,000 fee and the fact that he had to do without Dahms, Nation's representation cost Melvin in other ways. Not far from the surface, Nation held St. Joseph and its residents in low regard. He never vented his feelings publicly, at least not before Melvin's trial, but his attitude toward the city, its people, and its legal system, saturated his courtroom presence. The reporters who covered Melvin's trial detected it as soon as jury selection had begun. It was detectable in his manner of asking his questions, his general condescending attitude and his strained interaction with Insco and Circuit Judge Frank Connett, Jr. The reporters wondered how his attitude would affect the jury.

Years later, after Eric Christgen's killer was sent to prison, Nation described St. Joseph as a "decidedly feudal" city with "no present and no future." He thought there was no new wealth in the city, and that people with motivation, intellect and the will to achieve inevitably left.

"It is introspective; everyone seems to know everyone else," Nation said. "In such a fishbowl, conformity becomes a paranoia. Rumor is the ultimate avocation. Acceptance in this society demands strict compliance with the norm; everyone else is a pariah.

"The middle class is voiceless in its subservience to the old families. The scions of the old families are not obliged to do anything to keep their positions of power and respect. Largely, they do nothing. They are hedonistic and indulgent. Those who feel the need to succeed leave St. Joe; those content to live off their family name, stay. They drink, drive speedboats on the Missouri River and live to excess."

Nation thought St. Joseph still reveled in the Pony Express, an unsuccessful 18-month experiment in transcontinental mail service which originated in St. Joseph in 1860. He said the police department was still embarrassed over its inability to capture Jesse James. Missouri Gov. Thomas T. Crittenden had offered a $10,000 dead-or-alive reward for James, and a member of James' own gang

took the governor up on it in April, 1882. James'
home was later turned into the "Jesse James Museum," one of St. Joe's most popular tourist attrac-
tions.

Nation thought Melvin could not survive in St.
Joseph because of its intolerance and bigotry.

"The cruelty of children was magnified in St. Joe
by a society that encouraged childish suspicion. He
was not stupid, nor was he a problem child. Instead he had the wide-eyed innocence of a much
younger child. He was sensitive and effeminate—
an easy mark for ridicule and exclusion. In St. Joe,
he had as much chance of fitting in as a leper. Although his mother had remarried and his family
was loving and supportive, he certainly felt the
brunt of childhood's cruelty, the cruelty reserved
for those that are different.

"Growing up, Melvin found acceptance from
other St. Joe pariahs. He was friends with blacks
and with the poor. He was also welcomed in the
homosexual community. While homosexuality was
accepted in San Francisco, and even tolerated in
Kansas City, it was a perversion in St. Joe. The in-
tolerant children of St. Joe society would openly
show their bigotry and the community would ap-
prove. The politicians and the police would openly
deride gays and the rest of society would find their
own suspicions and antipathies brutally accept-
able."

It was surprising, considering his attitude toward the city and the heavy coverage the case had
received, that Nation did not have the trial moved
to another city. He said later that he thought the
news accounts of the description of the older man
seen walking with the little boy would be remembered by the St. Joseph jurors, which would help to
clear Reynolds.

CHAPTER FIVE

"The guy could still be out there and may strike again."

— Assistant Buchanan County Prosecutor
Tom Crossett

THE TRIAL BEGAN ON TUESDAY, OCTOBER 9, 1979. Judge Connett began the process of selecting the jury. Except for his years in law school at the University of Missouri and his service in the Army Air Force during World War II, Connett had spent all of his 57 years in St. Joseph.

The selection process lasted all day, and showed what a small pond St. Joseph really was. Nearly all the jurors either knew or were related to one another, or knew either Melvin, the Christgen family or Insco. Nation was the only stranger in the courtroom. All 50 potential jurors knew about the Reynolds case from the newspapers. One man said bluntly that the St. Joseph newspapers had already convicted Reynolds. When questioned, many of the potential jurors said they knew about Melvin's lifestyle. Nation had earlier asked the entire jury pool whether this would affect their ability to presume Reynolds' innocence. None indicated that it would.

Judge Connett scheduled opening arguments for the next day. Nation appeared unperturbed. He seemed to know something the rest did not. His frequent smiling nods to Reynolds reinforced the appearance of a secretly shared confidence. Whispered conferences between lawyer and client were nearly nonexistent, but Melvin talked frequently with the deputies who escorted him.

The case against Melvin Reynolds had attracted the attention of Harriet Frazier, a criminal law professor who enjoyed going from trial to trial in Missouri. She taught a criminal evidence class at Central Missouri State University in Warrensburg, and sometimes the trials provided material for her classes. She had become interested in the Eric Christgen murder case because of its disturbing similarities to an Illinois crime she had studied in her lawbook.

Frazier wondered whether either of the two lawyers was aware of the Illinois case and its possible application to Reynolds' situation. The case, known as *Miller vs. Pate*, involved a child murder, an incensed community and the confession of a man under intense police questioning.

On November 26, 1955 in Canton, Illinois, an eight-year-old girl died as the result of a brutal sexual attack. A taxicab driver, Lloyd Eldon Miller, was arrested and charged with the crime. He confessed to police after hours of questioning. He was later convicted and the Illinois Supreme Court upheld the conviction in 1958. On February 13, 1967, the conviction was reversed by the U.S. Supreme Court. The reversal was based on the disclosure that prosecutors had used false evidence in Miller's trial.

Frazier thought there were similarities between that case and Reynolds'. She wondered whether Reynolds could receive a fair trial in St. Joseph, given the intense community feelings.

"There's nothing that brings out community outrage like sexual molestation and murder of a child," she told a reporter. "You've got more outrage with this kind of a crime than with any other. Somebody has to pay for a crime like that."

Frazier had attended law school with Insco and Nation, graduating a few months before them. In fact, she had interviewed for an assistant prosecutor's job with Insco's predecessor. When she strolled into the corridor of the Buchanan County Courthouse, there was a three-person reunion of the University of Missouri-Kansas City School of Law, class of 1975.

"I have been studying how *Miller vs. Pate* could be applicable in this case," Frazier told Insco and Nation.

Both of them looked at her with amused expressions.

"We're lawyers, not professors," Nation said.

"We don't have time to read that stuff," Insco said.

The day after the jury selection, the opening arguments began. Insco told the jury what the state would prove. Nation did not have an opening argument. There was a parade of prosecution witnesses —everyone from Karen Carter, Eric's babysitter, to Dr. Bridgens, the forensic pathologist. Steve Greiner, a painting contractor, testified he saw Reynolds on the downtown mall at about 2:55, the afternoon Eric was abducted. There were plenty of pictures too, color slides of Eric's battered body and the autopsy results, which washed the color from the jurors' faces. There was an aerial view of St. Joseph. During a break, Nation told Frazier that the picture "looked like the inside of a stove."

Throughout the early part of the trial, Nation kept his seat. But when Sergeant Bob Anderson took the stand to testify about Reynolds' confession, Nation objected. He argued that the constant harassment Melvin had received over the weeks before his confessions made them inadmissible. The defense attorney pointed out that they had been made involuntarily, without a lawyer present and without an intelligent waiver of the defendant's rights. Judge Connett listened to the complaint, and then excused the jury for the rest of the afternoon to listen to what Anderson would say.

"What led you to investigate Reynolds?" asked the judge.

"I heard he molested his nephew," Anderson replied.

That old rumor still haunted Melvin. The story—rooted in a remark the little boy had made to his parents—wasn't true.

The little boy shocked his mother and father one night when he said: "Melvin said, 'Suck my cock.'" The family was unaware until later—when Melvin explained and the little boy affirmed—of the complete context in which the statement was made: While babysitting the little boy one afternoon, Melvin walked with him on a St. Joseph street. The driver of a passing truck shouted something to them or made a gesture that prompted Melvin to shout back.

"Suck my cock!" Melvin yelled.

The little boy startled his parents that night by repeating the statement. Although the context of the remark was later explained, neighbors had heard the incomplete version of the story, and one of them was a sheriff's deputy.

"Before talking to him, did you threaten or coerce Melvin in any way?" the judge asked Anderson, who was sitting on the witness stand.

"No sir. When he read the word *coercion,* he did not understand that word. It was explained to him by Sergeant Muehlenbacher."

Anderson described how Reynolds had answered Detective Jones' written questions, given the taped statements and finally written out his own confession. He stated that Melvin had found the location of the crime, but Anderson acknowledged under cross-examination by Nation that Melvin might have seen newspaper photographs of the crime scene. Judge Connett ruled that he would allow the jury to hear Anderson and the confessions. Nation filed a continuing objection. He said the statements were taken unconstitutionally after an arrest without probable cause and without adequate waiver of Reynolds' right to remain silent or have counsel. Judge Connett overruled Nation's objections.

Trial resumed, and Anderson, in his matter-of-fact way, repeated the entire story, and Nation made a continuing objection that the testimony was unfair. Copies of the written confessions were passed to the jury and Melvin's taped statements were played for them. The fact that the confessions jeopardized Reynolds' case was obvious, but the order in which they were presented to the jury was especially damaging. The prosecutor did not present the confessions that had been made early in the day—the ones with the inconsistencies and discrepancies, the ones in which Anderson's voice sounded loud and threatening. Instead, Insco relied on the tape-recorded statements Reynolds made later that day—the ones in which he seemed to have all the answers. Nation could present the other confessions later, during the defense phase of the trial, but it was the third and most damaging tape recording that the jury heard first. In it, Melvin graphically and explicitly described how he caused the boy's death through sexual assault.

"How long a time have you been scared about being caught?" Melvin was asked.

"I just felt like it was going to catch up with me sooner or later," he said into the tape recorder.

"How do you feel now that you've said this?"

"A lot better. I feel relieved."

"Melvin, was this statement given of your own free will?"

"Yeah."

"Has there been any pressure or coercion?"

"No, I'm just happy to get it over with—to get it off my chest."

Insco turned off the tape recorder, and said the state rested its case. A recess was called. As spectators in the courtroom stood up, the stiff faces of the jurors filed past. One young woman was in tears.

During the break in the trial, Professor Frazier told Insco she thought he had a flimsy case. She had listened to all the testimony and the confessions. Sitting next to her was a nurse, a high school classmate of Judge Connett's, who was familiar with the case because of her knowledge of the truth serum tests that had been conducted on Reynolds at the hospital. Both women seriously doubted that Melvin had committed the crime. They had driven the route Melvin said he took with the Christgen boy, and they said the pair would have been spotted by dozens of people that afternoon.

"But there are no witnesses that put the boy and Reynolds together," Frazier told Insco. "What are you doing with this case?"

"Are you questioning my integrity?"

"No. I'm questioning your judgment."

"Just keep the fuck out of my case," the prosecutor replied.

The two former law school classmates did not speak again for the rest of the trial. Another lawyer in the courtroom had questions about the case.

Thomas Crossett, the assistant Buchanan County prosecutor, had helped Insco present the case to the jury. Doubts had nagged his mind ever since two NOMIS investigators—people Crossett relied on and trusted—had told him that they did not think Reynolds was guilty. Crossett could not confirm Reynolds' guilt in his own mind, but he could not say he was innocent, either. There was no denying that Reynolds had confessed to the killing. But when Crossett listened to the tape recordings of the confession, he found that the third and last one was much stronger than the first two. That indicated that Reynolds was susceptible to suggestions made in the earlier tapes.

In addition, it appeared that Reynolds had been ready, just a few days after the crime, to admit he had killed Eric, but the police chief in charge then had turned the confession down. Crossett wondered why a new police chief had decided to use the confession nine months later. In addition, there was the problem with the crime scene. Reynolds had not picked out the exact place where the body had been found.

The fact that Melvin might be innocent of the murder was not Crossett's deepest concern. He thought Melvin was guilty of other, smaller crimes, and a trip to prison for him would not be a grave injustice. As he wondered about Reynolds' guilt, he was most concerned with the possibility that if he was innocent, the real killer was still at large.

"If this guy is innocent and gets convicted," Crossett said to himself, "the police will close the books on this case and never get the right guy. The guy could still be out there, and may strike again."

Crossett had joined Insco's office just two weeks before the Christgen murder. He thought it was a "politically explosive" case that would end Insco's political career. In his mind, the case was a loser. He believed Nation would nail the prosecution to the wall with the descriptions of the old man and the boy. Crossett also expected him to pick apart the crime scene identification. He thought Insco would end up like the prosecuting attorney in neighboring Platte County who had lost a high profile murder case and had been defeated in a subsequent election. The one thing that might save the prosecution, Crossett thought, was the jury.

"Will those 12 jurors, whose names had been printed in the newspaper, want to return home to their neighbors with a 'not guilty' verdict after hearing tape recordings of the guy's confession?" Crossett asked himself.

The trial resumed after the break. Nation called just three witnesses; defense testimony lasted for only 40 minutes. Earlier in the week, before the trial had begun, he told both Insco and the judge that he planned to call seven or eight witnesses. Among those Nation did call was Lieutenant Terry Boyer, who testified that during the two polygraph examinations he had given Melvin, the suspect denied killing Eric but offered to admit it. But Insco cleverly turned Boyer's testimony to damage Reynolds' case. While the prosecutor did not object to the first part of Boyer's testimony, he did raise an objection when Nation asked Boyer for the results of his polygraph tests. Because the tests are not admissible in court, Judge Connett sustained the objection, and the jury was not told that Melvin had passed the tests. Instead, the jurors could assume that Reynolds had failed them.

Melvin's friend Bunny Terry testified that she had seen Reynolds the night the boy was missing and that Reynolds had told her that he was unaware the crime had occurred. One reporter who covered the trial said Terry could not have convinced "a fly to leave her sandwich."

Jeffrey Davey and Carl Simpson, who had earlier told investigators that they had seen a bigger, older man walking with a boy who matched Eric's description, were not called. Neither was Etta Anderson, who could have been a reluctant alibi witness for Reynolds. Nation said later he thought that the jurors had been aware enough of the case and that they knew that Melvin did not look anything like the man who had been the early suspect in the case. He also said that Davey could not positively identify the little boy that he saw as Eric Christgen.

"He might have done Melvin more harm than good," Nation said later.

Nation did call Melvin, whose testimony was anticlimactic. In one- or two-word answers to Nation's questions, Melvin said he could not remember what he did on May 26, 1978, that he knew he did not kill the Christgen boy, and that he admitted doing it because he was scared of the police. Nation asked only 11 minutes' worth of questions of Melvin on direct examination. In his cross examination, Insco extracted from Reynolds an admission that the police had not beaten or threatened him physically. Reynolds admitted that his voice was on the taped confession, but stated that what he had said was not the truth.

When Reynolds was finished on the stand, Nation rested his case. At 9:00 A.M. on Friday, October 12, three days after the trial began, Insco delivered his closing arguments. He reiterated the facts the jury had heard and wove them together convincingly.

"Melvin Lee Reynolds told you he abducted and sexually assaulted Eric Christgen. He told you things only the real killer would know. He described in minute, painful detail just exactly how he did it. And then Melvin Lee Reynolds showed exactly the spot where the body was found on May 27, 1978."

He told the jury that the life of a healthy, four-year-old blond boy had just begun, and noted Eric's desire to enjoy a cloudless spring day on a sliding board.

Then Insco gave the police resounding credit for bringing the killer of Eric Christgen to justice.

"You heard Sergeant Anderson himself state the reason for the statements: check consistencies, check details, check with witnesses, check other investigators, so they could be sure they had the right person. So they checked and they double-checked. And after all of this, they finally checked again; they took Melvin Lee Reynolds to the scene. Or I should say Melvin Lee Reynolds took them to the scene."

The prosecutor then raised his voice slightly and concluded, "Melvin Lee Reynolds, the man seated there, took a life before it had even started. Melvin Lee Reynolds subjected Eric Christgen to pain and suffering no adult human being should have to endure, let alone a four-year-old child. Melvin Lee Reynolds should never be permitted to walk our streets again. Melvin Lee Reynolds should never be permitted to walk the downtown mall again. And he should be sentenced, and I'm confident he will be sentenced, to life imprisonment for the crime of second degree murder."

Lee Nation attempted to unravel Insco's carefully constructed argument in his final statement to the jury. He focused on the way that the police had questioned Reynolds and described the community pressure to solve the crime. He explained that Reynolds was an easy scapegoat for that purpose.

"The easy way is to say this is a horrible case. It's a bad crime. Everybody out there wants a conviction. My neighbors think this guy did it, and yet, he is sitting there and he made a statement so we'll convict him."

Nation challenged the believability of the state's two key witnesses, Dr. James Bridgens and Sergeant Bob Anderson. Nation said Sergeant Anderson lied on the witness stand when he said he had not threatened Reynolds.

"I think you can all infer from Melvin that he may not be as bright as we are. Listen to his first statement on tape. For 45 minutes he denies the crime. What was he threatened with? You want to get married, Melvin? Are you going to marry your wife in jail? Is she going to wait for you? You know we can make this hard on you, Melvin. We can slap all these charges on you. We can charge you with these crimes, like stealing ten bucks from the lady you talk to everyday. And if we throw you in jail, Melvin, is your girlfriend going to wait?

"That's the head of NOMIS. I believe that the jury should be perturbed when the head of that office comes up here and lies. Now, maybe he was mistaken. But listen to that tape and see what he calls Melvin when Melvin was mistaken: 'You lied, didn't you.' Listen to the tape and see if you hear Anderson saying this, and he denied it on the stand."

Nation told the jury that the day before Melvin led officers to the scene of the crime, he had been shown photographs of it by Anderson.

"Have you ever heard of a false confession?" he asked the jury. "Have you ever heard of people admitting to things they didn't do? It's easy. It was so easy here. Think about it. How many of our boys in Vietnam confessed to war atrocities when they weren't even tortured; they weren't beaten, but they were afraid sometimes to be beaten.

"How many hours was Melvin questioned? Sure he was relieved. How do you get a false confession? Remember the little boy and the little girl in each of you. Remember what it was like being young and afraid; someplace where it's dark; you know you're going to get spanked; you know something is going to happen. Remember the terror.

"Then we have the police saying: You can get hurt. You're going to go to jail. I can help you. It's going to be bad. You're going to be in trouble. We can help you. Can I go to the hospital? Well, I don't know, but maybe. We're going to hurt you. I'm going to help you. Somebody's going to hurt you. Somebody's going to help you. Come on, just tell us.

"How long could any of you continue to deny something. Isn't there a point when every human being asked the same questions over, over, over, over, and over again, and denies, denies, denies; how long before that person says, 'You're going to keep asking me this forever?' "

As he spoke, Nation paced slowly back and forth in front of the jury, looking at its members who were seated on a platform a foot above the level of the courtroom floor. He seemed to study each face as if measuring the effect of his argument.

"Maybe we don't know for sure whether Melvin did it or not. Maybe he might have done it. Maybe you think that in your own mind, maybe he might have done it. But you can't convict people on maybes. This is the biggest case, according to Muehlenbacher, in 20 years in St. Joe. The police have never had an unsolved homicide. Wealthy family. Big deal. What happens if they don't find somebody. The state wants Melvin Reynolds' blood. The state wants him. They want him to get up and go to trial. They ask for life. They want his blood."

Then Lee Nation stopped pacing and stared at the jury for a moment. He raised his voice and said, "They knew all along Melvin was innocent. They knew all along they had a patsy. They weren't even sure after the confession. They let Melvin go. They said, 'Well, go ahead and go, Melvin, we'll pick you up tomorrow.'"

This was Nation's last chance to convince the jury. In criminal trials, the defense gives one argument, the prosecution two. The amount of time they are allotted is the same. When his last turn came in rebuttal, Insco took a position at one corner of the jury box and stayed there to give his final argument. He said Anderson and the other police officers had not lied, but had solicited the absolute truth from Reynolds.

"Ladies and gentlemen of the jury, there was a witness, and that witness was Melvin Lee Reynolds," said Insco. "He told you exactly how he did it. The state has tried in every way to show that this man is guilty beyond a reasonable doubt and given you that amount of evidence; evidence beyond a reasonable doubt that Melvin Lee Reynolds, as he said on tapes which you heard, that he abducted and killed Eric Christgen."

The courtroom was packed. When the lawyers finished their arguments at 10:50 A.M., the judge had to ask the bailiff to forge a path so that the jury could make its way into the deliberating room. While the jury considered the evidence, Melvin was returned to his jail cell to await the verdict. He feared the worst.

Outside in the parking lot under Melvin's window, Bill O'Meara shouted up to his stepson: "We've got a highball waiting for you over in the car as soon as you get out. Pack your stuff and get ready."

"I'm going to be found guilty," Reynolds replied. "You might as well drink it yourself."

At 6:45 P.M., after seven hours of deliberations but only a single ballot, the jury returned. J. Michael Sturgeon, the foreman, handed the verdict to Judge Frank Connett. "We find the defendant, Melvin Lee Reynolds, guilty of murder in the second degree. We fix the punishment at life imprisonment."

The verdict brought celebrations and relief. The prosecutors went out to dinner. Some policemen looked forward to promotions for their work on the Christgen case. St. Joseph was relieved. A demented killer was being removed from the streets. Justice was done.

Norman Steward, the *News-Press* reporter and columnist whose writings had done so much to support Insco, wrote a column praising the Reynolds trial:

"I have never before seen a trial in a murder case which impressed me as much with the sincerity and hard work evidently involved in preparation, presentation and deliberation. In my opinion, no one can say that the defendant did not get a fair trial."

Steward wrote that Nation had done everything possible for Reynolds, and that Anderson had done a conscientious job as well.

"We are lucky to have law enforcement officers who work so hard to protect the innocent as well as to catch the law violators," Steward wrote.

But others were not so sure. Eaton, the police

detective who had never believed in Reynolds'
guilt, felt uncomfortable with the outcome of the
trial. He had been certain that the jury and Reynolds' defense attorney would keep him from being
convicted. He thought about stating publicly that
he believed in Reynolds' innocence. But he held
back, afraid of public ridicule.

A man in Kansas wondered how Reynolds could
be the murderer. The news of Melvin's conviction
traveled all over Missouri and into the neighboring
state, and Maynard Brazeal, the investigative hyp-
notist, read about it. He wondered about the accuracy of the description the witness Jeff Davey had
drowsily given him more than a year earlier.
Brazeal called the St. Joseph Police Department to
ask how close Melvin matched the description
Brazeal had obtained with hypnotism. He hung up
disappointed.

"He's not even close," Brazeal was told.

On January 2, 1980, Reynolds, with Nation
standing beside him, appeared before Judge Connett. Reynolds hoped that perhaps the judge would
reduce the sentence or send him to a mental hospital. Judge Connett sentenced him to a life term in
the Missouri State Penitentiary in Jefferson City.
Nation said Reynolds wore the face of a man who
had just learned he had terminal cancer.

When asked, Reynolds continued to say he was
innocent and that he had been framed, or that he
had framed himself.

"If I were you, I'd be pretty upset about being
sentenced for something I didn't do," a reporter
said to him.

"I am. But what can I do about it? There's not a
damn thing I can do about it right now. What really bothers me is that whoever did it, they're still
out on the streets, laughing about it."

CHAPTER SIX

"If you go in on a child molesting case, then most of the time you do not live."
— A prisoner telling Melvin Reynolds what he could expect in prison

A BLEAK WINTER SCENE PASSED BY THE WINDOW OF the gray police cruiser taking Melvin Reynolds to prison. In his last glimpses of freedom, he saw deserted streets in lonely, little country towns. Between the hamlets, fields wore coats of ice punctured with the stubs from last year's corn crop. At one point near Boonville, they passed along the bluffs of the Missouri River and the sight reminded him of the day nearly 11 months earlier when he had accompanied the police to the place along MacArthur Drive where Eric's body had been found. The scenery did nothing to distract him from the fearful thoughts that had plagued him since his days in the Buchanan County Jail. Thinking about the horrors that awaited him nearly drove him to suicide.

By the time the unmarked car swung around the Missouri Capitol's circular drive and turned for the prison two blocks away, the frightening stories Melvin had heard swirled through his mind. His slight build and youthful appearance would make Reynolds a likely target for the brutality of other inmates who would try to dominate or possess him. Reynolds had braced himself. But going to prison for the murder of a child dangerously aggravated his situation. Among criminals, a molester or a killer of children is the most despicable character of all. When he arrived at the Missouri State Penitentiary on January 8, 1980, Melvin Reynolds occupied the lowest rung of the prison ladder.

"If you go in on a child molesting case, then most of the time, you do not live," he remembered being told by cellmates in the Buchanan County Jail.

He had heard about the "shanks," long thin knives fashioned out of strips of metal discarded from the license plate plant, sharpened to a stiletto's point and fitted with a wooden handle. That's what Melvin feared, a cold shank driven into his chest by a nameless inmate. Melvin had also heard that the child molesters who were not killed in prison were frequent targets of sexual attack.

Melvin was about to enter one of the meanest lockups in the country. The Missouri State Penitentiary is a formidable fortress of rock walls and barbed wire fences. Guards carrying shotguns monitor the prisoners' movements from watchtowers. Most of the prison's buildings consist of antiquated 19th century structures. They are crowded, dingy, ovenlike in the summer and freezing in the winter. It is a maximum security institution, notorious for being the last place for convicts who are unmanageable elsewhere.

Once inside the gate, Melvin placed his watch, wallet and rings on a table. They were placed in an envelope, to be returned to him when he was released. That would never happen, unless his life sentence was reduced. The thought of spending the rest of his life behind bars brought tears to his eyes. He was stripped, showered and sprayed for lice. His long brown hair was cut to his scalp.

"Maybe the Lord has got His reason for putting me down here," he thought. "My mother has done a lot for me in her life, and, well, so has my stepfather, as far as that goes. And all I've ever did was cause her trouble. I love my mother with all my heart."

He began to weep.

After he had put on his gray prison uniform, Melvin was fingerprinted and photographed. He was assigned to H-Hall, a housing unit where inmates are kept during a 30-day evaluation period. He would remain there until a classification board reassigned him to a permanent cell. The board would decide whether Melvin could mix with the general prison population, or should be kept for his own safety in the Special Treatment Unit (STU). The unit would give Melvin protective custody, safe from the rest of the prison's 2,000 inmates. But it would amount to nearly total isolation. In STU, he would stay alive, but could he stand a life sentence in virtual solitary confinement? Melvin debated whether he should ask the board for protective custody or take his chances among the rest of the prisoners.

On the day he appeared before the board, one of its members suggested that he might need protection, since he was a child murderer. Melvin interrupted him.

"Let me tell you something. I don't give a damn what my case—what it says. I didn't do it."

Nevertheless, the board recommended he be assigned to STU. Melvin said he preferred the general population.

"I'll take my chances," he said.

After three weeks of classifications and tests in H-Hall, Melvin was moved to general population. His cellmate was a muscular 200-pounder named

Tim. Melvin braced himself for the worst, but Tim did not bother him. Instead, Tim offered friendship and protection. Another inmate, a boxer named Willie, did the same. Melvin began to believe his decision to live among the other inmates was the right one. But within a few months, both men were transferred. Melvin was left on his own.

He had been assigned a job in the prison kitchen, and it was there that he was given his official initiation into prison life. It was not much different from the one he had received at the boys' home 16 years earlier. Six prisoners jumped him one morning in a storage room where he had gone for spices. He was gagged, and each one took turns raping him. It happened again a day later, this time in a trash bin. Then, once more, in the gym. Each time, six or seven prisoners attacked him. The inmates were different every time.

Melvin was horrified, but he feared that if he reported the attacks, he would be killed. It seemed as if every inmate in the institution took turns jumping him. He wondered whether the attacks were organized. He suspected someone had gone through his records and had spread the word that he was a child killer. But it was more likely that the other inmates had learned about Melvin's crime through detective magazines, which are popular prison reading. In the months following his conviction, two of them had printed the details of the Eric Christgen case.

After the initial attacks, an inmate raped Melvin in the shower. The inmate claimed Melvin for himself. For awhile, Melvin accepted the protection that went along with the horrible arrangement. Eventually, he complained to a guard. He was branded as a snitch, which brought him a different kind of trouble. Melvin was warned that several inmates had decided to stab him to death. To Melvin, the rumor had a special kind of vividness, since he had expected such an attack all along. Just a few weeks before the warning, he had witnessed a prisoner having his throat cut. He considered remaining in his cell, never coming out. Again he thought about his previous decision against the protection of STU. But he thought he would look foolish by begging for it after having turned it down before.

Melvin had been transferred from the kitchen to the garbage detail. Early one morning, he and four other inmates clung to the side of the trash truck as it made the rounds of the 47-acre institution. Vince, one of the inmates riding with him, told Melvin that he did not have long to live because he had killed a little boy.

"I don't give a damn," Reynolds said. "I didn't do it."

The two men began grappling on the side of the truck. Vince was bigger and stronger. Melvin lost his grip, and at the same moment, the other inmate gave him a shove. Melvin fell backward, landing with his entire weight on the back of his skull. He awoke more than an hour later in the prison hospital. He was later released after doctors found no severe injuries.

A few days later, Melvin was in a recreation yard, watching an intramural baseball game. A spectator confronted Melvin with the familiar accusation.

"You're a child killer."

"I'm sorry to tell you I'm not," Melvin replied. The two argued. Melvin frantically tried to convince the man while other inmates stood nearby. Five prisoners attacked him. He was kicked in the stomach, head, back and groin. He spent three weeks in the hospital recovering from his injuries.

Lee Nation had begun work on an appeal of Melvin's conviction to the Missouri Supreme Court. But the process took months. The fact that Melvin's family had no more money for his legal defense contributed to the delay. Nation said he would continue to pursue the appeal; the family could pay him later. Nation believed he had good ground for an appeal in the way that Judge Connett had selected the jury. But before the appeal could be filed, a transcript of the trial had to be prepared, which took money too. Eventually, the court determined that Melvin was an indigent, and waived the fee for the transcript.

Corrections officers told Melvin that if he did not win his appeal, he would have to spend 30 to 40 years in prison because of the nature of his crime.

Since its gray rock walls were erected in 1836, the Missouri State Penitentiary had been the scene of unspeakable acts of brutality. In fact, for all his fear, pain and loneliness, Melvin Reynolds was fortunate when compared to other young men who had come to live in the maximum security prison. The stories that Melvin had heard about homemade knives piercing the flesh of smaller and weaker men were true. The threat of violence constantly lurked beneath the surface of prison life. After a brief scuffle, a man would lie bleeding. The weapon might be found, but it was never "on" anyone. It would be wiped clean. The witnesses, if there were any, would never "see" anything.

CHAPTER SEVEN

"We have an inmate presently confined in solitary confinement whom we believe caused your husband's death; however, we must secure sufficient evidence to prove our suspicion."
—Warden E.V. Nash discussing his suspicion that Charles Hatcher murdered a fellow inmate

NINETEEN YEARS BEFORE MELVIN REYNOLDS ENtered the Missouri State Penitentiary, a young man was murdered there in a way that was identical to what Melvin had imagined his fate would be. The murderer was the man whose crimes caused Melvin's imprisonment. The victim was Jerry Lee Tharrington, and he was a special "brother" to Melvin Reynolds. What bound Melvin Reynolds and Jerry Tharrington together was their relationship to the third man. In different ways, his evil shattered them both, and it also had the effect of freeing each of them from prison.

Jerry Lee Tharrington, like Melvin Reynolds, did not belong in the Missouri State Penitentiary. It was not that Tharrington was innocent of the break-in that he had admitted in a confession. But he belonged at a prison farm or medium security institution. He had only two years to serve, and if his burglary had been committed today, he would be back on the streets with probation and a stern warning from the judge. But it was 1960; judges were less lenient and the prisons had more space.

When Tharrington entered the institution on January 4, 1961, prison officials recognized that he would need protection from the general con-wise population. They assigned him the operation of an elevator that delivered foodstuffs to the main prison kitchen. With this job, he would have minimal contact with other convicts. But being kept out of the way also made Tharrington vulnerable.

Jerry's ticket to prison was $175 in mechanic's tools that he had stolen from a garage. The burglary took place on November 16, 1960, five days before his 26th birthday. When state police arrested him, he admitted the crime, explaining that he could not find a job and he needed the money. He told the police that his wife, Shirley, had lost a baby the month before, that he owed $350 in doctor bills, $750 in funeral expenses and payments on his car. Most of the story was true, and officers might have accepted it if Jerry had not left his job in St. Louis without word and been unemployed for the last month.

When Jerry Lee Tharrington arrived at the Missouri State Penitentiary, he had a mischievous grin on his face and 19 cents in his pocket. He had received a two-year sentence for the Raymondville burglary, but hoped that with good behavior he would be out much sooner. He was an elf compared to the rest of the prison population; he was five feet, six inches tall and weighed only 124 pounds. Like all incoming prisoners, he underwent a battery of tests to measure his chances for reform. He scored above average in the mental exams. The caseworker who interviewed him recommended Jerry for a job in the prison print shop.

Although Jerry wanted to be assigned to the print shop and was recommended for it, he began work on February 2 on the kitchen elevator. He spent his days hauling meat from the cold storage plant up to the kitchen and taking large pots and pans down to an outside dock where they could be washed.

Because his sentence was so short, the state Board of Probation and Parole had begun to consider plans to release him provisionally. On February 20, it scheduled a parole hearing for July. He had no conduct violations, and the kitchen supervisors turned in good reports on him.

On May 22, Jerry asked to be released from the maximum security institution.

Four days later, Jerry was interviewed on the request and at the same time, information was collected for a pre-parole progress report. Things were looking up. He was told that he could be considered for outside work "in about a month."

Jerry had begun to think about freedom again, which could occur as soon as August. His experience in prison had taught him a lesson, and he made big plans for his future. He told a caseworker he wanted to enter Dismas House, a halfway house in St. Louis. At that time, his wife Shirley was living with relatives in Jackson, a small southeast Missouri city. As he scratched the last days of June off the calendar on his cell wall, Jerry grew optimistic. July would be a big month for him. The farm assignment was scheduled to come this month, and possibly the parole hearing too.

And with a wife like Shirley Faye, maybe the dream would come true. She had written him regularly, one-page letters on loose leaf paper. The last one was written June 29. It was postmarked June 30, and became Shirley's last chance to communicate with her husband.

Thursday June 29, 1961

To My Dearest Darling Jerry,

Say, I have a seckret that I would like to tell you and the whole wide world, I Love You.

Well Darling after tomorrow I will have a week in at the shoe factory, but I wont get a pay check until next week darn it anyway. Bernice came over after me tonight, we all went down to the school yard and played badmiton for a little while, then we went over to the park to watch the little boys play ball. It was a good game. Indians 12 and the Yankies 8. The umpire was rotten. When the ball should have been a strike, he called them ball, then all of the balls was so close to the ground he called them strikes. Oh, that made me mad. I felt like telling him off, but I didn't.

Honey, that is how I spent my evening tonight. I just wish you could have been here with me.

Darling this is the only sheet of paper that I have left so I guess I'll close for tonight. May God Bless and Keep You Safe and Guide You all through the Night.

I'm sending You All of My
Love Darling, Your Wife
Shirley F. Tharrington

Jerry Tharrington never got the chance to read the letter. On Sunday, July 2, Jerry was found lying on his back on the kitchen loading dock, his lifeless eyes staring at an evening sky. A guard in the kitchen had noticed that the elevator was unmanned and after a brief search, Jerry was found with the point of a "shank" protruding from his chest. It was about 6:00 P.M. There had been no witnesses. Jerry had taken food containers to the dock to be cleaned, and he had been stabbed from behind, the knife entering his back below his left shoulder blade, coursing diagonally through his heart and exiting his skinny chest just below the right breast. He had been hit quickly and was dead before he knew it. Jerry was taken to the prison hospital. J.J. Maloncy, an inmate who worked in the prison hospital, said later that Tharrington had been raped.

Beyond the shock and grief expressed by his family, Jerry Tharrington's death attracted little notice. Prison stabbings were common. Every so often, one of the stabbings proved fatal. The incident earned five paragraphs on the front page of the *Jefferson City Post Tribune*, which saved its big headline that day for another violent death, Ernest Hemingway's.

Jerry's family pestered Warden E. V. Nash with questions about who killed him. Willis Tharrington, who had disowned his son months before, came forward to collect the body. Nash wrote to each member of Jerry's family, including his wife, Shirley:

> It has been determined that the instrument used to assault your husband was stolen from the office of our cold storage operation. At present, I cannot advise as to why your husband was attacked. We have an inmate presently confined in solitary confinement whom we believe caused your husband's death; however, we must secure sufficient evidence to prove our suspicion. As soon as we can definitely ascertain that this inmate was the person involved, he will be prosecuted.

While no one had seen Jerry Tharrington's murder, nearly everyone in the prison knew who had done it. It was easy to figure out. There were only so many suspects, and it was simply a process of elimination to narrow down the list. Tharrington's murder became known within the institution as "the cold storage killing," and within days, Major B.J. Poiry, a corrections officer, determined who was responsible. Poiry questioned 11 inmates who worked in the kitchen and the meat locker, and each identified the killer, although the inmates did not want their names connected in writing with the accusations because they were terrified of the man they were fingering. The inmates told Poiry that the man worked in the kitchen and was the only one missing at the time Jerry was killed.

The man who had been singled out was named Charles Ray Hatcher. After studying Hatcher's criminal record, Poiry suspected that he was capable of shoving a knife into Tharrington's back. Hatcher was a career criminal type who began by stealing cars and eventually turned to violence. His most recent offense—the one that sent him to the penitentiary for his latest tour—involved an attempt to abduct a newspaper delivery boy, using a butcher knife. The boy had fled and called the police. Hatcher was arrested a short time later. The crime had taken place in St. Joseph.

Poiry interrogated Hatcher, who stubbornly denied the killing. He would say nothing else. Poiry told Warden Nash that Hatcher had killed Tharrington, but that it could not be proven in court. They decided the best they could do to punish him for the moment was to put Hatcher in solitary confinement. They hoped it would soften him up, so that he would agree to talk about the killing. To most inmates, solitary—known to prisoners as "the hole" and known to officers as "administrative segregation"—is second only to death row in institutional nightmares.

When Hatcher was sent to solitary on August 21, 1961, the unit was known as "E-hall," a dungeon located in the basement of a cellblock. Heavy steel mesh covered the painted windows, and no natural light reached the inmates who soon lost track of night and day. Naked lightbulbs, that were never turned off, hung suspended from 17-foot high ceilings of peeling paint. They were too dim to read by but bright enough to keep one awake at night. The noise was deafening, as inmates attempted to carry on conversations between cells by shouting through their steel doors. Meals were eaten in the cells. Breakfast, lunch and supper marked the passage of time. The food came on metal trays shoved under the heavy cell doors across a concrete floor where cockroaches scurried. The only recreation consisted of a twice weekly, one-hour walk in a special, fenced-in yard. There were no trees there, and the birds struggled to make their nests in the crooks where the brackets supporting the barbed wire joined the wire mesh of the fence.

Some corrections officers believe that a man kept in solitary confinement will reflect on his sins and begin his own reformation. But the environment drives most prisoners to the brink of suicide. Men emerge from the darkness a little meaner than before. But Charles Hatcher thrived in this environment. In the musty darkness of his cell, he fed on anger, hate and memories that would have haunted an ordinary man. The picture of Tharrington lying bleeding on a dock was only one of the memories.

Over the deafening sounds of clanging steel doors and screaming curses, Hatcher carried on private conversations with the demons who visited and administered to him. They had commanded him before, and now they offered him reassurance and comfort. The stark deprivations of solitary had little effect on him. His existence up until that time had taught him to adapt and survive. His life had begun the same year as the Depression, and he grew up poverty stricken in an area where economic hardship was already the way of life. He learned about death very early. Solitary confinement couldn't throw much more at him than what he had beaten in life.

The other inmates were glad Hatcher had been separated from them. There were plenty of tough characters in the institution, but Charlie terrified them in a way that mere killers did not. He said and did things that set him apart. Between long, brooding episodes of silence, he told them stories of things he had done, which if true, indicated his crimes were cursed with a certain demonic possession. He was charming and intelligent at times, but there seemed to be a layer of unexpected violence lurking just beneath the surface. The crimes he described had strong sexual overtones. To his face, the other prisoners were respectful and accommodating, but behind his back, they called him "Crazy Charlie."

CHAPTER EIGHT

"I realize something's wrong with me and I need psychological treatment."

—Charles Hatcher

BY THE SUMMER OF 1961, WHEN HE MURDERED Jerry Tharrington, Charles Ray Hatcher had become more than just a tough rock-hardened convict. The perverse sexual behavior that was promoted behind prison walls had created emotional imbalances in him. He had just celebrated his 32nd birthday, and he had spent almost half of those years in Missouri jails and prisons. He had taken his first trip to the penitentiary when he was 18. His first trip to prison was supposed to "reform" him. But it had not. It had merely added to the bitterness, distrust and hate that he had displayed from his childhood.

Hatcher was the product of a broken home, but before his parents separated, he was influenced by his alcoholic father and unstable mother. From his birth until adulthood, Charles received attention from his mother that his brothers did not. His mother believed in him, despite his criminal ways, and over the years, each time he was released from prison, he would return to her. He adored his mother, but caused her much misery. He stole from her; threatened her and caused her many sleepless nights. But she always forgave him. Over the years, with different husbands and different homes in several small Missouri towns, she offered her youngest and special son a haven. She was always willing to help him pick up the pieces of his life.

Charlie's father drank heavily and physically abused his children. Charles Hatcher experienced a painful childhood, and grew up to inflict pain on children. Charlie's father moved the family constantly to keep ahead of creditors and the law. Charles Hatcher thus developed an aimless life pattern, filled with deception and violence.

Charles Ray Hatcher came into the world at 4:00 P.M., on July 16, 1929, the fourth and last child of Jesse and Lula Hatcher. There was not much waiting for him. Three boys had already arrived to a father and mother who did not have much to offer. His ex-convict father was 42 at the time; his mother 24. He was born in Mound City, 34 miles north of St. Joseph. Before Charles was 10 years old, the family had lived in a dozen rented houses and farms in Graham, Fillmore, Maitland and New Point, settlements that dot the rolling countryside that make up Holt, Andrew and Nodaway counties. This constant movement set a pattern for Charles Hatcher's later life, when he roamed the country like a lost nomad.

It was not just the physical side of his life that was threadbare and chaotic. Emotionally, Charles Hatcher had been planted in sterile soil. He was the last in a line of demanding babies who could not be satisfied with what was available from Jesse and Lula. They had no energy or will left—if there had been any to start with—to discipline him or provide him with the kind of emotional support he needed. Jesse and Lula, who snatched their pleasures where they could, had never taught their youngest son the difference between right and wrong. Perhaps because of this, Charles was unable to develop warm, genuine relationships with others, and instead, acquired a callous disregard for the rights and feelings of others.

Charles Hatcher did well in school. The criminal cleverness that he displayed in later life was a logical extension of the mental adroitness he exhibited in grade school.

Some psychiatrists theorized that Charles Hatcher inherited his criminality from his father. While Charles, his brothers and their mother are remembered as being quiet, Jesse Hatcher was another story. Jesse and his younger brother, Grover Hatcher, had served time together in the Missouri State Penitentiary, and neighbors feared them both, especially after they had been drinking.

As a child, Charles Hatcher could have learned to imitate the actions of his uncle and his father. But could his evil be tracked to his genes? Psychiatrists have said that children of petty criminals seem to inherit a tendency toward anti-social behavior. But that tendency would have touched Charles' brothers, also. One of them, young Jesse, did serve some time in the Missouri State Penitentiary, but none of the boys grew up to commit the atrocities that Charles did.

Charles Hatcher's family connections became more tenuous as the years went by. In his later life, he said he never knew his father. In the end, he disowned his family, and they him.

Psychiatrists would later agree that Hatcher's family had been a fundamental influence on his psychotic and criminal behavior. He was raised in a one-parent dominated clan and his father drank and abused his children. But they theorized that one traumatic experience that Charles Hatcher encountered at the age of six may have begun his fascination with death.

Arthur Allen Hatcher had been born in Maitland, just 15 months before his brother, Charles. He had been in school for two years and had just celebrated his eighth birthday when the accident occurred. It was a windy spring Sunday, the kind that boys, no matter how poor, can enjoy. They had made a kite and were flying it with copper wire they had unwound from the generator of an old Model T Ford. They argued over who would fly it first, but Jesse, being the oldest, easily won the honors.

As the kite danced in the breeze the boys took turns passing the tugging wire from hand to hand. The kite went from Jesse to Floyd and then to Arthur. Just as he was the last in line for the clothes they wore, Charles would be the last to feel the thrill of the kite straining at the wire. But before Arthur handed it to him, the wire made contact with a high voltage power line attached to a pole along the road near the home. Arthur was electrocuted. One of the boys ran up to a neighbor's house to call the doctor. It was shortly after 1:00 P.M. The Holt County coroner came and pronounced Arthur dead. Charles had witnessed the entire tragedy. Psychiatrists believed that this event might have left Charles Hatcher with an abiding sense of guilt and a deep seated need for punishment.

When Charlie was 16 years old, he moved with his mother and her third husband to St. Joseph. In those years immediately following World War II, St. Joseph was a good place to live. The city prospered and jobs were plentiful, even for an unskilled worker like Charles Hatcher. He set pins in a bowling alley and washed dishes. In the fall of 1947, he got a job driving a truck and hauling logs for the Iowa-Missouri Walnut Co. Hatcher's job lasted just two weeks. On the night of October 9, 1947, the company reported to the police that one of its trucks had been stolen. Hatcher brought the truck back the next morning. He was drunk, he said, and admitted taking the truck. He was given a two-year suspended sentence.

It was the first of many times in his criminal life that Charles Hatcher would be given a second chance. But shortly after the first of the year, Hatcher earned his first trip to the penitentiary. He was working at the St. Francis Hotel in St. Joseph, washing dishes and doing odd jobs. He stole a 1937 Buick, and on February 5, 1948, his probation was revoked. He was sentenced to two years in the Missouri State Penitentiary. Charles Hatcher was received at the prison for the first time on February 7, 1948. It was the first of many appearances.

He was 18 and still growing. He weighed 143 pounds and was five feet, eight inches tall, with dark brown hair, brown eyes and a fair complexion. He found that prison had an atmosphere of monotony, futility, hate, loneliness and sexual frustration. He was subjected to the same sexual humiliations that Melvin Reynolds later experienced, and they deepened the mean streak that already existed within him. If he had been required to serve his full sentence, Hatcher would not have been released from the penitentiary until February 1950. If he had to serve three-quarters time, his release date would have been August 1949. But Hatcher, in the first of many breaks he would receive from the corrections system, was set free on June 8, 1949. Before the year was out, he was back in prison for forging a $10 check at a service station. After serving additional time for an attempted escape and a burglary, he was released on July 14, 1954.

When they released Hatcher from the penitentiary in the summer of 1954, the probation officers wondered how long it would be before they saw him again. He never seemed to profit from his experiences. Shortly after the first of the year, he fell back into the familiar pattern. On February 5, 1955, he stole a 1951 Ford in Orrick, Missouri, a town about 50 miles east of Kansas City. He was sentenced to four years for the car theft and for another escape attempt, an additional two. In September 1955, he returned to the penitentiary to serve the fifth and sixth sentences of his criminal career. He was 26 years old. Hatcher was released on March 18, 1959.

That was the year the uglier side of Charles Hatcher emerged. Up until then, all of his crimes had involved property—thefts, forgeries and burglaries. The violent, physically aggressive nature of his personality, which was there all the time but unrecorded, made its presence felt in a way that would mark his later crimes. It was the year of his first documented attack upon children, and it marked a sharp turn in his criminal life. On June 26, Hatcher attempted to abduct Steven Pellham, a 16-year-old newspaper boy, by threatening the boy with a butcher knife. After Pellham reported the crime, Hatcher was arrested when the car he was driving (and had stolen) was identified by police.

The crime that exposed the darker side of his character was not explored in any great detail. What prompted him to attempt to grab a defenseless boy on a dark and lonely street? What had he planned to do with him? These questions went unanswered. Hatcher was not talking. When they arraigned him on the assault charges in Buchanan County Circuit Court, he remained mute.

He was charged with auto theft and assault with intent to kill and was tried in November. A young judge heard his case. Frank Connett Jr. had been on the circuit court bench for less than a year. During his two-day trial, Hatcher remained mute. He was convicted and sentenced to five years' imprisonment under the Habitual Criminal Act. On November 21, while waiting to be transported to the penitentiary, Hatcher unsuccessfully attempted to break out of the Buchanan County jail. On November 25, 1959, he arrived at the Missouri State Penitentiary for his fourth tour.

Hatcher had begun to stake his claim to the title of the most notorious criminal in northwest Missouri since Jesse James. His crimes, though not nearly as daring, had touched as many counties. Before he was finished, they would be more ruthless and depraved.

In "E-3," administrative segregation, the darkness of solitary confinement, the "hole" of the Missouri State Penitentiary, Charles Hatcher thought about the forces that were driving him. He had been placed there in solitary in August 1961 on orders of Warden Nash and Major Poiry. Nash included a "hold for investigation" memo in Hatcher's file, along with an inter-office communication that said Hatcher was to serve his full sentence until November 24, 1964. Prison officials felt that if they could not prosecute Hatcher for Tharrington's death, they would hold him for as long as possible. They hoped solitary would soften him up, make him talk. After nearly five months, Hatcher sent out a signal. He seemed to be asking for help. On the face of his request, Hatcher sought treatment for mental problems. The note was addressed to Major Poiry on official prison stationery and was dated January 18, 1962.

Dear Sir:

First of all, I want to say this isn't a skam to get out of E-Hall. I realize something's wrong with me and I need psychological treatment. I've wrote to Mr. Rook but never heard anything. I hope you can help me out on this as I do need help.

Yours Truly
Charles Hatcher

Leroy Rook was the prison psychologist, and Hatcher's letter was marked to his attention. Rook made two telephone calls and learned that Hatcher had been in solitary on suspicion of killing Tharrington. He forwarded Hatcher's letter to Warden Nash, but attached his own memo stating that he had not received the letter referred to by Hatcher in his note. Rook believed Hatcher was scheming to get out of administrative segregation; possibly trying to get out of the prison entirely and into a state mental hospital. Rook wrote to the warden eight days after Hatcher's request was made. Hatcher's letter was attached to it.

The attached letter is forwarded for your consideration. It has been Poiry to Lock to Rook.

I called E-3 since the man has not written me a letter which I received. I was told that, according to their records, he has been held since 8/21/61 for investigation, indefinite, signature of B. J. Poiry.

So then, I called Lock, who looked up the record and reports that he is 'your man' held in connection with the cold storage killing. Hence this referral.

Psychologically, the give away is in Hatcher's opening phrase, . . . 'this isn't a skam to get out of E-Hall.' Such a gambit is revealing since, as S. Freud taught, there are no negatives in the unconscious.

Leroy H. Rook

Based on Rook's diagnosis of his motives, prison officials did not agree to Hatcher's request for psychiatric treatment. They believed his request was just another attempt at artful manipulation by a career convict. Prison officials chose not to talk to Hatcher about his problems, even though through such discussions Hatcher might have admitted killing Tharrington and might have agreed to voluntary psychiatric commitment for the crime. If prison officials had responded to him, Hatcher might have been put on another path and perhaps things would have been different later on.

Instead, prison officials let Hatcher smolder in solitary confinement for nearly another year. It was not until the last week of October 1962, when Nash and Poiry realized they could not break the hard man from St. Joe, that he was returned to the prison's general population. Nash later rescinded his order specifying that Hatcher was to serve his full sentence. It was cut back to three-quarters time.

On August 24, 1963, Hatcher was released from the Missouri State Penitentiary. He would return again, many years later, when the circle that connected him to Melvin Reynolds was completed. The murder of Jerry Lee Tharrington was never officially solved. The man who had killed him learned an important lesson. Something as big as a murder charge could be beaten if there were no witnesses and you kept your mouth shut.

CHAPTER NINE

"I went with a man to get some ice cream."
 —Gilbert Martinez, a child molester's victim

ON FRIDAY, AUGUST 29, 1969, SIX YEARS AFTER Charles Hatcher's release from the Missouri State Penitentiary, and nine years before Eric Christgen's disappearance and murder, police officers in San Francisco were dealing with a missing child report. Officers Marion Jackson and Robert Guinn were looking for five-year-old Gilbert Martinez (not his real name). They had received a desperate telephone call from the boy's mother, Valenia, who said that her son had been abducted. Valenia Martinez said she had arrived home at about 5:00 P.M. At that time, Gilbert had been playing with other children on the block. But when she checked on her boy a short time later, she found he was gone. Denise Lieb, a six-year old neighbor with whom Gilbert had been playing, told Valenia that a man had approached them at a little park up the street. He had offered her candy to induce her to go with him.

"I didn't go, but Gilbert did," Denise said. The horrified mother immediately called the police and described her missing son. Officers Jackson and Guinn were looking for a dark complected Hispanic boy, three feet tall and weighing 50 to 60 pounds, in the area of 19th and Valencia Street. Gilbert had last been observed walking south with the man on Mission Street.

For Gilbert, a lifetime of nightmares had begun. A man had offered to take him to get some ice cream, but the torture had started almost immediately. First, there was the grueling, forced march to the remote site of his anguish. Then came the gagging and the painful probing. And finally, there was the incessant, methodical beating that knocked him to the brink of unconsciousness. Therapists later would assure Gilbert repeatedly that the incident was not his fault. His only mistake had been to occupy the same place and time as a man in the midst of a violent obsession. Like Eric Christgen, Gilbert had become a victim of opportunity. And Gilbert would have suffered Eric's fate had it not been for Roger Galatoire.

After work, Roger Galatoire returned to his home and had decided to exercise his aging dog with a walk up Bernal Heights, a steep hill four miles south of downtown San Francisco. Bernal Heights is a remote oasis inside the crowded city. From there, you can see the major buildings of San Francisco and San Bruno Mountain. At 7:00 P.M. there was still plenty of daylight remaining. At the point where Folsom Street crested the hill, Galatoire led his dog off the pavement and down a path that cut through a vacant lot. As he walked down the trail, he saw a man lying on the ground a few yards away. He did not pay close attention to him, thinking he was either drunk or asleep. The man did not notice Galatoire.

Galatoire followed the path for another two blocks and then turned around. He began retracing his route for home. When he passed the man again, Galatoire noticed he was in a sitting position and thought he saw something between the man's legs. At the same moment, he heard a thumping sound like a watermelon being struck. Suddenly, Galatoire was shocked to see a nude, male child jump up from between the man's legs.

As he later testified in court, Galatoire said, "The boy stood up, and when he did, the man grabbed the boy by the neck and forced him to the ground with a thud, with an actual thud. He grabbed him by the neck and threw him violently to the ground and began beating him."

The boy Galatoire saw was very small. He thought he was a Mexican boy, and that the man was going to kill him. Reacting instinctively, Galatoire sprinted away, hoping to find a telephone to call the police. Galatoire believed that the man had not seen him. He moved quickly, fearing that any delay could mean the difference between life and death for the boy. The dog could not keep up, so he scooped it into his arms and carried it as he raced three blocks to Bradford Street. At the first house he found, Galatoire called the police. Within minutes, four officers met Galatoire and he led them quickly back to the place where he had seen the man, hoping they had arrived in time. The police found the man lying on his back with his underwear around his thighs. His genitals were exposed and the man held the child's face there. When the man saw the uniformed officers, he threw the sobbing and frightened boy off his lap.

Gilbert had been beaten black and blue. Police found bruises on his cheek and forehead, swelling of the neck and gross anal bleeding. "There was blood all over the boy," Officer Paul Brown reported. "There was blood in the buttock area and blood on his legs. The blood was not centered in one place, but there were marks of it on various parts of the body."

As the officers collected the boy's clothing and dressed him, Brown arrested the silent man who stumbled drunkenly as he hitched up his pants. He appeared to be in his forties. Several days' growth of beard darkened his sullen face. His eyes peered from two narrow slits set wide apart from a thick, broad nose. He was a sinister looking man with heavy eyebrows and a thick head of greasy hair, and the officers wondered how such an evil looking character could have convinced Gilbert into going with him. He had thick arms and a narrow trunk, and appeared to the detectives to be in good physical condition. The man would not answer any questions except to say his name was Albert Price.

Two of the officers took Price to the Ingleside police station while the other pair went with the boy to the hospital. When officers began to advise Price of his right to remain silent, he began yelling and screaming incoherently. At the station, the police attempted to take his picture, but Price ran to a corner of the room and stood facing the wall, making whimpering noises. When the officers attempted to book him, Price's behavior became even more bizarre.

"The suspect, while waiting to be booked, took a double-edge razor blade from his pocket and cut his left wrist," Officer Brown said. Price was taken to Alemany Emergency Hospital, where the cut on his wrist was sutured.

Police thought that they had removed everything from the man's possession. They had found a five-foot length of wire in his pocket and a billfold that contained identification for a man named Hobert Prater. It was not until the next day, Saturday, that Price was released for processing. He was finally booked, but he refused to answer questions. Two decades of dealing with lawmen had taught the man who called himself Albert Ralph Price that the less said the better. Better still if they think you're crazy.

"We attempted to interrogate the suspect Albert Price at the city prison, where he is presently being held in isolation," wrote one of the officers who investigated the attack on the child. "However, we were unable to do so because of his comatose condition. This may be due to the fact that he attempted suicide after his arrest. He sat in a corner of the cell and was totally unresponsive."

Gilbert, meanwhile, had been taken to Central Emergency Hospital, where Dr. Curtis Long examined him and found he had contusions on his forehead and left cheek. His neck was swollen. His anus had been lacerated, causing gross bleeding. But Long's report covered only the injuries that could be seen. They would heal. But the invisible hurt, the emotional trauma that would linger, was there, too. The police realized the extent of the trauma when they tried to question the boy.

"We were unable to interview the victim as he was very shy and refused to talk about the incident," Brown reported. "The only thing he would say was 'I went with a man to get some ice cream.'"

The case was turned over to the juvenile bureau. Inspector Kelly Waterfield, who took personal interest in the case, said that the attack on Gilbert was "the worst case of child molesting" he had ever seen. Over the years, he had witnessed the devastating effect child abuse had wrought on victims and their families. For the lucky children, whose encounters were brief and nonviolent, the scars were barely visible. They might have trouble later making friends with kids their own age, or their performance in school might be affected. But generally, they would survive the experience.

Other children, whose circumstances were more violent, would have periodic nightmares. Over the long term, some victims might have trouble dealing with authority. Documented studies have shown that a high proportion of drug offenders and prostitutes were victims of sexual abuse as children. Finally, there were those children who never came back alive. Victims who disappeared one day and whose broken, strangled and violated bodies were found days, weeks or months later.

San Francisco police wondered about the crazy man they had locked up in City Prison. For several days, he had been hospitalized for attempting suicide. Albert Price had then been returned to police custody, and now sat in a corner of his cell, staring at the floor, saying nothing. His left wrist was wrapped in gauze where doctors had closed his self-inflicted wounds. Police had managed to take Price's fingerprints, and finally the FBI reported back that his real name was Charles R. Hatcher, a 40-year-old Missouri man. One California prosecutor studied Hatcher's criminal record and called him "a one-man crime wave."

It had been 10 years since Hatcher had attempted to abduct a newsboy in St. Joseph. In San Francisco, in the summer of 1969, Hatcher showed what he had had in mind for his earlier victim. During the decade in between, there had been car thefts, burglaries and assaults. There was no way for the 1961 murder of Jerry Tharrington in the Missouri State Penitentiary to show up in Hatcher's record. But Hatcher's Houdini-like escapes were there: a Missouri prison farm; county jails in Missouri and Kansas; and just a week before his arrest in California, his escape from a minimum security prison in Kansas.

Hatcher had also learned other ways to avoid the criminal justice system. As the next chapter will show, by the time he was tried in California, he had become quite adept at manipulating the courts and the psychiatrists ordered by the courts to examine him. Through his manipulation of the system, he would eventually regain his freedom from the California penal and mental health systems which tried to punish him, or alternatively, to treat him for the crimes he committed against Gilbert Martinez. Hatcher would surface again in St. Joseph nine years later, when Eric Christgen was murdered.

CHAPTER TEN

"I killed three men and you look like one of them."
—Charles Hatcher talking to a fellow patient in a mental hospital

ON SEPTEMBER 12, 1969, CHARLES HATCHER, USING the name of Albert Price, was brought before Judge Francis McCarty to answer the charges of assault with intent to commit sodomy and the kidnapping of Gilbert Martinez. The judge ordered psychiatric evaluations to determine whether Hatcher was sane enough to stand trial. Later that month, two court-appointed psychiatrists examined him.

To Dr. Arthur Carfagni's questions Hatcher returned a "dull, blank expression."

"It was impossible to ascertain his degree of orientation or to test abstraction or concentration," Carfagni reported.

Dr. Roland Levy found Hatcher in a catatonic state.

"The defendant had to be led into the interview room and only after being told several times, did he sit down," Levy said. "He sat sideways facing towards a wall and kept his head down and his arms hanging limply at his sides. He said nothing at all during the interview and did not respond to any questions or commands. His left arm showed numerous healed and fresh cuts from wrist to elbow, and his hands were blue and cold from being held in a downward position for so long."

Hatcher had impressed both psychiatrists. They found him insane and said he could not stand trial. Dr. Levy recommended a complete mental workup, and on September 25, Judge Byron Arnold ordered a 90-day evaluation at the California State Hospital. It was the first of five times that Charles Hatcher would avoid prison in California by feigning mental illness. Carfagni and Levy were the first of nine psychiatrists who were paid $50 to $75 to examine Hatcher and then explain his mental state to a judge. The doctors observed and interviewed him during sessions which typically lasted 50 minutes. The doctors made diagnoses, and wrote short reports which were delivered to prosecutors, public defenders and judges. It was assembly line psychiatry, and Hatcher merely had to maintain his charade for the interviews.

Experienced psychiatrists have written in scientific journals that practitioners should watch for malingerers who feign insanity to avoid prison. They believe it is a rare occurrence. The malingerers are most effective when dealing with psychiatrists working superficially. Clarifying the mental state of any individual takes time, especially when the individual has no desire to cooperate.

Hatcher was a habitual criminal who had learned how to artfully manipulate many of the psychiatrists he met. Experienced forensic psychiatrists say they need a very sharp intuitive faculty— a sixth sense—to diagnose a difficult case. But intuition is not enough. Thorough examination and research are always necessary. Many of the doctors who came into contact with Charles Hatcher for pretrial evaluations did not have the time, resources or experience necessary to expose his charade.

Hatcher never believed for a minute that he was mentally ill. In fact, he was offended when anyone called him crazy. But he was willing to be called just about anything to beat a charge. He knew that a hospital was far more comfortable and provided a freer environment than a prison.

Years of experience had taught him what symptoms were needed to convince someone he was crazy. Hatcher would proclaim that he heard voices commanding him to do evil. He feigned delusions of persecution, asserting that people were plotting to do him in or that poison was being added to his food. Often he pretended to be confused and disoriented. For effect, he would throw in a suicidal gesture. A wrist slashing with a crude, handmade knife or an inept job of hanging himself would compel others to take notice and do something to help him.

Hatcher was a professional at examining those who were appointed to examine him. He had an uncanny ability to know just what each examiner wanted to hear. The psychiatrists who examined him at the induction end of the California justice system were ill equipped for what they were dealing with. They did not always have a record of his previous charges with which to form a basis for their diagnoses. In addition to his strange behavior at the time of the examinations, the sordid nature of his crime added weight to the conclusion that the accused was mentally ill.

Thus, the examinations with Drs. Carfagni and Levy were the beginning of Hatcher's odyssey through California's courts, prisons and mental hospitals. At first, Hatcher cunningly turned the mental health system in California into his own sanctuary to avoid criminal prosecution. He hoped to use it as the path of least resistance back to freedom. Psychiatric exams and years in prisons and mental hospitals had taught him how to convince doctors that he was insane so that he could then gain entry into the mental health system. He would then turn the hospital into a revolving door by convincing doctors that he was "cured."

Nine years before the murder of Eric Christgen, on September 30, 1969, Hatcher began the first of his five tours of the California State Hospital. The hospital's 1,162 acres straddled the Salinas River three miles from Atascadero, a city midway between Los Angeles and San Francisco. California courts sent people to this hospital for observation and diagnosis.

The hospital also administered programs to treat sexual offenders. Three psychiatrists treated 1,000 patients. Many patients were dangerous sex offenders and sexual psychopaths. A study of hospital records showed that two-thirds of a group of 280 men committed to the institution had histories of previous sex offenses. Some admitted they had committed acts as many as 20 times prior to their arrest. Many of the victims were children.

When the hospital staff believed an individual was "cured," he would be released. There were no guard towers or cell blocks, and the people brought to the facility were called patients, rather than inmates. They lived in small individual bedrooms rather than behind bars. Each year, about 15 escaped.

Between August 1969, when he was charged in the Martinez case, and December 1972, when he was tried, Charles Hatcher took merry-go-round rides on California's mental health system. Four times, the hospital sent him back to court saying he was competent to stand trial. Psychiatrists appointed by the court would then reexamine Hatcher and determine him to be incompetent. He was found to be sane, then insane, then sane, then insane, then sane, then insane, and finally, sane. Those involved in his case thought *they* were going crazy.

At Atascadero, Hatcher was a Jekyll and Hyde kind of patient, quiet and cooperative one minute, hostile and violent the next. He was judged a suicide and an escape risk. To Hatcher, both were escape hatches from the terrible thoughts that bubbled in his brain. At times, the horrible thoughts plagued him; the sights seemed so real. He would see a motionless man lying on a blood-covered dock. Then, there was a naked bleeding child. And finally, there was another scene, the one that troubled him most of all. Actually, it was a series of mental pictures that began with a boy riding a bicycle. In the next frame, Hatcher would see himself driving a car with the boy sitting beside him. He would be talking to the boy. Hatcher would see himself driving the car and would look over at the boy "riding shotgun" and see a little of himself reflected there. The boy seemed so eager to be with him. So willing to go. So friendly and trusting. Then, the scene would change again. They were no longer in a car, but on a creek bank. The boy would be lying on the ground, and Hatcher would see himself over the boy, with his own hands wrapped around the boy's throat.

Each time the scene ended with a sight so horrible that Hatcher would tremble and flinch, as if trying to physically eject the thought from his head. At those moments, there was no escaping the mental pictures. In the ward dayroom, while other patients sat and watched television, he would pace back and forth, like a caged animal, haunted by what he was watching in his mind.

The other patients avoided him. One named Kovacs told a ward worker that he had asked Hatcher what he had done to get into the hospital.

Hatcher replied: "I killed three men, and you look like one of them."

Often Hatcher was quiet and sullen, but he was subject to wild mood swings at the slightest of provocations.

Once, for no apparent reason, he walked over to the television and abruptly changed channels. It angered the other patients, and a black man, who was the ward's "sergeant-at-arms," cursed him.

Hatcher called him a "mother-fucking nigger.

"No black nigger is going to tell me what to do," he said. As two thick-muscled aides wrestled him to the floor, Hatcher said, "That mother-fucker had better not fool with me anymore."

As they carried him off to seclusion, dressed him in pajamas and tied him to a bed, he declared: "I don't let anyone cuss me out, especially niggers. I'd just as soon stay back here than be out there with that nigger bastard."

Drugs—with names like mellaril, thorazine and stelozine—were pumped into Hatcher like liquid coolant. They lowered the temperature of the evil thoughts that plagued him. But the drug-induced escapes were only temporary, and when they wore off, the memories came roaring back, more powerfully than before. Seclusion then became a real nightmare for Hatcher. The burning heat in his head made him thrash in his bed, breaking the bindings that held him there. Hatcher would scream and kick at the door with his bare feet until his toes bled. When he came down from these episodes, his head would be dizzy and pained, and like Mr. Hyde, he never knew where he had been.

The hospital nurses observed it all, sometimes carefully recording, by the hour, the actions of this strange, demented man. They compiled reams of notes on him:

"Patient is sullen and verbally hostile."

"Patients in his dorm have become increasingly fearful of him."

"Mr. Price was surly. I told him it was time to take a shower and he replied, 'Fuck you.'"

"He sits quietly in group therapy with his hands covering his face and does not participate."

"Patient's previous behavior has been so unpredictable that the decision to seclude patient at this time seemed unavoidable in the interest of safety to other patients, staff and patient Price."

The hospital staff wondered about the thoughts that troubled him. They wanted to know about the secrets he was hiding. Some suggested that Hatcher be questioned under the influence of sodium amytal, a truth serum. A doctor tried to talk Hatcher into it, but he refused to sign the consent form.

"He felt that this would be used as evidence in court," the doctor said. "He was informed that it would not be, but he still refused to sign the form."

The Dr. Jekyll side of him was quiet and remote. He kept to himself.

"Mr. Price appears to be shunned by most of his peers with only one or two possible exceptions," the staff noted. "He participates in no table games and socializes only sporadically with other patients. He has formed no noticeable close relationships and spends most of his time on the ward in the dayroom, slumped in a chair. He belongs to no clubs, participates in no activities or religious services. Outside of the ward, the only place he visits is the library."

Hatcher looked for ways to escape. The staff discovered an electric cord missing from a floor buffing machine Hatcher had been using. They believed he planned to lasso a vent with it to make an escape. During a shakedown of his room, aides found a California state roadmap and an address hidden in his shoe. Each altercation with the staff and patients and each attempted escape earned him a round of medications and seclusion. It reminded him of the months of solitary confinement he had spent in the Missouri State Penitentiary eight years earlier.

Hatcher rode a roller coaster drug ride, hanging onto the highs and diving with the lows. He was moved from ward to ward and room to room—a compression of his nomadic life—as patients and staff complained about him.

Psychiatrists at Atascadero would repeatedly determine that Hatcher was competent to stand trial. Hatcher would be sent back for trial, and court-appointed psychiatrists would re-examine him. During these sessions, Hatcher either would be evasive to questions asked of him, or would answer in ways which tended to show insanity. Each time, the psychiatrists found him incompetent and sent Hatcher back to Atascadero for further diagnosis and treatment.

The first finding in Hatcher's case was delivered in December 1970 by Dr. James Hollingsworth, chief of staff at Atascadero. He found that Hatcher had a passive-aggressive personality, laced with sexual deviation and pedophilia. He said Hatcher refused to give his social history to the hospital staff, and that his actions indicated he was malingering. Hollingsworth reported to the judge that twice he had attempted to escape, and that when they had put him into a seclusion cell, he kicked the door.

"When questioned concerning this incident, he would become mute and refused to answer any questions," Hollingsworth wrote. "This has been the patient's usual pattern since being sent to the hospital." Hollingsworth said Hatcher was ready to stand trial.

"Since this man is a serious escape risk as evidenced by one probable escape attempt and involvement in two other alleged escape plots, we would appreciate it very much if you could pick him up at your earliest convenience for return to court."

Hatcher was returned to San Francisco to stand trial. Judge Walter Calgagno ordered two more psychiatric examinations.

Dr. David Kessler encountered Hatcher on January 21, 1971. Hatcher wore an angry expression for the interview, but Kessler found he could turn it quickly into a sarcastic smile. Hatcher would avoid direct eye contact.

"He tended to reply to many questions by stating that he either did not know the answer or could not remember or refused to go into details," Kessler said. "Even when he responded, he tended to give the briefest, most general answer, requiring the interviewer to ask a whole stream of follow-up questions in order to try to overcome what appeared to be the defendant's evasiveness and guardedness."

"They think I'm crazy, that's why I'm getting the runaround," Hatcher said.

"Why would they think such a thing?" asked Kessler.

"So they won't have to set me loose. That's why they sent me to Atascadero for a year and a half."

"How can they do that when you have these charges against you?"

"I don't know anything about no charges."

"You don't remember anything about why you were arrested?"

"The last thing I remember was living in Sacramento in July and August of 1969."

"Why can't you remember any more than that?"

"I don't know."

"You know you are charged with kidnapping and child molesting."

Hatcher twisted his face into an angrier expression and began breathing heavily.

"That's bullshit," he said forcefully.

"But you have discussed the charges against you with the people at Atascadero."

"They want me to admit these charges, kidnapping and child molesting. They'll do anything to get you to admit it. They kept me there for a year and a half for no reason. Why else would they do it?"

Hatcher told Kessler that he heard X-rays coming through the doors of his room at Atascadero, and that this was the "radar" that the staff had been using to observe him while he was in the hospital.

"He felt," Kessler said, "that by this means the staff was able to read his mind and to tell what he was thinking. He said the medication that he received there caused hallucinations and that he began feeling that colored people were trying to burn him up."

Kessler concluded that Hatcher was insane and required vigorous psychiatric treatment in a secure hospital facility.

The day after Kessler's examination, another psychiatrist, Dr. Edward Dean, met with Hatcher.

Although Hatcher was known in California as Price, Dean referred to him as "Mr. Prince."

"He had episodes of amnesia when drinking, would black out in one town and regain his memory in another," Dean said. "He also had a fear that he would be burned up by a group of colored men. He could hear them talking outside his room in the hallway, talking about what they were going to do to him. He also had episodes of visual hallucination, on one occasion seeing a person turn into an eagle. These were frightening experiences."

Based on his interview with "Mr. Prince," Dr. Dean found him unable to cooperate with counsel in his defense. Judge Calcagno pronounced Hatcher incompetent to stand trial, and ordered him returned to Atascadero for further diagnosis and treatment.

In April, Hatcher was one of a group of patients implicated in an escape plot. It involved a plan to take an employee hostage. He was placed in seclusion. A month later, he was returned to court, this time before Judge James Welsh in San Francisco Municipal Court. A public defender, Edward Mancuso, was appointed to represent him. The judge agreed with the request by Gerald Riggs, the deputy prosecuting attorney, that Hatcher be bound over for trial.

When he was arraigned on May 24, Hatcher pleaded not guilty by reason of insanity, and this plea prompted another round of psychiatric studies. To examine Hatcher, the judge appointed Dr. Carl Drake Jr. of the University of California Medical Center in San Francisco. The examination took place on May 27, and Albert Price lied about his life history to the psychiatrist, who was not familiar with Hatcher's background. He would do the same with many other doctors who relied on the unsupported word of the former convict.

Price told Drake he had been born in Los Angeles, was 35 years old, married but separated. Hatcher at that time was nearly 42. He had never been married.

"I was not able to review his record because they were not in the district attorney's record room at the time," Drake said. "Mr. Price was a very reluctant historian and was very difficult to interview. It is most unusual to find an individual with the kinds of memory defects that Mr. Price has. This is the first time I have interviewed someone who did not remember the name of his high school or the year he graduated. It may be possible that Mr. Price is suffering from a chronic organic brain disease which results in his being mentally impaired."

Drake concluded that Hatcher could not stand trial. He was the fifth psychiatrist to have come to such a conclusion. Drake made his diagnosis without the benefit of the records that showed Hatcher's lengthy criminal record and his history of never having been treated for an organic brain disease.

Hatcher had told his doctors that he wanted to argue his own court case, and on the day Drake conducted his examination, Hatcher filed a motion asking that the case against him be dismissed on the grounds that the victim had left the country and was not available to testify against him.

While Hatcher was getting plenty of psychiatric attention, his victim, Gilbert Martinez began developing a paralyzing fear of people. For months, he refused to go outside, afraid that the stranger who had attacked him was still there. Once, he finally did venture out, only to return screaming because he thought a car that stopped in front of his house was coming to pick him up for another journey to terror. Kelly Waterfield, the juvenile officer who had taken a special interest in Gilbert's case, wondered what the long term effects of the violent sexual attack would be.

"The victim suffered mental trauma and had to be relocated out of the San Francisco area," Waterfield said. "The kid was not talking for a year or two after that." Gilbert underwent psychiatric treatment until 1972, but the sessions with the doctor strained the family budget. No compensation programs for crime victims existed at that time, and there was no government money to pay for psychological counseling sessions. A request for help from the city was turned down. At the same time, taxpayers were paying for Hatcher's psychiatric tests and his room and board at Atascadero. The Martinez family concluded that leaving San Francisco might be the best thing for the boy. They moved to Guadalajara, Mexico.

On June 2, Hatcher escaped from San Francisco General Hospital where he had been taken for medical treatment. A week later, police in Colusa, California—90 miles north of San Francisco—arrested a man on suspicion of stealing a car in Sacramento. They turned the man, identified as Richard Lee Grady, over to authorities in Sacramento, where he faced charges of grand theft auto. Two court-appointed psychiatrists examined Grady at the judge's request. Both doctors told the judge that Grady's behavior was so bizarre that he could not face trial, and on July 15, he was committed to the California State Hospital at Atascadero for evaluation of his mental disorder. There, the nurses recognized Charles Hatcher: "This isn't Richard Grady," they said. "This is Albert Price."

Hospital physicians continued to recommend

that Charles Hatcher, now known as Price, be tried on the charges involving the attack on Gilbert Martinez. But court-appointed psychiatrists kept sending him back to the hospital.

In one psychiatric examination, Dr. David Cook thought it was possible that Price was faking and that he was capable of controlling himself and understanding what was going on around him.

But he added, "It must be recognized that as long as he persists in his present behavior, whether consciously motivated or otherwise, he cannot adequately cooperate with an attorney in making his own defense. Therefore, I am drawn to the conclusion that at this time the defendant is still legally insane and am recommending that he be returned to the Atascadero State Hospital for further observation and treatment."

The judge agreed.

The staff at the state hospital was incredulous. The gist of Cook's opinion was that as long as Hatcher could keep up his act, he would never come to trial. Dr. Hollingsworth, the chief of staff, could not believe what had happened.

"Why did they send you back here?" Hollingsworth asked Hatcher during an interview March 7, 1972.

"That's the only thing they can do," Hatcher replied. "Send me back here."

"What about the charges against you?"

"The only thing I ever done that was wrong was to steal a Hostess cupcake from a Safeway Store."

Hollingsworth decided that Hatcher had had all the chances he deserved at Atascadero. He assembled a chronology which showed that before his most recent visit, Hatcher had spent nearly two years total time there during three separate tours, one under the name of Richard Grady. During all the time there, he attended group therapy sessions, but refused to participate. He was administered tranquilizers, Thorazine, Trilafon, and a special mood elevator. But he was going nowhere.

The staff believed Hatcher would not benefit from psychiatric hospitalization. The escape attempts convinced them that Hatcher was "a severe danger to the health and safety of others." Their conclusion seemed to end Hatcher's run in the state mental health system. On April 4, the staff decided that Hatcher should be transferred to the state prison hospital at Vacaville, about midway between San Francisco and Sacramento. The corrections officers there quickly measured the experienced con man they had received.

In August 1972, Hatcher was transferred to San Quentin. In the three years since the commission of the crime against Gilbert Martinez—and six years before the murder of Eric Christgen—Hatcher had never been formally tried and convicted. But while the judges, defenders and prosecutors would not bring him to justice, the doctors and the prison guards who handled him recognized Hatcher for what he was and determined that he should be incarcerated for the public safety. A civil libertarian might object to the fact that Hatcher had been shuttled from jail to doctor to hospital to prison without the benefit of a trial by jury.

But those who dealt closely with him on a day-to-day basis, who knew his crimes and knew what he had done to Gilbert Martinez, concluded that Hatcher belonged in California's toughest institution. And by forcing him into prison, the doctors and the corrections officers brought about what judges and lawyers had not been able to produce— a trial. Two days after his arrival behind the walls of San Quentin, Hatcher wrote to Edward Mancuso, his public defender.

Dear Sir,

On January 10, this year, I was sent to Atascadero State Hospital from Department 22 by Judge Calcagno. On May 30, I was sent to California Medical Facility by the hospital, and on the 23rd of August, I was sent to San Quentin Prison. Is all this legal? I'm sure my transfer to the medical facility was, but is it legal for them to send me to San Quentin? They don't have medical facilities here that would come under treatment for a mentally disordered sex offender as I was sent to Atascadero for treatment under that status.

I agree that I don't need further treatment and am ready and willing to stand trial. Can you get me back to court with a writ of habeas corpus—as some of the people here and at Vacaville suggest I write you about this for the quickest way—and they all agree that I'm ready to return to court. Would appreciate it if you would file a writ for me on this matter.

Yours Truly
Albert Price B41814
San Quentin Prison
Tamal, Calif.

Charles Hatcher was terrified in San Quentin. He feared that Carl Lindy Pierce had connections there. Hatcher and Pierce had served time together at the Kansas State Penitentiary in Lansing in 1969.

Pierce had helped Hatcher get a job in the prison hospital and Hatcher repaid the favor by informing on Pierce's escape plot. Hatcher told guards that Pierce had a gun hidden within the institution and planned to use it to escape. The disclosure had complicated Pierce's prison life considerably but helped Hatcher move to a minimum security farm from which he later escaped. Hatcher was worried that Pierce would try some way to even the score. Pierce had served a term at California's Folsom Prison, and Hatcher believed that Pierce had connections there who could arrange to have him killed at San Quentin.

Hatcher's letter, proof in his own handwriting that he was capable of rational thinking, led to preparations for a trial.

Gilbert's parents, fearing that the stress of his appearance at a trial would deepen the emotional scars that already marked him, did not let him testify at the legal proceedings. But the prosecution believed it had a strong enough case without Gilbert as a witness. There was no question that Albert Price had done it. Galatoire was a solid witness, and the police had caught Price in the act. Hatcher's only defense could be that he was insane at the time he committed the act, and Richard Janoupal, his new public defender, petitioned the court for two sets of mental examinations. One examination would determine whether he was competent to stand trial, and the other would find whether he was legally sane at the time he committed the crime.

On October 24, 1972, Dr. Edward Dean performed the eighth court-ordered examination of Charles Hatcher. Dean, who had examined Hatcher the previous year, believed Hatcher had delusions while drinking alcohol.

"One night, he saw a corpse stretched out in the next room, and all night Indians performed a ceremonial dance over the body," Dean said. "At Atascadero, he saw them move a large incinerator opposite his room, make a big fire in it, and continually put people into it. He thought they were just outside his room, waiting to take him next. He could hear them talking about what they were going to do to him."

But Dean determined that Hatcher understood the charges against him and was able to cooperate with his defense counsel. Dr. John Glathe of Palo Alto also examined Hatcher and rendered an opinion that Hatcher was probably sane at the time the crime was committed.

Thus, on December 12, 1972, Charles R. Hatcher was finally tried for the abduction and molestation of Gilbert Martinez. Judge S. Lee Vavuris presided over the trial in the Municipal Court of the city of San Francisco. Galatoire told the story of the scene he would never forget. Two police officers recounted that they caught Hatcher in the act of sexually molesting a child. Three psychiatrists testified as to Hatcher's mental state, and the written reports of two others were read into the court record. Hatcher did not take the stand. Five days after the trial began, and more than three years since he attacked Gilbert Martinez, Hatcher—under the name of Albert Price—was convicted on charges of lewd and lascivious conduct.

CHAPTER ELEVEN

"This report is to inform the judge that in my opinion this man is still a mentally disordered sex offender, has not recovered and remains a danger to society and should not be given a new opportunity to victimize others."
—Dr. A.J. Rucci describing Charles Hatcher

HATCHER WAS MORE COOPERATIVE AFTER HE WAS convicted of the attack on Gilbert. He opened up a little more, hoping to become classified as a mentally disordered sex offender. He no longer denied the attack, and explained that it happened as a result of drinking and taking drugs.

While the doctors differed on whether Hatcher's sexual deviancy could be treated, there was no doubt in Warren Jenkins' mind. The court's chief probation officer knew that Hatcher could not be returned to society. When Jenkins gave Hatcher a probation questionnaire form to complete, Hatcher tore it up and threw it in the wastebasket.

On January 9, 1973, Judge Vavuris committed Hatcher to the California Mental Hospital at Atascadero as a mentally disordered sex offender. This time Hatcher, still known as Albert Price, was sent not for evaluation but for treatment. Atascadero, with financing from the National Institute of Mental Health, was pioneering programs for treating sex offenders. The idea behind the programs was that the sex offender could be treated and perhaps rehabilitated. The offender was retained for as long as it took to cure him. When he was no longer dangerous, the man was returned to society.

Dr. M.J. Reimringer interviewed Hatcher on his readmission to Atascadero and thought the prognosis for him was "very poor."

"It is highly probable that this man will be institutionalized most of his life," Reimringer predicted. That was wishful thinking.

Over the years, statistics had shown that of the individuals sent to Atascadero by judges for 90-day evaluations, about half were determined to be not amenable to treatment. They were customarily returned to the court system for processing and conviction, followed by a sentence in California's prison system. These individuals formed a group that was somewhere between crime and disease, and the reports the doctors provided on each patient were designed to help the judge determine whether the offender belonged in the mental health treatment system or in prison.

Hatcher had become another case history in the continuing debate over whether a violent sex offender should be imprisoned or treated for rehabilitation. Psychiatrists and psychologists were sharply divided on the effectiveness of rehabilitation programs. Some argued that the sexual psychopath laws, passed in the 1930s and 40s, should be repealed because no method of treatment had proved successful. They cited studies showing that psychiatric treatment for sex offenders had not been more effective than confinement without treatment. But others maintained that treatment could prove effective.

More than half of the states in the United States have sexual psychopath laws that were enacted when many psychiatrists predicted that all criminals would one day be treated successfully. But the laws were not adequately funded or fairly applied. While one group of offenders went to state hospitals for treatment, another group was sent to prison where sexual attack, rather than treatment, was the norm.

The extreme brutality of Hatcher's crime was a rarity among child molesters. In fact, child molesters were considered to be among the most nonviolent of sex offenders. Of the three types of child molesters, the class that Hatcher fell in was the most difficult to treat.

The most common type of molester was the relatively normal man, who, under stress, might perform a sexual act with a child, perhaps his own child. Psychiatrists agreed that this person was treatable.

A second class of molester included the man whose psychological development was arrested before adolescence. He had no normal sexual relationships with women and had no desire to do so. This person appeared to be fixated on children; he would not rape them in a violent sense, but would have love relationships with them. This type was more difficult to treat, but some success had been reported.

At Atascadero, one way the men were tested for sexual deviancy was to measure their sexual arousal while they were shown slides of nude children. Forms of treatment ranged from participation in group therapy sessions to exposure to heavy doses of pornographic tape recordings. Because alcohol abuse almost always played a role in molestations (many offenders said they were drunk at the time they committed their crimes), treatment for alcoholism was part of the program.

The third type of molester, the very small proportion that included Hatcher, were men who raped children. Sexuality and aggression were fused together in a sadistic desire to get pleasure out of hurting people. The men who preyed on small boys exclusively were the hardest to treat. Hatcher was probably 14 years past the point of being treated. In 1959, after he attempted to abduct a St. Joseph newsboy, intensive therapy might have made a difference. But instead of being treated then, he had been sent to prison where he had satisfied his compulsive desire by stabbing another inmate to death.

In many states, public mental facilities reluctantly accept people like Hatcher. Since the study of sex offenders in the field of forensic psychiatry is not as prestigious or financially lucrative as other psychiatric specialties, the hospitals often face personnel shortages of individuals trained to treat sex offenders who require intense observation and therapy.

Atascadero, like hospitals in other states, was ill-equipped to satisfactorily treat Hatcher. Given the nature of the offense, his social background and his criminal history, Hatcher could have been an interesting specimen for study at Atascadero. Eager scientists, hungry to observe the demons who drove him, could have been expected to line up anxiously for the chance to treat Hatcher. But in this setting, Hatcher was not unique or unusual. Hundreds of men with similar sexual deviancies were processed through Atascadero every year. Only the best prospects were chosen for treatment. Hatcher became a numbered unit who blended into the background, biding his time, waiting for release or a chance to escape.

Hatcher thought he had his chance on March 28. Shortly after 5:00 P.M., security guards found him hiding in a cooler near the main courtyard of the hospital. Two sheets were stuffed in his pants. He admitted to them that he planned to make a getaway. Hatcher was placed in seclusion. A few days later, Dr. A.J. Rucci, the medical director of the California State Hospital, asked the court to take Hatcher back.

> This report is to inform the judge that in my opinion this man is still a mentally disordered sex offender, has not recovered and remains a danger to society and should not be given a new opportunity to victimize others. He has not benefitted from therapy and should be returned to court for resumption of criminal proceedings. He is antisocial, has severe sexual deviation and aggressive sexuality. He is an extremely sociopathic and dangerous person.
>
> His offense is a rather brutal sexual assault on a five-year-old boy. This appears to be an isolated incident in an extremely sociopathic and dangerous person. It is the staff's opinion that this man is unamenable to the treatment program here and that he remains dangerous and is an extreme escape risk.

Rucci's report finally closed his hospital's door on Hatcher. He was returned to court for sentencing, and Judge Vavuris gave him an indeterminate sentence of one year to life in prison. The judge was careful to advise Hatcher that he had the right to an appeal of his conviction and that the state would take care of his bills.

Hatcher was sent to the California medium security prison at Vacaville on April 27 for a determination of which custodial setting would be appropriate for him, given his background. The sentence allowed prison officials to determine when Hatcher could be returned to society. But the prison system had no programs to treat him. If Hatcher could not be rehabilitated at Atascadero, where programs were established to treat people like him, how could a prison prepare Hatcher for his eventual return to society?

The California prison system offers inmates education, vocational training, medical services, group counseling and other rehabilitative activities. The system combines diagnosis, evaluation, treatment and classification at its hospital clinic prison center at Vacaville. Education, vocational, medical, social and psychological evaluations are made for each inmate, and a board determines where a prisoner should be placed. The superintendent of the facility is customarily a psychiatrist. Group psychotherapy is available and is participated in by nearly all of the prisoners. Hatcher liked Vacaville but corrections department counselors believed that he deserved maximum security treatment.

W.D. Lewis, who interviewed Hatcher at the reception center in May, 1973, found him to be a "manipulative institutionalized sociopath."

Lewis recommended Hatcher be assigned to maximum security custody at Folsom Prison.

But Hatcher told staff psychologist Raymond McDonald that he was afraid of being sent to either Folsom or San Quentin because he would be targeted as a snitch and killed. He also hinted that darker secrets locked in his brain were troubling him, but he would not discuss them.

Despite his worries, prisons officials, on June 15, 1973, recommended transfer to Folsom. Ten days later, Hatcher cut his left wrist and the right side of his neck with a razor blade. Doctors in the prison hospital sutured the wounds. Hatcher was placed in psychiatric segregation in the prison hospital.

He told doctors there that his drinking was to blame for his criminal behavior.

Dr. M.F. Stock, a staff psychiatrist, examined Hatcher and reported that he was suffering from paranoia and schizophrenia with "catatonic features." He recommended that Hatcher be placed in psychiatric segregation. This recommendation kept him out of Folsom Prison.

The thick medical reports that had been compiled on Hatcher had finally concluded that he had been faking all the symptoms; the voices he heard came and went depending on where he was, which indicated that Hatcher was able to control them. The voluminous dossier on his mental treatment showed his delusions were simply malingering. Yet, the prison staff psychiatrist either ignored these reports or did not bother to study them. As a result, Hatcher remained at Vacaville.

His considerable case file fell into the basket of William Henry, a correctional counselor who would observe and work with Hatcher for four years. In the controlled setting of the prison, without the possibility of escape and other temptations, Hatcher became a model prisoner. Freedom in the immediate future was remote. An appeal of his conviction had been rejected on all grounds. But the reports Henry compiled on the man he called Albert Price began turning favorable in the summer of 1974.

"He shows determination and self confidence in his work. Price has been in the Intensive Treatment Center Program for approximately nine months. During this period of time he has been no custody problem at all."

But Henry did not believe Price could safely be paroled. He said he was not ready to accept responsibility for his crime.

"Today, he tried to present himself in a complimentary way but did not succeed," Henry wrote. "Violence potential outside a controlled setting in the past is considered to have been greater than average and at present is estimated to be the same. Subject is not psychiatrically ready for parole at this time."

Price told Henry that he would have to give some thought to his destination after release from prison, because he had learned that Kansas had dropped its detainer on him for prison escape. The Kansas penal system was considerate enough to forward to Hatcher two checks, totalling $45.75. It was the amount that remained in his prison account at the time of his escape.

Each year, Charles Hatcher was eligible for parole review. Counselors, caseworkers, guards and psychiatrists would offer opinions regarding Hatcher's readiness for release. It was an orderly review process that also diluted individual responsibility for releasing someone who was not ready. Hatcher was making steady progress, according to the various reports written about him.

In August of 1975, the guards stated for a parole review that Hatcher was not a custodial problem and had performed his tasks well in the hospital kitchen. The guards described him as a loner, although he seemed to get along with everyone. He met Henry for one-on-one counseling sessions, but did not offer any information on his crimes.

"He now describes himself as an alcoholic as well as his parents being alcoholic. He volunteers that he will not get into trouble if he does not drink. Price now volunteers that he believes he can control his behavior as long as he leaves alcohol alone. It is most important that Mr. Price seek help from someone whom he has confidence in. He keeps himself at a distance and fails to get involved. He is not a management problem."

On June 25, 1976, the California Parole Board determined that Hatcher had accumulated two years, seven months and 17 days for time spent in jail. The board also found that in the three years since doctors had determined that he was a dangerous, sexual psychopath, Hatcher had improved dramatically while undergoing treatment and incarceration at Vacaville. They began to talk about paroling him.

He had impressed them by making admissions that he might have attacked the little boy. The counselors believed that these admissions constituted a critical step in his rehabilitation.

"Reports indicate he is doing outstanding work," Henry wrote. "His effort, conduct, cooperation and initiative have also been excellent. There are several academic chronos on file from the intensive treatment program teacher, and all indicate that Mr. Price continues to do outstanding work in the school program. He is repeatedly described as an outstanding and dedicated student. All grades of all phases in the academic program have been in the above average range.

"Subject is certainly more outgoing and his progress has been commented on by staff members as well as his peer group. Mr. Price has certainly become more responsible and shown signs of accepting responsibility for his behavior."

Henry's final report on Hatcher ended with a conclusion that he was not as dangerous as he had been: "Violence potential outside a controlled setting in the past is considered to have been greater than average and at present is estimated to be decreased."

The psychiatric council that interviewed Hatcher

that Bicentennial summer believed his schizophrenia and paranoia would be in remission as long as Hatcher remained on medication.

In reaching their conclusion that Hatcher might be ready for life on the streets again, the caseworkers measured his performance, attitude and activities in the California prison system for the previous three years. The prognosis was hopeful. But there was no discussion about whether he had gained control over the strong sexual desires that psychiatrists had been told about three years before. (There had been hopeful prognoses about Charles Hatcher before. The first was in Missouri in 1951, when prison officials thought Hatcher was ready for an assignment at a prison farm. He escaped 20 days later. The last was in Kansas in 1969, when prison officials assigned him to an honor camp, where he lasted 17 days before escaping.) The California Parole Board decided Hatcher could be released in 17 months under certain conditions. It set a parole date of December 25, 1978, which would have freed him seven months after the day that Eric Christgen was abducted and murdered.

But Christmas came early for Charles Hatcher. The California Legislature had approved a bill that gave prison inmates credit for time spent not only in county and city jails but also in hospitals and mental health facilities. The change in the law was made while Hatcher was still in prison, and it was originally considered to be prospective—applying to those arrested, jailed and convicted after the law went into effect. But an inmate filed a suit that resulted in application of the law for those serving sentences at the time the law was approved. As a result, on January 3, 1977, Hatcher received a modified parole date that led to his release 19 months earlier than expected.

On May 20, 1977, the man California authorities knew as Albert R. Price—the man who had been described four years earlier as "an extremely sociopathic and dangerous person" and "a danger to society" who "should not be given an opportunity to victimize others"—was released to the custody of the Home Care Services Center, a San Francisco halfway house.

Parole is a relaxed version of custody. Hatcher was free, although there were special conditions attached to his parole. He had to promise to abstain from the use of any alcoholic beverages and to undergo narcotic testing.

He left the California Medical Facility at Vacaville with a three-weeks' supply of tranquilizers, anti-psychotic medication, anti-anxiety medicine and a prescription to combat various side effects caused by the medication. At 9:00 every night, Hatcher was supposed to take nine pills. The state of California paid for them. It also gave him $100 for expenses and placed additional money in his account at the halfway house.

This assignment was cheaper than keeping him in the state's prison system, which costs $15,000 to $18,000 per year per inmate. But the real human costs of Charles Hatcher's freedom were staggering. The bills for the emotional distress, psychological damage, physical injury and loss of life could never be calculated, but many would pay.

Gilbert Martinez had continued to make installments. Several years after the attack, Kelly Waterfield, the police juvenile officer, attempted to track down Gilbert in San Francisco to monitor his progress. Waterfield culled school district records, and because Gilbert would have been of age, ran a

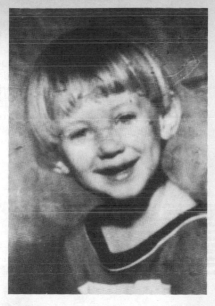

Eric Scott Christgen, abducted and murdered on May 26, 1978, in St. Joseph, Missouri. Of sixteen people killed by Hatcher, three were children. *(Courtesy* St. Joseph News-Press/ Gazette*)*

The play area in the St. Joseph shopping mall where Eric was kidnapped. *(Photo by the author)*

Composite drawing of the man witnesses saw with Eric Christgen on the day of his abduction, which bears a striking resemblance to Charles Hatcher. *(Courtesy* St. Joseph News-Press/Gazette*)*

Despite the fact that Melvin Reynolds, right, did not resemble the police profile of the suspect, he was arrested, tried, and wrongly convicted for Eric Christgen's murder, and spent four years in prison. *(Courtesy* St. Joseph News-Press/Gazette*)*

St. Joseph Police Chief James Robert Hayes, who was in charge of the investigation leading to Reynolds' conviction and imprisonment. *(Courtesy* St. Joseph News-Press/ Gazette*)*

Buchanan County Prosecuting Attorney Michael Insco, the man who prosecuted Reynolds and who later prosecuted Charles Hatcher for the same crime. *(Photo by the author)*

Lee Nation, Melvin Reynolds' defense attorney. *(Courtesy* St. Joseph News-Press/ Gazette*)*

FBI Agent Joseph Holtslag, Jr., the man who finally brought Hatcher to justice. *(Photo by the author)*

William Freeman, the first child known to be murdered by Charles Hatcher. He was abducted on August 28, 1969, in Antioch, California. *(Courtesy Josie Freeman)*

Michelle Steele, abducted and murdered on July 29, 1982, in St. Joseph, Missouri. *(Courtesy* St. Joseph News-Press/Gazette*)*

Charles Hatcher's school picture, taken in 1938 at the Pine Hill School, Maitland, Mo. Charles Hatcher, the smallest boy, is in the first row, on the far left. Also shown are his brother Floyd, second row, second from the left, and his brother Jesse, second row, third from the left. *(Courtesy Ruth Allen)*

Portrait Of A Killer

1982
St. Joseph, Mo.
Michelle Steele 11, is murdered

1981
Des Moines, Iowa
Hatcher pulls a knife on a man in a Salvation Army center.
Davenport, Iowa
James L. Churchill, 38, is murdered.
Bettendorf, Iowa
Todd Peers, 11, is snatched from a grocery store.

1978
St. Joseph, Mo.
Eric Scott Christgen, 4, is murdered.

1961
Jefferson City, Mo.
Hatcher stabs to death fellow inmate Jerry Lee Tharrington in the Missouri State Penitentiary. No charges are brought against him.

1947-1959
Northwest Missouri
Hatcher commits a series of crimes including burglary, forgery and auto theft. Much of this time is spent in the Missouri State Penitentiary. He makes several escapes.

1978
Omaha, Neb.
A 16 year old boy is sexually attacked.

1980
Omaha, Neb.
Hatcher assaults a man during an argument over payment for sex.
Lincoln, Neb.
Hatcher molests a 17-year-old retarded youth.

1959
St. Joseph, Mo.
Hatcher attempts to run over a police officer, threatens a 16-year-old newsboy with a knife and attempts to force him into his car.

1969
San Francisco, Calif.
6 year old Gilbert Martinez (not his real name) is sexually attacked; William J. Freeman, 12, is murdered in nearby Antioch.

This diagram tracing Hatcher's violent trail is based on an earlier one published in the *St. Louis Post-Dispatch*.

The old St. Joseph and the new. Above, the Jesse James Museum, which is located where Jesse James was shot on April 3, 1882. Below, downtown St. Joseph as it looks today. *(Courtesy Eric Keith)*

ST. JOSEPH NEWS-PRESS

ST. JOSEPH, MISSOURI, THURSDAY EVENING, OCTOBER 13, 1983

Hatcher guilty of Christgen murder, given life sentence

Hatcher says Melvin Leo Reynolds was framed

St. Joseph Gazette

St. Joseph, Missouri, October 13, 1983

New Reynolds case hearing to be asked

St. Joseph Gazette

St. Joseph, Missouri, October 14, 1983

...ayes disputes confession

ST. JOSEPH NEWS-PRESS

ST. JOSEPH, MISSOURI, MONDAY EVENING, OCTOBER 17, 1983

Aftermath
Insco: Hayes turned down chance to question Hatcher

ST. JOSEPH NEWS-PRESS/Gazette

St. Joseph, Missouri, October 16, 1983

Community deserves answers to murder case flip-flop

Commentary

Special squad was list shy of Hatcher

St. Joseph was shocked to learn that Charles Hatcher, not Melvin Reynolds, had murdered Eric Christgen. The headlines above show how St. Joseph newspapers covered this and other stories.

These mugshots and fingerprints of Charles Hatcher were taken from November 25, 1959, to July 23, 1981. *(Courtesy Missouri Department of Corrections, Kansas Department of Corrections, California Department of Corrections, Bettendorf Police Department)*

computer check of state drivers' licenses. The results were all negative. The only record discovered was in the police computer. A boy with the same name and the same birthday—March 24, 1963— had been apprehended for shoplifting in 1975. He had been released with a lecture.

On May 25, 1977, five days after he arrived at the Home Care Service Center, Hatcher violated the terms of his parole. Halfway house officials called him a "walk away," but Hatcher was running, and he covered a lot of ground very quickly. On the morning of June 6, a teletype was received by San Francisco police from Willmar, Minnesota. The sheriff in Willmar asked whether a man named Charles R. Hatcher was wanted. San Francisco police responded affirmatively and requested that a hold be placed on him. But Willmar police said he had been released June 3, because there had been no local charges pending against him.

Police waited for Hatcher to surface again. On June 13, he was declared a "parolee at large" and a warrant was issued for his arrest. The handwritten notes in Hatcher's file encouraged those who might deal with the case in the future to be diligent. The notes warned: "very serious commitment offenses. . . . long criminal record. . . . long term drug abuser. . . . includes crimes against children."

Within the year, Eric Christgen was murdered.

CHAPTER TWELVE

"I don't know how you stop a guy like that."
—Nebraska Prosecutor Sam Cooper describing
Charles Hatcher

IN THE MONTHS IMMEDIATELY FOLLOWING THE
murder of Eric Christgen, Charles Hatcher roamed
the Midwest like a violent nomad. The FBI profile
had said that the Christgen boy's murderer would
commit another crime by October or November of
1978. On September 4, 1978, Hatcher was arrested
in Omaha, 150 miles north of St. Joseph, for a sexual attack on a teenage boy. It was the first in a
series of violent crimes involving Hatcher in
Omaha, Nebraska and Iowa. Between the fall of
1978 and the spring of 1982, Hatcher was arrested
for molesting a teenage boy, attempting to stab a
seven-year-old boy, and fighting over payment for
sex with a young man—all in Omaha, molesting a
man in Lincoln, Nebraska, and attempting to stab
a man in Des Moines and to abduct an 11-year-old
boy from a shopping mall in Bettendorf, Iowa.

But despite all of the charges, Hatcher never
spent a day in prison. After each arrest, he convinced law enforcement officers that he was insane
and avoided going to jail. None of the jurisdictions
that encountered Hatcher bothered to process his
fingerprints. As a result, authorities never discovered his violent past, which had included sexual

attacks on children. When sent to mental hospitals for treatment, Hatcher managed to convince psychiatrists that he was sane and was repeatedly released.

In February 1979, as Melvin Reynolds was arrested and charged with the murder of Eric Christgen in St. Joseph, Charles Hatcher, using the name Richard Clark, was released from the Douglas County Mental Hospital in Omaha, where he had been placed for the September 1978 sexual attack.

"When he was jailed, he curled up into a ball and wouldn't talk to anybody," said Sam Cooper, the deputy Douglas County prosecutor. "They got him to a county hospital and he was committed. He was in and out through our state mental institution. I don't think we ever had him identified here as Hatcher.

"I don't think it's rare that someone is arrested and then let go," Cooper said. "Cities all over the country release people wanted in other jurisdictions, if you have no particular reason for holding them. I suppose if he stayed in the criminal system here, ultimately we would have tried to do some background on him and tried to confirm who he was. He was in and out of our clutches so quickly, I think everybody thought, 'He's crazy, and he's not coming back to court,' and that was the end of it. I don't know how you stop a guy like that."

The pattern repeated itself in Lincoln, Des Moines and finally Bettendorf, Iowa, where Hatcher was arrested on July 16, 1981—his 52nd birthday—for attempting to abduct 11-year-old Todd Peers from a grocery store. The boy had gone into the supermarket at his mother's request to retrieve a bag of ice that she had forgotten. As Todd picked up the bag of ice, a man grabbed him by the shoulder and accused him of stealing.

"I'm a security guard," the man said. "Come with me."

The man began marching Todd down an aisle toward the rear of the store. They walked through an "employees only" door, through a storeroom and out a rear exit. Todd walked along, but protested that he had not taken anything. He showed the man the receipt that his mother had given him, proving that the ice had been paid for.

"You just come with me," the man replied. "We'll get that all taken care of later."

Once out the rear of the store, the man and the boy quickstepped across a parking lot and headed toward a wooded area.

"Where are we going?" Todd asked.

"I'm taking you to see your mom," the man replied.

Todd became suspicious. He knew that his mother was waiting for him in front of the store. Terrified, the boy broke away and sprinted for freedom. He found a security guard who called the police. The man was arrested, and he identified himself as Richard Clark. Child abduction charges against him were later dropped. On March 18, 1982, Hatcher, using the name of Richard Clark, was sent to the Mental Hospital Institute in Mount Pleasant, Iowa on an involuntary commitment. After 49 days, on May 7, 1982, he was released.

Two months later, a young woman named Stephanie Richie was accosted by a strange man on the downtown shopping mall in St. Joseph, Missouri. The man wanted to take her for a walk to get a cup of coffee. The stranger appeared to be in his fifties, was well-groomed and clean shaven. Stephanie was frightened by the man, whose eyes seemed to smolder. She told him to leave her alone. The encounter took place half a block down

the tree-lined mall from where Eric Christgen had
been abducted four years earlier.

The day after the stranger approached Stephanie
Richie on the downtown mall, a 10-year-old boy
named Kerry Heiss was grabbed at a mall on the
outskirts of St. Joseph. The attempted abduction
occurred in the same way that Todd Peers had
been snatched in Bettendorf, Iowa, the year before.
Kerry had been browsing in a record shop at the
East Hills Shopping Center in St. Joseph when a
man grabbed him by the shoulder and announced
he was a security guard. The man attempted to escort Kerry outside the store, but the boy bolted
away. Kerry found his grandmother, who had
brought him to the store, and together they notified
the St. Joseph police. But by the time officers arrived, the man was gone.

The next day—Thursday, July 29, 1982—there
was a brief report on the attempted abduction of
Kerry Heiss in the morning *St. Joseph Gazette*. Annette Steele, who lived in St. Joseph, with her two
children did not notice the short item in the paper
that morning. As she left for work at 7:45 A.M., her
11-year-old daughter, Michelle, and 13-year-old
son, James, were still asleep. The night before, Annette reminded Michelle that she had an appointment with the dentist the next day. She gave
Michelle bus fare for the trip downtown, money to
buy candy and a warning to be careful.

In that summer after the sixth grade, Michelle
enjoyed long days of bike riding with friends.
Freckle faced and red haired, she was known as
"Mary Poppins" to her many friends. They considered her special; the numerous "friendship beads"
on Michelle's blue tennis shoes indicated her popu-
larity. Teeth-straightening dental appointments
were not the only things that interrupted Mi-

chelle's summer play. There were babysitting jobs as well. All her mother's friends considered Michelle to be mature, and there were many requests for her babysitting services.

Her mother was aware also of Michelle's cautious approach to life. Once, when the two of them were watching television, Michelle pondered the predicament of a woman who had been kidnapped on the show.

"If something like that happened to me, Mom, I'd holler until someone paid attention to me and came to help me," Michelle said. "And, if that didn't work, I'd run."

Michelle had resumed living with her mother just a month before. Annette had separated from Leonard Steele in May 1981. Michelle had stayed with her father until June 1982, when Annette obtained custody. The move back to her mother's home was not a big one for Michelle. Leonard lived at 2712 Jackson and Annette lived just three blocks away.

Before Michelle left for the dental appointment, she put on a pair of earrings from a set her grandmother had given her two months earlier. Her grandmother had pierced her ears, and the earring set contained 12 pairs with birthstones, one for each month of the year. That day, Michelle chose the red stones.

Michelle's appointment was at 10:30 A.M. at the Kirkpatrick Building downtown, a three-mile bus ride from the family's home. Michelle had taken the bus downtown five or six times before, but never alone.

Helen Smith, the receptionist for Dr. Robert Day, greeted Michelle when she arrived promptly for her appointment at the fourth floor office. Michelle left at about 11:25. For the trip home, Michelle would have boarded the bus one block down Francis Street from the Kirkpatrick Building, right in front of Skaggs Drugstore where she could spend her candy money. Skaggs stands around the corner from the site where Stephanie Richie had encountered a strange man two days before.

When Annette Steele returned home from work at 3:15 P.M., her daughter was not at home. When Michelle's brother, Jim, said he hadn't seen her all day, Annette became concerned. She began calling her friends, who said they had not seen the girl. The dentist's office confirmed that Michelle had made her appointment. Annette called Leonard to see if Michelle had gone to visit her father. He said he hadn't seen his daughter all day, and now he became worried.

Together they anxiously retraced the route the bus would have taken to return their daughter home. They went to Skaggs and the Kirkpatrick Building, but found no trace of her. At 4:11 P.M., Annette Steele reported her daughter missing, and police officers dutifully took down the description: four feet, eight inches, 85 pounds. An organized search was not launched immediately, but police broadcast the bulletin about the missing girl.

The distraught couple told the police that Michelle was a very outgoing person who would talk to anyone who spoke to her. But she was not the type to go anywhere with a stranger. Annette said that Michelle could easily have gotten lost if she strayed off the main streets, but added that the girl was an "A" student, and if lost she knew enough to call her mother. She told the police that she and Michelle had a very good relationship, that they had had no major arguments and that Michelle had never attempted to run away before.

At 7:15 P.M., five police officers began to search

the Kirkpatrick Building. The search provided no clues to Michelle's disappearance. That night's summer reruns were interrupted by a televised bulletin about the missing girl, which prompted many tips. Girls matching that description had been seen at a snack bar, at a shopping center and riding a banana-seated bicycle. Later, the police discovered that there was another girl by the name of Michelle Steele living in the city, and police collected several reports on her whereabouts.

As the summer's day drew to an end, a scene from an unforgettable nightmare was recreated in St. Joseph. Sixty-five volunteer searchers began fanning out from the downtown area. By 9:00 P.M., 24 extra officers had joined the 4:00–12:00 shift. The police officially declared Michelle a missing person at 11:00 P.M., since it had been more than 12 hours since she had last been seen by anyone. The detectives said they would work 12-hour shifts until she was found. Michelle's picture appeared on the 10:00 news. At midnight, Chief Hayes took personal charge of the case, arriving at the Steele home to question the parents.

"It's possible that she ran away to teach you both a lesson," Hayes told the Steeles as they sat in the living room. Before he arrived, the police had searched the entire house, to be sure Michelle was not hiding there.

"If she was here, she wouldn't be hiding," the girl's brother said.

Annette repeated the story to Hayes. She told him that Michelle had gone downtown for a dental appointment.

"What kind of a mother are you to let your little girl go down there alone?" Hayes said. "Don't you know about all the perverts down there?"

Annette was stunned. No one had ever told her

that the downtown area was dangerous. When the reality of Hayes' remark sunk in, she and Leonard began to cry.

Lieutenant Loren "Buck" Powell was the police watch commander that night, and he processed the reports on sightings of Michelle Steele from all over town—at the park, at the swimming pool, on a bike, at a shopping center. But every report was checked thoroughly and none of the girls spotted was Michelle.

"You'd be surprised how many little red-headed girls there are," he said. Four years earlier, he had supervised the attendants who removed Eric Christgen's body from the bluffs near the Missouri River. Powell had bad vibes about this new disappearance.

Powell directed the searchers to cover the area between downtown and the river. He thought she must have gone that way, since someone would have seen her if she had traveled through downtown or the city's residential areas.

The orange sun sunk into Kansas and a bright moon turned the muddy river into a silver, shimmering stream. Searchers with flashlights scattered through the brush calling Michelle's name.

The upper Missouri was dingy that day, the state Conservation Department had reported. But it also reported that carp and catfish fishing were good. That night, Raymond Shubert was proving the department's report to be inaccurate. Shubert, his 15-year-old son, David, and Billy Fleck, a 12-year-old neighbor, were not having much luck.

Shubert noticed a man approaching from the woods that lined the downstream bank. As he came closer, Shubert could see that the man was carrying a radio in one hand, and in the other, a canteen that he frequently brought to his lips. The

man ignored Shubert, but sat down on the riverbank, about 10 yards from the boys.

"How are the fish biting tonight?" the man asked.

"Not like they usually do," young Shubert said.
"My dad usually catches plenty right here."

Another couple nearby also noticed the man.
Donald and Janet Niedel did not think he was a
fisherman. He was wearing tennis shoes and a
baseball cap, but carried no fishing equipment. He
looked odd, walking behind them, and stopped
without saying anything.

Later that night, about a mile downstream from
the fishermen, Max Bartram was behind the wheel
of a car that inched along the dirt road adjacent to
the riverbank. Bartram was a mechanic, but in his
spare time, he served the community as a reserve
deputy for the Buchanan County sheriff's department. He had been asked to help in the search for
Michelle. At about 10:00 P.M., Bartram was looking
toward the Missouri River when he spotted a man
walking underneath the Interstate 229 overpass
that runs parallel to the river. Bartram brought the
car to a stop and pointed a spotlight on the man,
who now hid behind a pillar.

"Hold it right there!" Bartram ordered, jumping
from the vehicle. A six-foot-high chain link fence
separated the two men and Bartram scrambled
over it. He approached the pillar.

"I'm a deputy sheriff. Come out of there."

The man emerged from the shadows. Bartram
noticed he was carrying a canteen.

"What have you got there?" Bartram asked.

"Just some of my things," the man replied.

"Come with me and bring them with you."

When the two men came to the fence, Bartram
shined a light on the man and asked him for identification.

"Have you seen anyone down there?" Bartram asked, motioning over the man's shoulder toward the river.

"No, I haven't. I've been down there almost all day and I haven't seen anyone."

"We're looking for a little girl."

"I haven't seen one."

"What's your name?"

"Richard Harris. I've been here most of the day, except at about 7:00 or 7:30 when I went up to Skaggs for beer."

Bartram let the man go, but noticed him again about an hour later near the spot where the Niedels were still fishing. Two St. Joseph policemen, also searching for Michelle, questioned "Richard Harris" there.

Detective Steve Fueston asked the man for identification, and he slowly reached into his wallet and displayed a card that identified him as Richard Harris. The card showed his date of birth as July 19, 1929. His address was 612 South 6th Street, which was the location of the Salvation Army Headquarters. Harris also showed the officers a Kansas City bus ticket which indicated that he had been in the area for almost a week.

"I've been fishing here all day. Except at about 7:30, when I went to get some beer at Skaggs," the man repeated.

"Skaggs closes at 6:00," said Fueston.

"Then it must have been earlier."

Fueston returned to his patrol car and radioed a request for outstanding warrants against "Richard Harris." The results of the check were negative, and the police gave no more thought to Harris that night.

Early Friday morning, there was an ominous re-enactment of an eerie St. Joseph scene. A search party formed in the parking lot of the downtown Civic Arena, two blocks from the river. A highway patrol helicopter hovered over the area and officers on horseback covered the rugged terrain. Fifty searchers began working north from the Pony Express Bridge and another group began sweeping south from the Civic Arena. Ten volunteers combed the area between the Arena and the river, all the way to the St. Joseph Power and Light plant. There, they turned south and headed downstream.

As the search resumed Friday morning, Ray Hector, a security officer at the St. Joseph State Mental Hospital, received a call from the switchboard operator. She told Hector that a man in the administration building was talking very loudly and kicking the information desk. Hector went to the building lobby. He found a man sitting in a chair, bent forward and holding his head between his hands.

"Make the voices quit," the man said. "Stop them. Make the voices quit. I can't stand it. They're scaring me."

The man was sobbing and would not answer Hector's questions. Two nurses began trying to calm the man down, and as they did, Hector searched through the man's duffle bag. Hector found a billfold that held an identification card in the name of Richard Clark of Davenport, Iowa. Hector asked the man if Richard Clark was his name. The man nodded "yes." The nurses asked him if he wanted medical help, and he nodded his head again. Richard Clark was voluntarily admitted to the mental hospital.

In 1978, Dennis and Kenneth Christgen had searched between downtown and the river for their missing nephew. Now four years later, Roy Montgomery was an uncle looking for his missing niece. He moved slowly. The "shingles" virus had prevented him from hunting for Michelle the night before. He was in pain. Each hundred yards he covered, in weeds over his head, seemed like a thousand. He was hurting inside too. He loved Michelle and feared for her safety. He was also angry. He believed that the police had been a bit cavalier about the search for Michelle.

Montgomery had begun just west of the arena, and proceeded south along the river. He felt that the others in the search did not take him seriously because he was having trouble keeping up. He was not with the other searchers when they discovered a blue "Pro Wing" tennis shoe. It was wet and was found six inches from the water's edge, as if it had been washed ashore.

When Montgomery caught up with the others and examined the shoe, he told them that he believed it was Michelle's. Clipped to the shoelace was a safety pin filled with "friendship beads." The police took the shoe to the Steele home.

"That's hers," Annette said when the police showed it to her.

Montgomery began to trudge along the muddy bank and he noticed a place where the weeds had been pushed aside, as if someone had created a path to the riverbank. He followed the vague trail until he found footprints, which he skirted.

"I don't know how far I walked, but I came to a tree I could not get around, so I went down to the river and walked along the river until I saw a broken tree and I went back up the bank," he said. "Just a little north of there, I saw what looked like a hollowed out place like maybe a tree had fallen. I looked over there and saw something white between the two logs and I walked over to it. I looked down between the logs and I saw Michelle laying there."

It was a picture he would try to forget for the rest of his life. Peering between stacks of branches, Montgomery saw the naked body of his niece lying in a fetal position. He sprinted up the riverbank, screaming.

"She's down there. She's underneath the brush. She's dead."

The news quickly reached Annette Steele at her home. Television crews were covering the morning's search efforts. The police at the scene confirmed for the reporters that the body was Michelle. Since Montgomery, the husband of one of Annette's sisters, had found the body, the police reacted as though the family had already been notified. No one softened the news for the Steeles the way that Holtslag had notified the Christgens of Eric's fate. Police confirmed the finding for the television crews, which broadcast the message that the body of Michelle Steele had been found. Annette Steele thus learned from a television announcer that her daughter was dead.

After finding Michelle's body, Montgomery, in a fit of rage and sadness, had sprinted down the riverbank. Police officers ran after him, and he reacted angrily when they stopped him. Then, in a bizarre turn of events, they arrested Montgomery and took him to the station to be questioned. Montgomery was considered a suspect simply because he had found Michelle's well-concealed body. In addition, the police theorized that Michelle would not have gone willingly to such a lonely spot if she did not know and trust the person who led her there. The police released Montgomery later that day after one of Annette's sisters vouched for his whereabouts on the previous day.

The discovery of Michelle's body brought a new set of demands on police resources. What had begun as a search for a missing person immediately turned into another child murder investigation. It was the ugliest of crimes, and as detectives began noting the evidence and taking photographs, they wondered how a city the size of St. Joseph could have hosted two fiendish killers within a four-year period. The chance of two psychopathic child killers operating within the city in so short a time was beyond the realm of possibility.

The body was found about 20 feet from the water's edge and 10 feet from the top of the bank. It was about 10 yards from the edge of the Interstate 229 overpass. It was less than a mile downstream from where Eric Christgen's body had been found. As the police wrestled the covered stretcher that carried Michelle up the slippery riverbank, one of the searchers wept openly.

"It's happening all over again," she cried.

CHAPTER THIRTEEN

"Maybe we ought to go back and see where Hatcher was at the time the Christgen boy was murdered."
—St. Joseph Police Detective John Kreiser

DR. YORK SILLIMAN, THE YOUNG BUCHANAN COUNTY medical examiner, said Michelle Steele had been beaten, bitten and raped. He believed she had been asphyxiated, and like previous pathologists who had studied the killer's work, he too had trouble determining how the asphyxiation had occurred. His first conclusion was that Michelle had died of "positional asphyxiation." He said she had been placed with her head pressed against the riverbank in such as way as to cut off oxygen. He also believed the girl had been tied up at one time, judging from the one-quarter-inch wide binding marks on both wrists. He estimated the time of death as sometime between 1:00 and 7:00 P.M. of the previous day.

Immediately after the discovery, the police issued a wanted bulletin for "Richard Harris," the man who had been observed the night before. When Bartram and the other officers compared notes, they realized that Harris had first been seen within 100 feet of the spot where Michelle's body was discovered. Other witnesses added information to the description, and from the police reports, it appeared that Harris had hovered around the murder scene for several hours.

The St. Joseph State Mental Hospital is 20 blocks from the river, but its security office operates on the same radio frequency as the St. Joseph Police Department. Hector heard the broadcast of the bulletin which described "Richard Harris." At 1:10 P.M., he called the police and told them that a man matching Harris' description had checked himself into the hospital under the name of Richard Clark. Hector gave the information to John Muehlenbacher, who had been promoted to lieutenant after the Christgen murder case was solved. Muehlenbacher dispatched two detectives to the hospital. One was Steve Fueston, who had questioned Richard Harris by the river the night before. That afternoon, the chief of staff, Dr. Richard Jacks, met the detectives and allowed them to see Clark.

Fueston identified Richard Clark as the man he had seen on the riverbank. Max Bartram, the reserve deputy who had seen "Richard Harris" at the underpass, went to the hospital and also recognized him. The police ordered the hospital to detain the suspect for them. They seized his clothes and the other property he carried in his knapsack. They found two lengths of nylon cords that they believed could have been used to bind Michelle's hands. They took Clark's picture, and mixed it with four photographs of other middle-aged men.

By this time, Stephanie Richie had reported to police that a man had tried to talk her into going with him on the mall. They showed the photographs to Stephanie and to Kerry Heiss. Both picked out Richard Clark as the man who had approached them in the two days before Michelle was abducted. The police also showed the photos to Raymond Shubert and his son, and they agreed that Clark was the man they had seen while fishing that night. The police learned that Clark had been living at the Salvation Army Headquarters, and when he had not been sober enough to check in there, he had camped along the riverbank.

On Saturday, Fueston and Muehlenbacher went to the hospital to pick up Clark for questioning. On the way to the station, Clark moaned, rolled his eyes, clutched his head and ignored everyone around him. He was photographed, but the police could not take his fingerprints. He was returned to the hospital two hours later. Dr. Jacks told the police that he thought Clark was feigning mental illness.

By August 3, the police believed that they had enough evidence to take the case to Michael Insco, the Buchanan County prosecuting attorney. Eyewitnesses had placed Clark near the scene of the crime. Nylon cords had been found in his possession. A dental impression taken from his teeth appeared to match the bite marks on the girl's body. In addition, Clark's shoes, seized when he entered the mental hospital, had a sole pattern consistent with the prints left on the riverbank where the body was found.

On August 3, 1982, Clark was charged with first degree murder, and bond was set at $250,000. Insco said the charge was first degree murder, because the death had taken place during the commission of the felony of rape.

For the next 10 days, Clark lay in a fetal position in the Buchanan County Jail, not saying a word and moving only when he had to use a restroom. Deputies were forced to carry him to the courtroom on August 13, where Associate Circuit Judge Donald Parker ordered a mental examination for him. When Clark first checked into the St. Joseph

State Hospital, he had admitted that he had been treated for mental illnesses in Nebraska and Iowa. Dr. Jacks obtained copies of Clark's medical records from those two states, and Jacks compared his present actions with his prior behavior.

Sheriff's deputies managed to obtain Clark's fingerprints and sent them to the FBI for processing. But even before the results arrived from Washington, some of the oldtimers who worked in the clerk's office in the Buchanan County Courthouse thought they recognized Clark as a notorious St. Joseph character from the 1950s. They recalled that his name was Charlie Hatcher.

As police began to plumb the depths of his criminal life, they learned that he had been released just months before from a mental hospital in Mount Pleasant, Iowa.

Stephen Anfinson, assistant superintendent at the Iowa State Hospital, said Hatcher had apparently tricked the system.

"I don't think we had any way of suspecting the extensive criminal history or involvement that this person had," Anfinson said. "Certainly, if there had been any inkling that there was something like that, our approach would have been different. To a large extent, the level of information you get depends on the honesty of the patient. Unless it's documented, we don't have a way of running a check like the police do using fingerprints and the FBI. That's not an option in the clinical setting. It's possible to fool the system to get in and out."

There had been no fingerprint check of Richard Clark when he was arrested in Iowa. When St. Joseph Police contacted the police in Bettendorf for information on the man named Richard Clark, there was an emotional explosion.

"That girl never needed to die," said Decker

Ploehn, a Bettendorf police detective who was enraged to learn that the man he had known as Clark had been released from the state mental hospital. Clark's fingerprints, which Bettendorf police had taken several months after he was arrested, were never sent off to the FBI. Thus, police there never learned of his history of sexual attacks on children or that he was a wanted man in California.

"We really screwed up," Ploehn said after learning of Michelle's death. "There are so many transient people. Who's to know who they are and what they are? He knew the game and played it perfectly. We just didn't play it as well."

Dr. Jacks did not fall into the same trap as psychiatrists had in California, Nebraska and Iowa. He benefitted from their observations, and he included them in his report to the court:

> I believe he is mute by deliberate choice as his mutism is observed to have a sudden onset after legal difficulties. There is a prior history of similar behavior. He has displayed coherent, relevant and purposeful speech to deputies even to the point of changing stories on the day of the offense. His exaggerated mouth movements with squinting of the eyes and muscular resistiveness and head banging without injury occur only when he believes he is being observed. I know of no neurologic or psychiatric disease which describes the above findings. I also believe that it is virtually inconceivable that a grossly mentally disordered individual walked the streets of St. Joseph for several weeks and lived with the Salvation Army without being brought to the attention of police, state hospital, or both for civil involuntary detention procedures.

Jacks concluded in his report that Clark had the capacity to understand the proceedings against him and to help in his own defense. He stated that Hatcher did not need to be held in a state hospital.

"It is my opinion that the accused does not have a mental disease or defect," Jacks concluded. "It is my opinion that at the time of the alleged criminal conduct that the accused did know and appreciate the nature, quality and wrongfulness of his conduct and was considered capable of conforming his conduct to the requirements of the law."

On September 12, Clark pleaded not guilty by reason of mental disease or defect. The plea was entered by Joseph Morrey, the assistant Buchanan County public defender who had been appointed to represent him. Morrey asked for a second test to determine Clark's competence to stand trial. Clark refused to talk to Morrey. Clark shuffled into the interview room and kept his head bowed on his chest. During the hearing on the request, Clark, gaunt and bearded, swayed in a wooden chair. His eyes were closed as he fidgeted with his thumbs. Occasionally, a cough would break his silence. He seemed oblivious to the sound of voices in the courtroom.

Clark was sent for a second mental examination at the Missouri State Hospital in Fulton, where Melvin Lee Reynolds had been examined for several weeks in 1979. A trial date was set for December 6. It was the first of many that would be set and missed.

As St. Joseph police began assembling the evidence against Charles R. Hatcher, aka Richard M. Clark, some detectives wondered whether there might be a connection between the Steele murder and the Eric Christgen case. They wondered if it was possible that Hatcher, who had launched his criminal career in St. Joseph 34 years earlier, had returned to his home in the summer of 1978. Judging from the records, it was possible. It had been 23 years since he was last in their custody. In 1959, he had been arrested for attempting to abduct a newspaper delivery boy. He had covered a lot of ground since then. There had been thefts, burglaries and escapes in Kansas and Oklahoma. There had also been sex offenses against children. Hatcher had covered more ground than Jesse James.

The suspicion was raised during a discussion of the Steele murder among detectives John Kreiser, James Brooke and Lieutenant John Muehlenbacher.

"Maybe we ought to go back and see where Hatcher was at the time the Christgen boy was murdered," Kreiser suggested.

"That case has already been taken care of," Muehlenbacher said. "This hasn't anything to do with that."

During the examination of Hatcher at the Missouri State Hospital in Fulton, psychiatrists used sodium amytal, a "truth serum," in an attempt to determine whether he was physically able, or simply refusing, to speak. Dr. Sadashiv D. Parwatikar, the "Dr. Sam" who had examined Melvin Reynolds three years earlier, obtained permission for the drug test from Richard Dahms, the public defender.

On December 2, 1982, Hatcher was strapped to an examination table while Parwatikar injected the drug into Hatcher's right arm. Dahms sat a few feet away and the only other person in the room was the man operating the camera that videotaped the session. Hatcher at first resisted the effects of the drug, shaking his head from side to side, and in a state of semi-consciousness, refused to respond to Parwatikar's questions. But then the fluid began to seep into the crevices of his brain and the evil stored there began floating to his consciousness.

Parwatikar's patient probing broke down Hatcher's resistance. Hatcher's answers were long in coming, and Parwatikar would often have to tap him on the forehead to bring him up out of a foggy sleep. Between the questions, he would inject more drops of the drug from the syringe still inserted in Hatcher's arm. Often Hatcher's answers were barely audible, and Parwatikar would repeat them so the microphone attached to the camera could record them.

"Where were you before you went to jail?" the doctor asked.

"By the river," Hatcher responded.

"What were you doing by the river?"

"I was hearing voices."

"How long were you hearing these voices?"

"For a little while."

"What would these voices say?"

"Sacrifice a maiden."

"What were you doing down by the river?"

"Drinking."

"How much would you drink on a given day?"

"A fifth."

"A fifth of what?"

"Whatever I got my hands on."

"Why don't you talk to us now?"

"The voices tell me not to."

"How long have you had the problem of not speaking to people?" Dr. Sam asked. "How long have these voices told you not to speak to people?"

"A year or so," Hatcher replied.

"So, for a year you have not been talking?"

"No, it comes and goes."

"What makes it come and what makes it go?"

"The gods are angry at me."

"Why are the gods mad at you?"

"My mother is white and my dad is black."

"Is that the truth that your father is black and your mother is white?"

"I have never seen my father."

"What were you doing on July 29? Can you remember?"

"I was down by the river."

"Do you remember seeing a girl at all?"

"I was watching girls."

"What do they look like?"

"They are beautiful."

"What are you doing?"

"I hear the voices."

"What are the voices saying?"

"Sacrifice a maiden."

"What are you doing next?"

Hatcher's head rolled back and forth on the pillow, as if he were trying to shake from his skull either the effect the drug was having on his brain, or the horrible memory of what he had done. He became still again, and would not respond to Parwatikar's questions. But the doctor would not let him sleep. He tapped him on the forehead again.

"Mr. Clark. Mr. Clark," Parwatikar said in a loud voice. "What are you doing next? Go back. Concentrate."

"I am talking to them," Hatcher responded, in a low, thick voice.

"To who?"

"The girls."

"What are you saying?"

"What are you doing in school?"

"What are you doing now?"

"I can't remember."

"Tell me what you can remember."

"I talked to girls downtown."

"What was her name?"

"She told me, but I forgot."

"Where were you?"

"Down by the river."

"Then what?"

"I can't remember."

"Concentrate. Concentrate."

"Then, I heard the voices."

"What are they saying now?"

"Sacrifice the maiden."

"Then what did you do?"

"We got into an argument."

"What kind of argument?"

Hatcher's chest heaved as he sucked in great gulps of air. He licked his lips repeatedly as if they were parched. He brought his head up and tried to rub his face with his hands, but they were held down by the leather straps. He was silent for a few moments and then Parwatikar thumped him back into the conversation.

"Richard, Richard," the doctor persisted. "What kind of argument?"

"She didn't want to drink," Hatcher said.

"So you wanted her to drink and she didn't want to drink."

"Yeah."

"Think hard. What's the next thing you remember?"

"Going up to town."

"What happened to the girl?"

"She stayed there."

"You don't remember what happened after the argument?"

"No."

"What were the voices saying?"

"Don't talk to anyone."

"But they were saying 'sacrifice the maiden.' Had you taken care of what they said?" Parwatikar asked. "Did you do what they asked you to do? Did you follow the command?"

"Sometimes I think I did," Hatcher replied.

"What makes you think you did?"

"I didn't hear those voices anymore."

Based on the test results and their other observations, Dr. Sam and the other psychiatrists did not believe Hatcher had really heard demons speaking to him. The voices came and went depending on where Hatcher was. It indicated that Hatcher was able to control the demons and their voices rather than their controlling him. He had clearly constructed the demons in order to provide himself with an explanation for his violence. The demons were a product of his conscious, deliberate thoughts, appearing at his beck and call. The hallucinations had not come to him; Hatcher had created them.

In the spring of 1983, Dr. Anasseril Daniel, a psychiatrist at the Missouri State Hospital, delivered a finding to the court regarding Clark's competence: "I don't believe he is suffering from any mental disorder. He might be suffering from a minimal depression, but nothing of psychotic proportions. Based on my lengthy observation with Mr. Clark, I am of the opinion his not communicating with me is voluntary. This person has benefited from remaining mute in the past. He's using the same symptom now when he is faced with serious criminal charges. The only time he can break his muteness, probably, is when everything is over."

On April 19, 1983, Clark was ruled competent to

stand trial for first degree murder in the death of
Michelle Steele. A new trial date of June 6 was set.
Clark had been returned to the Buchanan County
jail, and the guards noticed that dramatic changes
had taken place in him during his stay at the state
hospital. He was not the same man who was originally brought there in a catatonic state.

He now returned eye contact with the deputies
and communicated with them by gesturing with
his hands and head. He whistled religious songs.
Sometimes he would get up out of bed and scurry
around his cell like a mad mouse. The deputies
thought, at times, that he was exercising. When
they came to his door to observe him, Clark would
flip them the bird. Sometimes he laughed at them.
Once, he threw cupfuls of water at a jailer and another time he threw a glass of milk at a trustee. His
obscene gestures included unzipping his fly, taking
out his penis and shaking it at whoever was observ-
ing him. The jailers watched Clark like a mad mon-
key at a zoo.

At other times, Clark would lie flat on his back,
with his hands clasped behind his head. He would
try to keep his eyes open by staring at the ceiling.
He fought sleep because of the nightmares it
brought. When he closed his eyes, ugly scenes
danced in his brain. There were so many pictures
of bodies—on a river bank, on a bluff, along a
creek bed, on a concrete slab, on a loading dock.
They were so numerous that it took several minutes to count them all. Then there was that other
picture . . . the innocent man denied freedom
. . . suffering sexual humiliation . . . looking out
the cell door. The establishment Clark had grown
to hate, the St. Joseph justice system which had put
him away so many years ago, was responsible for

an innocent man's imprisonment. They are as guilty as I am, Clark thought.

Jack Christopher, a sheriff's deputy, never knew what to expect from his unusual prisoner. He was making his rounds at 8:00 A.M. on May 3, 1983. He went into Clark's cell and asked whether he wanted his window opened. Clark shook his head. As Christopher was leaving, Clark was exercising his arms by swinging them. Just before the jailer closed the door, Clark handed Christopher a scrap of paper. It was a laundry slip, and on the back it said: "Please call the FBI and tell them I would like to see them today. Very important case."

CHAPTER FOURTEEN

"Sixteen total that I know for sure from the midwest to the west coast."
   —Charles Hatcher discussing the murders he
had committed

THE NOTE THAT CHARLES HATCHER HAD WRITTEN
was passed through the hands of jail supervisors,
the sheriff and then Patrick Robb, the assistant
county prosecutor who was responsible for the
state's case against Clark.

"If he wants to see the FBI, there's nothing we
can do to stop him," Robb told Hatcher's jailers.
"You better call Joe Holtslag."

In the spring of 1983, Joe Holtslag was spending
his 16th year on his St. Joseph assignment, much
longer than he originally intended. When he and
his wife, Sandy, arrived from the east coast, they
nearly cried their first night in St. Joseph. They
kept telling each other, "Well, it's only for three
years." But during the weeks and months that followed, they found the community appealing. The
people were definitely friendlier. It was a quick
trip to get to work. They easily made friends. And
once their three children, Jay, Tracy, and Eric,
were all in school, there was no moving them.

Joe and Sandy had been high school sweethearts
in Albany, New York, where Joe's father owned
and operated a service station. Joe's ambition was
to become a partner with his dad after high school,

but his father encouraged him to attend college. Joe and Sandy were married in 1962, a year before he received a Bachelor of Science degree in economics from St. Bernadine of Siena College. He went through the Army ROTC program and was commissioned a second lieutenant in 1964. He was sent to Vietnam, and every day he was there he received letters from Sandy that were 10, 12, 15 pages long. He was a forward air observer until a premature jump from a landing helicopter severely injured his knee in January 1966.

Recuperating in a hospital at Ft. Benning, he thought about a future in law enforcement. He thought about the FBI but believed that one would have to be an accountant or lawyer to qualify. Sandy inquired with the FBI office in Columbus, Georgia, and the timing could not have been better. J. Edgar Hoover, eager to hire Vietnam veterans, sought 500 new agents under a modified hiring program. Holtslag saw three doctors before finding one who would state that Joe's knee was 100 percent functional. He entered new agents training on April 25, 1966.

His first assignment was in Charlotte, North Carolina, where he investigated cross burnings and the intimidation of blacks. Holtslag felt like the Lone Ranger—a Yankee, a Roman Catholic, prosecuting the Ku Klux Klan in North Carolina. Later, they moved to Raleigh, and then in June, 1967, he was assigned to the St. Joseph office. Holtslag liked the variety of the work. He spent his days performing background checks, supervising police training, reacting to bank robberies and investigating car theft rings. Much of his duty fell under the heading of "liaison with local police departments." This was how he categorized his early work on the Christgen murder case. But before the case reached its conclusion, it reminded him of his days in North Carolina. He felt like an outcast.

When Holtslag received the call to see Richard Clark, he thought, "Oh shit, here we go again. It's another police brutality case. Somebody thinks their civil rights have been violated."

At 10:30 A.M., on the morning that he heard about the note, Holtslag visited Clark in the dark bowels of the Buchanan County Jail. The yellow and gray paint, which four years earlier Melvin Reynolds had spread on the walls and cell bars, was now covered with grime and was flaked and chipped. Holtslag had heard about what Clark had done to the Steele girl, and he was not looking forward to meeting this man and listening to his whining complaints about unfair treatment. Holtslag was prepared for revulsion as Clark shuffled into the interview room, handcuffed and shackled.

Nine months in captivity had turned Clark's skin the color of a lizard's belly. His watery brown eyes dripped like a pair of gleaming ball bearings that had been dipped in motor oil. The eyes darted wildly back and forth between a thick band of eyebrows and a matted thicket of a grey, red and brown beard. Greasy streaks of black hair were pasted down on his forehead, and one side of his drooling mouth hung lower than the other, as though he had suffered a stroke.

If Clark was not crazy, and they had pronounced him sane at the Missouri State Hospital, he sure looked the part, Holtslag thought. But Holtslag was not startled or revolted by Clark's appearance. He felt instead an eerie fascination. The first emotion Holtslag felt was recognition, and he riffled through mug shots in his memory wondering where he had seen Clark before.

"I know this guy," Holtslag thought. "But from where?"

He kept staring at Clark as he sat clumsily down at a table across from him. He was still wondering where he had seen Clark before when the prisoner began a series of movements indicating that he could not talk.

"That's a bunch of bullshit," Holtslag said loudly. He was anxious to get the meeting over with. "I know you can talk. Everybody knows that. The police talked to you that night under the viaduct. If you've got something to tell me, tell me man to man."

Clark, looking paranoid, glanced self-consciously around the empty room as if it were filled with people watching him. Apparently reassured he reached into his sock and pulled out a piece of paper folded tightly into a one-inch square. He handed it across the table to Holtslag, who carefully opened and studied it. The top half of the document was a map of a region of eastern Iowa and western Illinois, separated by the Mississippi River. The map indicated Davenport and Bettendorf, Iowa, and Moline and Rock Island, Illinois. The area is known as the "Quad Cities." In the river between the two states was an island where the U.S. Army Arsenal was located.

The bottom half of the document contained directions to be followed on the map:

Going from R.I. toward Davenport on the right side of the bridge on the Arsenal side of the bridge theres a guard rail on the right side. About the middle of the rail look toward the bank. There's a level area. Walk about 10 feet to the bank. Look down the bank about five feet. There's a steel rod sticking out. Go under the rod and look to your left about two feet. Dig under the rocks. You will find a body.

After Holtslag read the map he looked up at Clark, whose brown eyes burned brightly.

"Will you answer some questions about the note?"

Clark quickly nodded and at the same time motioned as if he were writing. Holtslag got the idea and handed him a pen.

"You find the body, then we will talk," Clark wrote. "This isn't bullshit. This is all for now. OK?"

"Is this on government property?" the agent asked.

Clark took up the pen again. "The Arsenal. There's three bridges at the Quad Cities. This is the Arsenal area."

"Is the body a male or female?"

Clark scrawled the word "male."

"Is he an adult or child?"

"Adult," Clark wrote.

"When was the body buried?"

"June 1981," Clark wrote, and he immediately followed it up with: "Come back after you find it."

Clark then stood up from his chair and shivered uncontrollably. He turned and walked to a corner of the room and faced the wall. He stood there while Holtslag watched his back. The agent wondered momentarily whether he could get more information from Clark, then got up and left Clark staring at a corner of the Buchanan County Jail. The entire interview had taken 12 minutes and Clark had not said a word the entire time.

With Clark's map in his pocket, Holtslag drove to the FBI office in Kansas City. He faxed the document to the FBI office in Rock Island.

Jack Lewis, the agent who received the map

copy, took it to the security office of the Rock Island Arsenal where he was joined by local authorities. At about 5:00 P.M., they followed the map to Sylvan Slough, a chute of the Mississippi River on the Illinois side of the island. They came to the bridge marked on the map, and the agent climbed over a guard rail and went down a hillside. About four feet from the river's edge, the agent saw a steel post sticking from the ground. And just to the left of the post, he saw something else protruding from the rich, black soil.

Holtslag was still in his car returning to St. Joseph from Kansas City when he received a radio message instructing him to telephone Rock Island agency. When he did, Lewis told him he had found a human thigh bone growing from the mud along the riverbank. The agent had not even had to dig as Clark had suggested. High water had uncovered part of the body for him.

When Holtslag returned to St. Joseph, he went to see Patrick Robb, the assistant prosecutor, and told him about the discovery of the body in Rock Island. Both men agreed that Clark was gearing up to make a statement about the Steele case.

"He's smart enough to know the system," Holtslag said. "He knew he had to do something of a magnitude to get the FBI to listen to him. What better way than to give us a body?"

"I wonder why he didn't just tell the deputies about it?" Robb asked.

"I don't know. I guess he figured since it was on military property, it would be a federal case. Maybe he just didn't want to involve a middleman. Whatever the reason, he's established credibility now."

Over dinner, Robb briefed Holtslag on the details of the Steele murder case and plied him with questions he needed answers to. Hundreds of miles away, detectives began the work of carefully removing bones from a watery grave on the Rock Island Arsenal.

Eugene Sullivan, the Rock Island County coroner, told reporters that the body would never have been found without the map. At 11:00, police officers began removing the bones. They found a skeleton that was semi-clothed with a light colored shirt, what appeared to be the remnants of blue jeans and a reddish colored jacket. They also found light colored athletic socks and one running shoe. They placed the bones in a body bag and took them to a funeral home in Rock Island, where Sullivan began examining them.

"The only flesh which appeared to be remaining on the body was on the anterior area of the skull," the coroner later reported. "Also recovered were seven teeth from the area of the skull and what appeared to be hair."

"There was no skull fracture, no fractured ribs," Sullivan said in his report. "We had no way of knowing what might have been the cause of death. If there was any evidence at the gravesite, it has all deteriorated by now."

At about the same time, Holtslag met again with Clark. Deputies had brought him to an interview room in the county courthouse. The room was equipped with a two-way mirror, which permitted observation by a person in an adjoining room. From inside the small, dark room, where the prosecutor's office kept its files, Robb watched and listened as Holtslag began questioning Clark.

Holtslag began by telling Clark that the FBI had located a body at the exact spot indicated by his map. Then, Holtslag read him his Miranda rights, which Clark quickly signed as if he knew them by heart. Once the paperwork was out of the way, Holtslag sat for nearly a full minute, just looking at the prisoner.

Finally he said: "You've got my complete and undivided attention."

For the next 90 minutes, Richard Clark furiously scratched answers to Holtslag's questions on a yellow note pad on the table between them. The agent would ask a question, and if it required a "yes" or "no" answer, Clark would indicate with his head. A more detailed answer would be written on the paper, with Clark's face grimacing intently as he fashioned the words. He ignored the even inked lines and covered the page at wild angles. Sometimes the words were misspelled or unintelligible, and sometimes the sentences rambled.

Holtslag thought he could read insanity between the scribbles. When this interview was over, the agent knew that the most disturbing case of his entire law enforcement career had been dropped in his lap. And as wild as Clark's story was, he believed it immediately, and knew that his biggest problem would be convincing St. Joseph that it was true.

The FBI man in Rock Island had told Holtslag on the telephone that the body found there appeared to be that of a child, with very small bones and a small skull. That's where Holtslag decided to start.

"Is this person in Rock Island a teenager?"

Clark shook his head.

"Is he an adult male?"

Clark nodded.

"Was he in the military?"

Again Clark shook his head and then wrote: "James Churchill, 34 years old, from Galesburg, Illinois, 130 pounds or so—Police at Galesburg know him or sheriff dept."

When he disappeared in the summer of 1981, James Lewis Churchill was a 38-year-old man with the mind of a child. He had been born in Farmington, Illinois, and as a child, he had been diagnosed mentally retarded and developmentally disabled. Doctors believed his condition was caused by a bout of German measles his mother contracted when she was pregnant with Jim. When Jim was 11, he was placed in an Illinois mental institution. But when he was 31, the state determined he was not a danger to society and, over his family's objections, he was given his freedom.

Police in Rock Island, Moline and Galesburg got to know Jimmy from minor scrapes with the law. He was never the ringleader of the trouble, but he was always open to the suggestions of others. Then, in June 1981, he disappeared. His telephone calls to his family stopped. A nurse who frequently checked on him noticed that he no longer was living at his apartment in Galesburg.

"Did you kill him?" Holtslag asked Clark.

Clark looked at Holtslag with a blank face and gave no response.

"Was he a friend of yours?"

Clark nodded.

"Well, do you know who killed him?"

Clark nodded again.

"Who killed him?"

Again Clark did not respond.

"Why was he killed?"

Clark wrote: "Robbery."

"How did you know the exact directions to locating the body?"

Clark wrote: "You will get what you want, but give me time. That was one of my reasons."

As Holtslag read the answer, he became concerned. He wanted to establish a rapport with Clark. He knew Clark had something to say, but wondered how to tap the information without turning him off. He worried that he might say something that would conclude the bizarre conversation. He wracked his brain for questions that would keep the dialogue moving, wondering the whole time where it was going. Only Clark knew. Holtslag felt the interview was getting away from him, that he was losing control of it.

Clark pointed to the part of the Miranda warning that mentioned he was entitled to a lawyer in the event he needed one.

"This lawyer you talked about. Is he federal or state?" he wrote.

"You've already got a lawyer appointed to represent you on your pending murder charge. There has been no federal violation established, so the only attorney you would have access to now would be the public defender who is now representing you."

Clark seemed satisfied with the answer, and then abruptly wrote "Bathroom" on the paper. Holtslag knocked on the door, and the two deputies waiting outside took Clark away. With Clark out of the room, Holtslag turned to the mirror on the wall and shrugged his shoulders to Robb. Clark returned 10 minutes later, and Holtslag asked the deputies to remove the shackles. When the two had settled down again, Holtslag returned to the subject of Churchill's body.

"Why did you give us the directions to the body?"

"That's because it leads to yet another one like you just found. More than one, but I'm thinking about it. OK?"

"Well, how did Churchill die?"

"He was killed."

"Why do you want to tell the FBI about it? Why not the local cops?"

"That's because these fuckin' state and city cops lie too fuckin' much. I have more than one reason."

"These other bodies that you referred to; have they been found?"

"I know that one of the other bodies were found. I don't know if any of the others were or not. One of them should have been found, but I don't know for sure. I don't know just how far I will go. Probably in time, I will tell them all, but back to my number one reason in telling you about body number one is about the one that was found, but first I have to get things straight in my mind."

Holtslag stared at the answer. He read it again and again wondering if he'd be able to get it straight in his head. If he read Clark correctly, it seemed he pointed the FBI in the direction of the body in Rock Island so that the agent would then listen when he told him about other bodies, one in particular, that had been found.

Before the briefing with Robb, Holtslag had talked with the FBI agent in Rock Island, who suggested that perhaps Clark might know about the death of a 12-year-old boy who was found across the river in Davenport in August 1979. Holtslag brought that up, hoping it might jar something loose.

"No, I can prove where I was at that time," Clark wrote. "What date was that?"

When Holtslag repeated that it was August 1979, Clark scribbled: "No, I was in the hospital at that time."

Holtslag was getting desperate. Here's a guy you've got to be careful of, he thought. Say the wrong thing, and he's going to feel the same way about me as he does about all these local cops. The agent wondered if he should ask whether this other body was that of Michelle Steele. Then another idea struck him.

"How many bodies are there, altogether?"

Clark looked at the agent for a long time, then turned to stare at a wall, totally motionless. He remained that way for a long time. It became totally still. The man known as Richard Clark began thumbing through the pictures in his mind. Each scene was familiar to him. He had relived them over and over again. Holtslag thought he could hear the man thinking back over the years, counting the bodies. For 10 minutes, Clark sat that way, going over what had been carefully logged in his mind.

Finally, he took up the pencil again and wrote: "Sixteen total that I know for sure from the midwest to the west coast. All adult except three, all males, 13 adults, all males."

When Holtslag read the answer, he had to force himself to stifle a reaction. Ordinarily, in cases like this, he wore his computer face, an unflinching, almost remote look. But he had to fight now from showing the shock he felt. He had been prepared for something terrible, but nothing like this.

"Do you know what cities the bodies were located in?"

"I know about the locations of most of them, but not as sure as the one you found."

Holtslag looked back at Clark, more confused than ever. What in the hell does he mean? he thought. The one I had found. Does he mean Michelle Steele's body?

Holtslag was getting tired of the game. He wanted to reach over and grab Clark by the throat and choke him into talking clearly about his crimes. What in the hell are you talking about?, Holtslag wanted to say. Clark was indicating Holtslag had known about one of his bodies. But Holtslag knew he had not been involved in any murders Clark might know about.

Just as Holtslag was preparing to pose another question, Robb moved his chair in the adjoining observation room, and the noise caused Clark to glance sharply at the mirror on the wall. He looked at it for a long time and Holtslag held his breath. Clark then turned a knowing face to Holtslag and began writing again.

"They are over there. I could hear them. But it don't matter. First, I have to get the one that was found out of the way. I don't want these county dicks to know my business for now anyway."

Holtslag tried to bluff and played dumb.

"Would you be more comfortable in another room?" the agent said agreeably. "I can go next door and check to see if anyone is in there."

Holtslag stood up and stepped into the adjoining room. He told Robb to be quiet and instructed him to step out of the observation room for a moment. Holtslag returned to the interview room and told Clark, "I checked in there. There's no one in there now."

He resumed the interrogation.

"When was this other body found that you keep referring to?"

"I know. So do you know about it."

For a long moment, Holtslag looked at the written answer. He doubted whether he would be able to solve this puzzle tonight. It was almost midnight. It had been a long day. Perhaps if he slept on it, he would be better equipped to unlock the ugly secrets in this man's twisted mind. Initially, Holtslag believed he would be dealing with an ignorant criminal. He had come armed with questions for the prisoner to answer. But the agent had found himself dealing with a very disciplined man who had methodically offered up a body to gain his attention. Holtslag was beginning to feel as if *he* was the prisoner.

Now, Clark was asking the questions, and the FBI agent was out of answers. Holtslag looked at the scrawled sentence again— "So do you know about it"—and he filed through the murders he had studied in his 16-year career: the victims' bodies that could not be connected with a killer, the bones that could not be identified. As he stared at the sentence, Holtslag realized the answer was not on the page, but in the enigmatic face of the man sitting across the table from him. Holtslag raised his head and stared at it.

Holtslag's mind suddenly divulged the case. From the crevices of his mind the image emerged. It wasn't a photograph or a shadowy recollection of a face seen long ago. It was a mental picture, dictated by a drowsy, droning voice five years earlier in an interview which had been conducted using the technique of "investigative hypnotism." Holtslag raised his eyebrows and sat up straight in his chair. He looked directly in Clark's eyes.

I *have* seen this man before, Holtslag thought. The agent realized where it had been. Jeffrey Davey had described in vivid detail the man he had seen walking with a small blond boy down the railroad tracks along the Missouri River on May 26, 1978.

This is that guy, Holtslag thought. Right down to the stoop shoulder and the crooked arm.

Finally, the FBI agent had the answer that Richard Clark wanted.

"Eric Christgen."

For the first time in the interview, Clark smiled. Then he started to write. It would be a long time before he stopped.

CHAPTER FIFTEEN

"Don't you understand what has to be done to prevent this ever happening again?"
—Charles Hatcher

"FOR NOW, KEEP WHAT I HAVE SAID TO YOURSELF OR I clam up," Hatcher wrote. "You are smart enough to know what these bastards in St. Joe will do for a conviction, even if they have to frame someone to get it. They lied under oath on me about this deal I'm charged with. Also they got other witness to lie, so why wouldn't they do it on somebody else? I know that you probably have kids of your own and you wouldn't want some innocent person paying for it."

As he wrote, Clark's face would swing between contortion and animation. A twitch or change of expression would accompany each word. Holtslag watched his face but also tried to read the words as Clark wrote them.

"Before I say more, I want to be sure of something first," Clark wrote. "Why did you say the person you did? You must not have been satisfied with what was done on that deal."

"You're smart," Holtslag replied after he read the sentence.

"No, I'm not smart. I'm annoyed at the fix I'm in."

"Is there an innocent man in jail who did not kill Eric Christgen?"

"I didn't say that, but you're in a place and smart enough to get things rolling in the right direction. We're getting to reason number one."

"Do you know for sure the man in prison for killing the Christgen boy didn't do it?"

"People who did the thing on that guy isn't going to want to hear about this, but can get around it, I'm sure. I won't talk to any of these county or city cops and I may say more if the prosecuting attorney wants to file capital charges, otherwise, forget it."

Holtslag had to read the sentence twice, before he thought he understood what Clark was trying to say. If he understood him correctly, Clark was saying that he wanted to face the death penalty. The first degree murder charges he faced in the death of Michelle Steele could not get him a trip to the gas chamber. But capital murder charges could. Clark was saying he wanted to be put to death. In Missouri, if he were convicted on capital murder in the Michelle Steele case, he could be sentenced to either death or 50 years imprisonment.

As the agent read, Clark continued writing on the pad: "Don't you understand what has to be done to prevent this ever happening again?"

Holtslag read the sentence and then stared at Clark's impassive face.

"I don't think a person should be in prison for something he did not do," Holtslag said.

"I doubt if he ever did anything wrong in his life. He's just a harmless nut, or so I understood. I don't know him."

"How do you know he didn't kill the Christgen boy?"

"You're leading again."

"You appear to have a conscience and you are concerned about that guy."

"No, that's the problem. If I had one, I wouldn't do the things I have done."

"That's not true. You're sick."

"Very sick son of a bitch. But not insane."

"Well, do you want to talk about the Christgen case?"

"No. I can get what I want on any of these deals. Like I said before I may talk about them all in time I don't know yet. Maybe. Does the deal you found today carry the death penalty? I heard the federal government doesn't have the death penalty except on one thing and that isn't murder."

"The reason you are not charged with capital murder on Michelle Steele is because she may not have died until after she was left by her assailant. Do you want me to call the prosecuting attorney and ask him what the law is on capital murder?"

"He's probably sound asleep and wouldn't appreciate being waked up over that."

"The reason you're charged with first degree murder of Michelle Steele was probably because she died in the commission of a felony rape."

"You see, I may be guilty of murder, but not rape regardless of what the doctor said. I can't even get a hard on. So, this isn't going to get that kid out of the pen, and I want that most of all. I know what he has had to put up with down there. It's bad enough if he was guilty, but he isn't."

"You're the only person who can get Melvin Reynolds out of the pen. But you would have to prove Reynolds did not do it and furnish specific details of the Christgen case."

"I can do that and I think I can prove it to anyone except those bastards who put him there."

"Will you tell me about the details of the Christgen case?"

"Like I said, only if the D.A. agrees to a capital offense."

"Do you want to talk to the D.A. about the Christgen case?"

"Well, if the D.A. wants to talk about it, OK, and only the D.A. No assistants, no county or city cops around to hear what I have to say. I would like for you to be there because I know in my mind you won't lie about anything."

"You want to do it now?"

"Let's get some rest and we will do it tomorrow. OK?"

"What time do you want to do it?"

"Let's make it right after lunch." Then, he turned the paper over and wrote some more.

"I know how you feel about these things as most people would feel, but you have a job to do. Again, I would appreciate it if you would keep what was said here tonight between us until tomorrow anyway."

The interview ended at 1:13 A.M. Clark was returned to his cell. Holtslag and Patrick Robb, the assistant Buchanan County prosecutor, went to an all-night restaurant where they talked rapidly about the new development. Robb had been expecting Clark to disgorge the awful knowledge of the Steele murder, but instead he spoke of something that had been bothering Clark even more—the Eric Christgen case and the conviction of Melvin Reynolds.

Robb knew about the case. He had been a law school student in Kansas City when it first broke, and he had read about it in the newspapers. He joined the Buchanan County prosecuting attorney's office in March 1980, two months after Reynolds had been taken to prison. The man he succeeded, assistant prosecutor Thomas Crossett, told him that questions remained about Reynolds' guilt, and that some police did not think that he was Eric's killer. At one time, Robb had been interested enough in the case to retrieve the thick file and read through it. Now Robb was devoting nearly all of his time to the Michelle Steele murder case. With the interview between Holtslag and Clark, the case had taken a wild turn and Robb did not know where it was going.

From the restaurant, Robb telephoned Mike Insco and asked him to join them. At 2:00 A.M. the county prosecutor arrived, and after a cup of coffee, began to comprehend what Robb and Holtslag told him. They explained that Clark knew about the Christgen murder. Insco laughed at the idea.

"This guy is conning you," Insco said. "He's taking you on a trip."

"He wants you to file capital murder charges against him," Holtslag replied. "He wants to trade his information on the Christgen murder for the death penalty."

"He's playing some game," Insco said. "I don't know what he has in mind, but he's up to something."

"Will you talk to him?"

"I can't talk to him," Insco said. "I'm the prosecutor. He is represented by a lawyer. Do you think his lawyer is going to let him sit there and talk to me . . . tell me he is good for another murder?"

The three men discussed the case for an hour. They agreed that Holtslag would continue to meet with Clark, but Insco told the FBI agent that he was wasting his time. When Holtslag got home he spent an hour telling his wife everything that Clark had told him. Then he tried to go to sleep. He lay there a long time, with the events of the day running through his head.

Had the tiny scrap of paper "Please call the FBI" been an invitation to play a game? Or was it a summons to solve the most perplexing criminal case he'd ever encountered? For Holtslag, the suspicion that Melvin Reynolds was innocent, which had festered inside him for years, had been reawakened. He did not have the proof in his hands, but he could feel that Clark had committed the murder. Could the knowledge be extracted from him?

Holtslag relived the one sided conversation that had twisted and turned around the obstacles Clark had set up. He realized that Clark had not once said that he had killed Eric Christgen. His repeated references to the "body you know about" had finally prompted Holtslag to mention the boy's name.

Clark had prodded Holtslag until finally he had said it. Clark had not mentioned the subject; it was Holtslag who had suggested that there was an innocent man in prison.

Who was leading who? Holtslag wondered. This guy is shrewd. I underestimated him. He needs special handling. Holtslag knew he would have to be more careful with Clark in the next meeting.

"I've got a tiger by the tail," he said to himself.

Why had Clark singled out Joe Holtslag for his confessions? If Clark was the one man who knew the whole story of Eric Christgen's death, Holtslag happened to be the man who would most easily be motivated to question the guilt of Melvin Reynolds and be in a position to do something about it. If revealed to any other agent or lawman, Clark's allegations might have been ignored or even buried. The interrogator's reaction to Clark was critical. A listener's disinterest or rejection might have discouraged him from telling the story.

Clark had been in the county jail for nearly a year before he had extended his little feelers. Holtslag thought that Clark decided to talk after he realized the insanity ploy would not work. It was no coincidence, he thought, that Clark had asked for the FBI less than two weeks after a court had ruled him competent to stand trial. But how long, Holtslag wondered, would he be in the mood that compelled him to wish for death?

The initial contact had been a success, but the agent knew he had to carefully build upon it to produce the complete truth. What was the complete truth? Could there really be 16 bodies? Clark had revealed only a few pages of his life's book of crime. Holtslag knew from just those few pages that there were two or three bodies—this man named Churchill in Rock Island, Michelle Steele in St. Joseph, and maybe "the body you know about," Eric Christgen. Would it really take the death penalty to get the rest of the story?

The fallout from this story could be staggering. Clark had supplied Holtslag with information which could discredit the entire St. Joseph criminal justice system. Holtslag knew that that was one reason why Clark had come forward. Sure, Clark might want to get Reynolds out of prison. He might even hate himself enough to want the death penalty. But Holtslag knew enough about Charles Hatcher's background to know that he had grown up hating the St. Joseph police department. Holtslag believed that Hatcher would be willing to jeopardize his life to embarrass the St. Joe criminal justice system.

Holtslag occupied a high place in its system. Many of its other members were his friends. He hunted with Skip Jones and played cards with Bob Anderson, the two police officers whose investigation helped convict Reynolds. He played golf with Judge Connett, who had sent Reynolds to prison for life. If there had been a mistake in Reynolds' case, or worse, a deliberate injustice, the credibility of the law in Buchanan County would be open to question for a long time.

The idea of spending more time with Clark disturbed Holtslag. He knew that he would have to sit across the table from him for hours playing mind games and pretending that he understood and sympathized with him. And he knew that Clark was manipulating him, using him, to chip away at the local legal system that Holtslag had worked with for most of his professional life. Holtslag was the knife Clark was using to stab the justice system in St. Joseph. And while he was being used, Holtslag remembered what this man had done to Michelle Steele. He remembered Eric Christgen. And how many others were out there? "I'd like to put the gun between his eyes and pull the trigger myself," Holtslag thought.

Holtslag drifted off to a restless sleep, hoping to learn the complete truth quickly.

At 10:00 A.M., he returned to the jail to see Clark. He was rushing. The two men had agreed in the early morning hours to resume their meeting after lunch, but Holtslag, anxious for more information, had arrived early. He went to the cell where he found Clark lying prone on his cot, covered up. Like Holtslag, he had slept very little the previous night.

"Are you awake?"

Clark nodded, but did not turn over.

Holtslag approached him with a form titled "Interrogation; Advice or Rights." Clark turned over and looked at it. He took a pencil and wrote.

"I'll sign, but I'm really very tired. No sleep yet. I was hoping to get some."

"Well, I won't ask you any questions if you're tired. I'll come back later after you've had some sleep."

"What did we agree on last night before this afternoon?"

"Do you mean about the prosecuting attorney talking with you?"

Clark nodded.

"The prosecutor will not talk to you, he said, because you're represented by counsel on the first degree murder charges."

"How long has this guy been prosecuting attorney?"

"About six years," Holtslag replied.

Clark grinned. He now knew that Insco was the prosecutor in office when the Christgen murder had taken place. He was the prosecutor who had filed charges against Melvin Reynolds. Insco was that last man on earth who would want to hear or believe that Clark had killed Eric Christgen.

"I understand it," Clark wrote. "So you see, I'm not accomplishing what I started out to do, and I know by what you said last night that you do believe what was true."

"You can't just say you killed Eric Christgen. You're going to have to convince me that you were responsible for the killing."

"You're already convinced. Too bad. It don't matter. I don't know how much I can tell you or will say at this time."

"You want to talk about it later?"

"See me later. Maybe tomorrow. Maybe, if you want."

The interview was over by 10:14 A.M.

Word of the FBI contact with Richard Clark could not be kept quiet, because authorities in Rock Island talked readily about the discovery of James Churchill's body. They said they had been led to it by a map drawn by Richard Clark who was held by police in St. Joseph. When reporters asked Morrey, Clark's public defender, what Clark was telling the FBI, Morrey said he did not know. He said Clark was not talking to him.

"It's easier for us to read the newspaper to find out what's happening," Morrey said. Richard Dahms, Morrey's supervisor, exploded when he heard that the local FBI agent was interviewing his client. Dahms called Holtslag and told him to leave Clark alone. Holtslag replied that Clark was not talking to him about the Steele case, but about other matters. When Dahms asked the agent what the other matters were, Holtslag said he could not discuss them. Dahms warned Holtslag that he would seek a protective order from Judge Connett. Dahms called Connett and the judge then called Holtslag. He told Holtslag that he could not discuss the Steele case with Clark, but that he could interview him "about the weather, Hitler or other crimes."

Dahms then asked the sheriff's deputies in the jail to inform him whenever Holtslag talked to Clark.

Later that day, Clark gave a note to Lieutenant Charles Alldredge of the sheriff's department that said: "Please tell that FBI man I will see him after 6:00 tonight. He is expecting this. R.M.C."

But that night, when Holtslag arrived at the Buchanan County Jail, Dahms was there to meet him. Dahms told Holtslag that he had advised Clark not to talk to him or to anyone else. Holtslag then met

Clark for a few moments to tell him that he had received his note but that no interview could take place for now. He told him to consider his attorney's advice, and said that if he wanted to talk to him again, he should send out another note through his jailer. Holtslag began to worry. He felt that Clark was slipping away and was taking the truth with him.

The next day, Holtslag filed a report with the FBI office in Kansas City, which summarized his contacts with Clark. He wrote that Clark had decided to come forward with the information to free an innocent man and to get the death penalty for himself.

Holtslag reported: "The bureau should note that widespread and intense media coverage erroneous in many respects has severely damaged the potential of discovering the locations of the 16 other bodies Clark has alluded to. Also it is felt Clark will confess to the Christgen murder in time. Clark appears extremely intelligent and he knowingly established his undeniable credibility in locating Churchill's body. He has not confessed to any murders to date. The media has said he did confess to these murders and it is felt special agent's credibility will be destroyed if Clark hears of this. Inquiries at the jail determined Clark is in solitary confinement and does not have access to news media. It is felt, however, Clark's attorney will advise him of what is being reported by the media in an effort to discourage his contacts with the FBI.

"If future contacts are possible, it is anticipated Clark will provide information as to the locations of the other bodies, confess to these murders and furnish information that he was responsible for the Christgen killing instead of Reynolds."

For the next several days, Holtslag waited anxiously for Clark to contact him. But no messages came from the jail. By May 9, Holtslag could wait no longer, and he returned to the jail. He asked Clark whether he still desired to communicate with the FBI.

Clark gestured for a pen and wrote:

"You get the information you need; I have to be in the right frame of mind to do it. If you can, leave me some paper and pen, I'll put it all down upstairs and let you know when it is ready if that's okay by you. If you have an envelope so I can seal it, so these guys can't get it before. First wait. I'll let you know. It may be a week or so. These guys may not bring that envelope up to me, so make sure I get it."

"Now you know" said Holtslag, "before I can accept any written communications from you, you have to sign the waiver of rights against self incrimination and another waiver of your sixth Amendment rights."

Clark nodded his head. Holtslag then gave Clark the tools that could free Melvin Reynolds from prison: several pencils and felt tip pens, a tablet of white lined paper and a plain white envelope.

Two weeks elapsed, and Holtslag heard nothing from Clark. During that time, deputies felt a tension in the jail. It was much like the charged atmosphere that accompanies rumors of inmate riots or escapes. The deputies received unusual orders. In addition to Dahms' request that he be notified whenever Holtslag talked to Clark, Robb instructed the deputies to keep a detailed log of Clark's actions. They kept an eye on him 24 hours a day, noting his every movement.

Sheriff Mickey Gill told Holtslag that Clark is "only eating and writing. He is not mailing these writings. No one has seen these writings but the prisoner himself as far as I know. I have issued strict orders that none of my deputies look at these writings."

Clark had two sealed envelopes, and jailers told Holtslag that he kept them with him constantly. He had put them in his shirt when he met with Dahms, but the deputies did not know whether Clark had given the envelopes to his attorney. Holtslag was desperate for the information, but he knew Clark was not a person to be rushed. He visited Clark again on May 23 and asked him if he had given the envelopes to his attorney, and he shook his head "No."

It was not until May 28, ten months after his arrest, that Clark was charged under his real name. The prosecutor filed a first amended information in court correcting the name to Charles Ray Hatcher. It also listed his other aliases: Richard Martin Clark, Richard Harris, Richard Mark Clark, Richard Lee Grady, Richard Lee Price, Earl L. Kalebough, Albert Aire, Charles Marvin Tidwell, Hobart Prater, Ronald Springer, Doris Mullins, Carl L. Kalebough, Albert Ralph Price, Doris Mullins Travis and Dwayne Lee Wilfong. Hatcher had six Social Security numbers.

Holtslag told his supervisors that he planned to contact Clark again on June 6: "It is felt that if Clark is pushed, the rapport previously established will break down," Holtslag reported. "Clark may now wait until after his trial on June 20 before initiating contact, depending upon the results of that trial."

Dahms and Morrey had obtained a change of venue for Clark's trial. It was set for June 20, 1983, in St. Louis, but the lawyers said that it would not commence until at least September. The defense could not be ready in June, since Morrey, who had to defend Clark, had resigned his post and the defense could not be prepared without him. On June 14, his attorneys asked for more time. Another delay was granted and the trial date was set for August 22, 1983 in St. Louis.

Early in June, only Dahms was visiting Clark. Clark sent no letters and received none during that time. He ate regularly, but said nothing to anyone. As each day passed, it seemed as though the delicate negotiations between Holtslag and Clark were unraveling. The agent was repeatedly rebuffed during his visits. They seemed to collapse entirely on June 3.

It was on that day that deputies searched Clark's cell. They pulled Clark out and looked through all of his belongings. They said they were looking for contraband, but Clark believed they were looking for the paperwork he was preparing. Who were they working for? The police? The prosecutor? The defense? The FBI? Clark suspected either Insco or Dahms. The search failed to turn up any of Clark's writings. Clark believed that Holtslag had betrayed him either to the defense or the prosecutor.

When Holtslag came to see him on June 6, Clark told the frustrated agent he had written a detailed diary on his murderous activities, but that all of it had been "flushed down the toilet." But he had saved one piece of writing for Holtslag. It was a poem he had written that seemed to close the door to further contacts. It indicated that the final truth about Eric Christgen, James Churchill and the unnamed others would never be known.

> Everyone likes to play a part,
> 　In your life from the start.
> Everyone wants to have their say
> 　About you before that day.

But if they only knew,
  What is really happening inside you,
They wouldn't be so quick to say,
  The things they do on judgment day.

They will even tell a lie,
  But who's to know as days go by.
Except only me, and I won't tell,
  Because I'm on my way to hell.

That day is drawing very near,
  The one you all want to hear.
That time has come, I have to go,
  And now no one will ever know.

                    Richard Clark.

CHAPTER SIXTEEN

"It's an uncontrollable urge that builds and builds over a period of weeks until I have to kill."
—Charles Hatcher

FOR ALMOST TWO MONTHS, JOE HOLTSLAG WAITED for Richard Clark to disclose his dark secrets. The FBI agent had begun to wonder whether Clark would ever reveal more information about the Christgen case. Holtslag had promised himself to check with Clark periodically, wherever he was, to see if he would talk. But at times Holtslag questioned Clark's veracity. Perhaps Holtslag had been all wrong. Maybe Clark did not have the key to the crime. Maybe he had just heard about the Christgen murder from another inmate and had decided to amuse himself at the FBI's expense. Seven sultry weeks went by, and on the morning of July 27, Holtslag got what he had been waiting for.

It was in an envelope mixed in with the law enforcement magazines, FBI bulletins and other government packages whose return addresses promised boring contents. It had no return address, but Holtslag recognized the handwriting immediately. He had seen it several times during interviews in the county jail in May and June. Holtslag fingered the envelope as if it were a long-awaited treasure from a mail order house. It had been postmarked two days earlier from St. Louis, where Richard Clark was being held as he awaited trial on the Michelle Steele murder. Holtslag quickly but carefully opened it. Two documents were inside: a short introductory note and a longer handwritten narrative on white, unlined letter paper. The writing was small and neat and contrasted with the wild scrawls the man had penned in the past.

Holtslag read the short letter first: "Here's what you wanted, I hope you can use it in the right way," it began. "The only reason I waited so long was those people there from the county were trying to cut theirselves in and put bullshit in the game like they did when I started this thing, and when they sent that other guy down for this thing.

"As far as the others I told you about, they're still running over in my mind and may come out later. But this one is the most important one to me, so I would get it out of the way first. What a waste. R.C."

Holtslag turned to the second document: "I came to St. Joseph the first of May, 1978, from Minnesota," it began. "I checked in the St. Charles Hotel under the name of Richard Grady and went to work out of the state employment office under that name on temporary jobs."

Clark related how he worked at a packing company until a few days before the Christgen boy was murdered. He wrote that he had been drinking for three days and had consumed a half pint of whiskey the morning Eric was abducted. Clark saw Eric while walking near the downtown mall.

"I saw this young boy there playing by the slide," Clark wrote, adding that he took the boy by the hand and began leading him away from the downtown mall. He recited his route, which led him to the wooded spot on MacArthur Drive, northwest of downtown. He described witnesses who might have seen him along the route.

"At this point, I noticed a truck parked on Mac-Arthur Drive, a little to the north of this street that runs down to the tracks," he wrote. "I believe that it was a dump truck and it was backed up with its back toward the east and its front toward the west. I noticed, I believe, one man in the back either loading or unloading something. I really didn't pay too much attention to it."

Clark recounted how he walked Eric another quarter of a mile to a spot where they turned into a thick forest. They continued walking until they reached a small clearing.

"At this level area, we stopped, and I told this boy to take his clothes off. He didn't want to at first but then he said he would and asked me to help him with his shoes. He started to take his clothes off, then I changed my mind and told him to put them back on, but not before I had seen his shorts, which were white and seemed pretty well worn and were jockey type. After he got his clothes back on, I told him to give me oral sex, which he did.

"Then after I finished, I grabbed him around the neck with both hands and chocked him until I was pretty sure he was dead," Clark wrote. He described how he placed the body on a ledge and then attempted to leave by going up a steep bank which he climbed by grabbing onto saplings. But then, he spotted a house and he turned around and went back down the bank.

"So I left then the same way we came, across MacArthur Drive to the tracks, down the tracks to the road that runs to the river and when I got to this road, I noticed the truck that was there was gone. And just as I got about 50 feet or so from this road, a police car came out of this road that goes to the river with one officer in it, going back toward town. But I don't believe he saw me.

"At the time I picked this boy up at the mall, was around 12 or after P.M. It could have been around 1 P.M. When I drink, I lose track of time. This kid had blond hair, light complected and kind of a funny mouth, or so it seemed to me. I believe he wore jeans and t-shirt and some kind of lace up shoes and I figure he was approximately five at the time. He told me his dad worked at St. Joe Wood, and his mother's name and that he had a dog and that either his mother's name was Vicky or that was his dog's name. He told me both his mother's and dog's name, but I can't remember which was the right one. I left the following Saturday after this happened, going to Omaha by bus.

"That's the way this happened as I best can remember it. I was with no one else that day except the boy. I seen no one else except the ones that I spoke about. About two years after this happened, I read a police magazine that some one else had been convicted of this crime. And that was the first time I knew about some one else being suspected of it. But I and I alone am responsible. I found out later that the kid's name was four-year-old Eric Christgen, and Reynolds was convicted of this."

Holtslag read the confession thoroughly twice. It took him nearly an hour, because during the second reading, he traced on a city map the route Clark said he used. In all his experience, the FBI agent had never been so startled both by the horror of a crime and the precision in which murderer recalled it. It was as if Clark had relived the murder a hundred times in his memory until the details of it were engraved in his mind. It was not a matter of regurgitating facts that he had learned somewhere else. The way Clark laid out the intricate details of a murder now five years old left no doubt in Holtslag's mind that Clark was the murderer of Eric Christgen. Clark knew things no one else could know about the killing.

It was an evil document and it chilled him to read such a cold, detached description of the murder of a child. But there was a good side to the paper, too. It was a perfect confession; complete, well written, uncoached. Holtslag knew he was holding in his hands the foundation of a claim that would correct an injustice. There was no comparison between the confession that sent Melvin Reynolds to prison and Clark's letter. Holtslag realized that there were some problems with it. He recalled that Eric had been abducted late in the afternoon, but Clark's confession put the incident closer to 1:00 or 1:30 P.M. This was not a major discrepancy, since intoxicated people often lose track of time.

The biggest discrepancy concerned the description of how Eric Christgen had died. Clark said he had killed the boy by strangling him. Melvin Reynolds' confession that the boy had died during a sex act had been consistent with the cause of death set forth by the pathologist, Dr. Bridgens. According to Clark, Bridgens had been wrong. The little boy had died with the man's two strong hands wrapped around his throat.

Melvin had said that on the day of Eric's murder he had seen no one and no one had seen him, but Clark said that as he and the boy walked along MacArthur Drive, he had seen a man loading or unloading something into a truck parked beside the road. Holtslag believed that the man Clark referred to must have been Jeff Davey. Other small details in the document, such as Clarks' attempt to climb the steep bluffs by grabbing onto the branches of saplings, convinced Holtslag that Clark had been there.

"What are Bob Hayes and Mike Insco going to do when they read this?" Holtslag wondered. "Now they are going to have to pay attention to this guy."

Holtslag realized that he would have to go see Clark, and soon. Holtslag did not know how long Clark would remain in this clear and communicative state of mind, but he knew that he would have to act quickly for the written confession to be of any legal value.

The day he received them, Holtslag took copies of the letter and confession to both Hayes and Insco. The police chief said he would study them, but displayed no visible reaction. The prosecutor said there was nothing in the confession that Hatcher could not have learned from the newspapers. But Holtslag and Robb began comparing the confession with the prosecution's case against Reynolds.

"Can't you see that this guy is a manipulator and a bullshitter?" Insco told them. "He's taking you on a trip."

"This guy is going to be your killer, not Reynolds," replied Robb.

The prosecutor laughed.

"Don't be led down the primrose path," Insco said. "He's a con artist. That's all he is is a con artist. There is some detail there. But there are generalities. It's all too vague. This doesn't tell us anything you couldn't get out of the newspaper."

Four years earlier, Mike Insco had searched for ways to believe Melvin's confession. Now he searched for ways to disbelieve Clark's.

Insco could not understand Robb's reaction. Insco, long ago, had been convinced of Melvin Reynolds' guilt and thought that Robb concurred in that belief. This was not the time to be digging up Melvin Reynolds, Insco thought. He was irritated with Holtslag, whom he thought was distracting the young assistant prosecutor. The FBI agent had caught a fever from Richard Clark and now was trying to pass it on to Robb. Running the prosecutor's office was Insco's responsibility. The Michelle Steele case was the top priority in the office, and Robb was directly responsible for it. Insco did not want Robb's attention diverted to a matter that had been concluded.

On August 3, Holtslag traveled to St. Louis to interview Clark. Before he left, he asked Chief Hayes if he wanted to send an investigator along. Holtslag suggested John Muehlenbacher, but the chief turned down the invitation. He also would not let Holtslag take the police file on the Christgen case.

Holtslag was accompanied by FBI Agent Thomas Den Ouden, a psychological profile coordinator. Den Ouden would collect Hatcher's mental quirks and assemble them into a report explaining what made him tick. Holtslag wanted him to answer the question, "How do we handle this guy?" He hoped Den Ouden could outwit Clark and extract more information from him than he had planned to give. Holtslag wished to exploit Clark's cooperative mood while it lasted.

The "Richard Clark" that Holtslag interviewed at the St. Louis County Jail was not the same man he had met three months earlier. When Clark greeted the two agents, he was cleanly shaved except for a neatly trimmed mustache. His hair was combed and he wore a gray jumpsuit and a new pair of brown shoes. A quick step had replaced his shuffle, and a pair of bright, clear eyes were set in the sockets where paranoia had reigned before.

Holtslag saw that Clark could change quickly from a slovenly skid row bum to an alert and perceptive person. It reminded Holtslag that he had to be wary of Clark. Clark shook hands with Holtslag and talked verbally for the first time. He stiffened when he was introduced to Den Ouden, but when Holtslag asked whether Clark would mind if the second agent sat in on the interviews, Clark said, "That'll be all right."

For the first time, Holtslag was hearing Clark speak. Holtslag breathed easier. Not only would FBI agent Den Ouden be allowed to remain, but Clark would converse, rather than write, during the interview. In the earlier meetings, Holtslag had always felt at a disadvantage, because the time Clark took to write after each question gave him more time to think about the answers. But even when Clark responded verbally, Holtslag felt that Clark was still a step ahead of him.

Clark was primed to tell a story, and his delivery of Churchill's body and the detailed written confession in the Christgen case had brought him eager listeners.

Clark's appearance was not the only thing that had changed. Holtslag found it more difficult to muster the contempt for him he had felt before. The new man sitting across the table from Holtslag seemed like "just another guy," witty and intelligent with a good sense of humor. He was almost sophisticated. The man's educational deficiencies, so readily apparent before in the mispellings of his answers, were no longer so obvious. Only occasionally did Holtslag feel the cold chill that reminded him of the kind of man he was dealing with, a person who could squeeze the life out of a child.

Richard M. Clark had gone through a metamorphosis since he had last seen Holtslag. The man who emerged had made a decision from which there was no retreat. Previously, he had delivered the body of James Churchill, but would not say who killed him. And he had only hinted that the wrong man was in jail for the Christgen murder. But since then, he had put into writing and signed the document that contained murder details no one else knew. There was no going back now. He had taken a major step towards convicting himself of the crime. Even if he stopped now, there was sufficient doubt raised about Reynolds' guilt and enough circumstantial evidence to implicate him in the murder. In a sense, Richard Clark was dead, and Charles Hatcher had succeeded him. The man of many names was prepared to assume his real identity. He would no longer deny who he was, or what he had done.

That's what has changed him, Holtslag thought. He's gotten it off his chest. There is no turning back for him. He is committed to his course.

Holtslag knew that Hatcher was manipulating him to humiliate the Buchanan County justice system.

"He is the ultimate selfish person," Holtslag later told his wife, Sandy. "He relates with people for self gratification—to either kill someone or to manipulate them. He likes me to the extent that he can use me. I am doing what Charlie Hatcher wants me to do. I know what we are doing is the right thing. I don't care that I am his pawn in this thing. Justice is being served."

The two agents' first interview with Hatcher began at 9:30 A.M., with Holtslag writing a one-page waiver of Hatcher's rights to be represented by an attorney:

I, Charles Ray Hatcher, also known as Richard Martin Clark, having been advised by my attorney

Richard W. Dahms, that I did not have to communicate with the Federal Bureau of Investigation (FBI), have given this advice sufficient and considerable consideration and have decided to communicate with the FBI and specifically waive my Sixth Amendment right to have an attorney with me during questioning or while furnishing any writing or other communications. No pressure, threats, promises or coercion has been used against me or made to me. I have read the above and told this orally by SA Joseph F. Holtslag, Jr., who is known to me as a special agent with the FBI and I desire to continue communication with him.

Hatcher signed the document "Richard Clark." Holtslag and Den Ouden witnessed it.

"Your confession is super," Holtslag said after the paperwork was out of the way. "You've got me convinced. You killed the Christgen boy. But they're not going to believe it in St. Joe. If we are going to convince people in St. Joe that you killed the Christgen boy, you're going to have to clear up some discrepancies and answer some questions. And we've got to come up with some more of these bodies you've been talking about. You say it was 16 people. Get your credibility really established. Tell us about the others."

"You'll get them all eventually," Hatcher replied.

Before he discussed the Christgen case, Hatcher gave other, more general information to Holtslag and Den Ouden. Both agents took notes as he described his nomadic life. He told the agents that he had killed 16 people. He said there had been three children and 13 adults, and that the killing began in the early 1960s.

"I kill on impulse. It's an uncontrollable urge that builds and builds over a period of weeks until

I have to kill," Hatcher said. "It doesn't matter if the victims are men, women or children. Whoever is around is in trouble."

Hatcher said the killings were not sexually motivated. He said he picked his victims with the intent to kill them, not for the purposes of committing sexual acts with them. Hatcher said that just before Eric's disappearance the urge to kill had been growing in him. He was in Willmar, Minnesota, and had gone to the local sheriff's office and told deputies he was probably wanted in California for a parole violation. The lawmen in Minnesota asked him, "Have you done any crimes in Willmar's jurisdiction?" When Hatcher said he had not, Hatcher said the police told him to "get lost."

Hatcher then recited the details of his written confession.

"When I saw the boy playing on the sliding board on the mall, I had an impulse to go back and take him. He did not attempt to leave me or appeared scared. At one point he asked me, 'Where are you taking me?' And he started to cry. I told him I was taking him to his mother. The boy quieted then. He was a smart kid. He asked me if I knew his mother's name and I told him I didn't. I knew the boy of this age could not be used as a witness against me and would not be able to make an identification. But I had an uncontrollable urge to kill the boy and I did so by putting my hands around his neck and squeezing just hard enough to cut off his air. I don't leave marks on any of my victims. I don't know how long I choked him, but it was long enough to kill him."

Hatcher said he received no sexual enjoyment from killing the boy, and he had done it merely to satisfy his urge to kill. He said that initially he was not consciously looking for someone to kill, but the impulse had probably been there. He also said that he must have intended to kill the Christgen boy when he initially picked him up.

"I know this from past experience," Hatcher said. "It doesn't matter. Whoever is available."

Holtslag told Hatcher that there were two things that were sexually done to the boy, according to the pathologist's report. Holtslag did not tell Hatcher what they were.

"I told you everything I remember. But it's possible I could have done other things while I was angry. But I can't remember."

"According to the pathologist, the boy was not strangled," Holtslag said.

"That damn pathologist is wrong. I know how I killed him."

Holtslag asked him about the time of the crime. Hatcher said he could be no more specific than to say it was sometime that afternoon. He said he did not have a watch, was drinking and that he lost track of time when he drank.

Hatcher emphatically denied knowing Melvin Lee Reynolds, but said he knew his name from reading of his conviction in a detective magazine. He said his primary reason for confessing to the Christgen killing was to have Reynolds released from prison.

"That's why I told you where you could find the body of James Churchill," he said. "It was a way to gain acceptance for this confession."

Hatcher then explained that he met Churchill in the "Quad Cities" area in early June 1981. They had become drinking buddies. He would not say whether he had a homosexual relationship with Churchill because "I wouldn't want to degrade Jim."

According to Hatcher, the Mississippi riverbank where Jim's body was recovered was used by transients as a place to drink. On Saturday, June 20, 1981, he and Jim were drinking there alone when Churchill became "drunk and silly." It was after dark, at about 9:00 P.M. Hatcher said he had been carrying a butcher knife and that he felt the impulse to kill growing inside him.

"I just walked over to Jim and began stabbing him over and over in the chest until the knife became imbedded in a bone to the right of center in his chest, near the heart. I needed two hands to pull the knife out. I must have stabbed him 10 or 12 times."

Two weeks went by and nobody noticed Churchill was missing and no one discovered his body. Hatcher said he returned to the scene of the killing to see if Jim was still there.

"I don't know why I went back there, but I did it on impulse. I had been drinking that day and I went back while it was still light. I went to the same spot, but the body was not there. I thought at first, the body had been found, but then I smelled him. Jim apparently wasn't dead when I left him. He crawled about 10 feet away and was laying on his side. I didn't touch the body, but covered it up with stones and a board that was about 10 feet long."

Hatcher then said he had lied when he told Holtslag that robbery was the motive for Churchill's death.

"I want to correct it because I don't want to tell any lies about this thing. It will hurt my credibility. I killed Jim to satisfy my impulse."

Hatcher's long, rambling narrative on the murders of Eric Christgen and James Churchill had taken most of the day. The interview on the Christgen case had ended at 2:05 P.M. The agents had stopped for lunch and then returned and discussed the murder of Jim Churchill until evening. They decided to continue the interrogation after supper, and stopped a second time.

As they prepared to leave, Hatcher studied the "Hoover sheet" on the table between them. The sheet listed chronologically the crimes Hatcher had been convicted of in jurisdictions across the country. It was several pages long, a depressing diary of a life of failure. It began with the October 27, 1947, arrest in Holt County, Missouri, on auto theft charges and ended with the July 29, 1982, arrest for the murder of Michelle Steele.

While the two agents were gone, Hatcher studied the outline of his criminal history for more than an hour. It filled in the blanks of his alcohol-soddened memory and prodded ugly recollections out of the recesses of his mind. Charles Hatcher could see and relive many of his killings, but the exact times and places of many of them were lost in a black fog. He could remember the victims' faces, but many were people like him and Churchill, wanderers of the nation's landscape. Hatcher had told Holtslag they were people who would "never be missed." Churchill's murder was easy to recall because it had been so recent. The others were spread out in several states over more than two decades. But the "Hoover sheet" helped Hatcher to recall the timing of one murder in particular.

This incident had troubled him for a long time. Of all his killings, it was the hardest. And he knew this child was someone who would be missed. He believed that this boy's body probably had been found but that the crime had not been solved.

Hatcher could still remember what the youngster looked like and what he was wearing. In a way, the child reminded Hatcher a little of himself as a young boy.

CHAPTER SEVENTEEN

"Sometimes the system makes a very bad mistake."

— Charles Hatcher

BY THE TIME THE AGENTS RETURNED FROM DINNER, Hatcher was primed to talk again. When the agents sat down, Hatcher leaned across the table between them and reached back in time to solve a killing that had puzzled police in a small California city for 14 years. He pointed to a notation of his August 29, 1969 arrest in San Francisco under the name of Albert Price for a sexual attack on six-year-old Gilbert Martinez.

"The day before this, or maybe two days before this, I abducted a boy in a town near Antioch, California," Hatcher said. "The boy was riding down the street on his bicycle and he had a tennis racket with him. I gave him some bullshit story and talked him into going for a ride with me. He left the bicycle and tennis racket on the sidewalk. He told me he was 13 years old. He was wearing jeans, a white t-shirt and tennis shoes. He had light brown hair. He did not act scared at any time."

Hatcher described how he had driven until he found a roadside stop beside a creek.

"When I told him I was getting out of the car to take a leak, the boy followed me to the river," Hatcher said. "I didn't perform any sexual acts on the boy, and I did not have the boy perform any sexual acts on me. I strangled the boy with my hands while he was lying on the bank near the creek. I strangled him from the front, with my thumbs over the boy's Adam's apple while the boy was lying on his back. After I was certain the boy was dead, I placed the boy in a drinking position. I put his hands and knees underneath his body and his face touching the water as though he were taking a drink.

"Of all the people I killed, this was probably the hardest one because of the way I felt about it both during and afterwards. The impulse to kill someone was inside me before I found that boy. The boy just happened to be available at the time. He was either my sixth or seventh murder victim."

Hatcher said he then drove to San Francisco in the car, a green Ford Ranchero that he had stolen, and ditched it there. He said that a few days later he was arrested for an attack on a young boy. He admitted that if he had not been interrupted by a witness, the result of that crime would have been the same as in the Eric Christgen case and he would have killed the boy he abducted. Hatcher said that he had an "impulse to kill" at the time which had not been satisfied with the killing of the boy in Antioch. He said he sometimes killed people on successive days to satisfy his urges.

The interview lasted until 10:00 P.M., and it was nearly midnight by the time the agents returned to their motel rooms. As soon as he got to his room, Holtslag called the San Francisco FBI office. He asked the clerk on night duty to inquire about the murder of a young boy near Antioch, California in late August 1969. He told the clerk to call him back with the information as soon as possible.

By breakfast, Holtslag had heard nothing. He

called the FBI in San Francisco again. The message was read to him: "There were no murders in or near Antioch in August 1982."

"No, no. I didn't say 1982," Holtslag said. "I said 1969."

The agent on the other end said he would check again with the authorities in Contra Costa County. Twenty minutes later, he called Holtslag and reported to him that a boy named William J. Freeman had been abducted and murdered there.

"They knew exactly the crime you were talking about," the agent said.

On August 28, 1969, William Freeman and Kenny Zimmerman had been riding bikes down an Antioch street after a day of playing tennis. William was 12 years old, over five feet tall, and weighed 100 pounds. The California sun had turned his brown hair to the color of sand, and behind the strands of hair, his gray-green eyes squinted from an open, freckled face of an All-American boy. As the two boys raced their bicycles down the street, a green car came up behind them, and the two boys parted to let it through. But the car slowed and veered to the curb, forcing the Freeman boy to come to a stop. As he pedaled on, Kenny Zimmerman saw his friend talking to the man driving the car. When Kenny arrived home, he told his mother what had happened. She and Kenny got in their car and returned to the place where he had last seen Will. There they found his bicycle and tennis racquet.

Late that night, William's mother, Josie, reported to the police that her son was missing. His body was found two days later beside a creek about 20 miles from where he was last seen alive. The Freeman boy was lying on his stomach at the base of a steep creek bank. His legs were tucked under him, as if he were resting on his knees, and his head was bent forward to the edge of the creek, his hair just touching the water. There were no marks of violence on Will's body except for long scratches that ran the length of his back. The pathologist who performed the autopsy said that William had been asphyxiated, but the manner of asphyxiation could not be determined. The murder had never been solved.

As the agent read the police report over the telephone, Holtslag was shocked by the details Hatcher had recalled more than 14 years after the crime.

"He had it right down to the position of the boy's body and the color of the car," he thought.

The police report noted that there were scratches on the back of the boy. Hatcher had not mentioned that there were marks on the body. He said he had strangled the boy and had done nothing else to him. When Holtslag returned to the St. Louis County jail to interview Hatcher again, he asked him whether there were any marks on the body of his victim. Hatcher thought for a long time and said there might have been cuts on the back of the boy because he had dragged him down the rocky bank after he killed him.

"The scratches could have been made at that time," Hatcher said.

Holtslag asked Hatcher if he knew anything about the murder on August 26, 1978, of Christopher Chapin in Atchison, Kansas. Melvin Reynolds had confessed to killing the boy, but Kansas Bureau of Investigation agents had discounted it. The murder remained unsolved. Hatcher denied killing the boy and said he was in Omaha at that time.

Hatcher said he had written down the details of most of his other killings while he was in the Buchanan County Jail, and had placed them in two thick envelopes. He said he had given a note requesting to see the FBI to deputy Jack Christopher. But instead of an FBI agent showing up, Richard Dahms, his attorney, had appeared. Hatcher said that he later destroyed all his writings by tearing them up and flushing them down the toilet. He said he then gave another sheriff's deputy a note notifying the FBI not to come because he had changed his mind. It was at that time that Hatcher sent Holtslag the poem which said that he would not divulge the details of his crimes.

Holtslag did not know what had prompted Hatcher to change his mind now. Nor did he care. He knew only that he had much work ahead of him, and the first item of business was to release Melvin Reynolds from prison. Hatcher concluded the St. Louis interview by stating that he did not want to furnish details of any other killings for the moment. He said, however, that he felt certain he would tell Holtslag about all the others at a later time.

For now, Hatcher believed that he had done all he needed to do. He believed that his confession would set Melvin Reynolds free. He relished the thought. He could not wait to see what happened when St. Joseph citizens realized that their police, prosecutors and judges had made a tremendous mistake by convicting the wrong man for the murder of Eric Christgen.

It was at about this time that editors at the *St. Joseph News-Press* received a mysterious letter. Later, they realized that it had been sent to them by Hatcher. It read:

Sometimes the system makes a very bad mistake. Not in all cases, but some. And I'm not just blowing steam as you will find out soon enough. It's a real stinker and should really shake up some of those of the criminal justice system in your fair city. It's been in the making for some time, but just beginning to get ready to blow. Keep your ears open.

When Holtslag returned to St. Joseph, he took the notes of his session with Hatcher to the prosecutor's office. He recounted Hatcher's story and explained that Hatcher was certainly Eric Christgen's murderer. But Insco continued to express doubts. Pat Robb continually brought the case up during their morning staff meetings.

"Pat, you have to keep an open mind about this," Insco told him.

"Me," Robb said. "What do you mean, me? You're the one who has to open up his mind."

Insco did not want to believe it. Prosecutors everywhere, everyday, live with the fact that the guilty are set free through various legal technicalities, lack of evidence or reluctant witnesses. A prosecutor's nightmare is sending an innocent man to prison. Of course, there had been doubts about the Reynolds' case, but Insco had managed to convince a jury of Melvin's guilt beyond a reasonable doubt.

By this time, Melvin Reynolds had spent more than four years behind bars.

"You can imagine the difficulty I had convincing myself that Melvin Reynolds didn't commit the crime," Insco said later. "I was the one that prosecuted Reynolds and I was the one prosecuting Hatcher. I was pretty reluctant to believe it."

Insco retrieved the Eric Christgen murder case file and reviewed the FBI psychological profile of the killer. As he studied it, Insco noticed how closely the profile resembled Charles Hatcher—a poorly educated man, a repeat offender, a man who had attempted to abduct children before, a murderer who selected victims at random, a man who was physically strong. Hatcher had told Holtslag that he had consumed a half pint of whiskey before killing the Christgen boy. The FBI profile said that the killer had probably been drinking heavily before the crime. Insco concluded that 21 points of the profile matched Hatcher's lifestyle. In contrast, only nine fit Reynolds.

"It really amounts to a description of Hatcher," Insco said to himself.

Insco assigned Wilt Lewis, an investigator from his office, to look into the case. Insco thought that Robb was caught up in the same excitement that seemed to hypnotize Holtslag. He thought Lewis, who was a former Iowa highway patrolman, was removed enough from the case to be an objective factfinder. Lewis had not been a member of the prosecutor's staff at the time of the Eric Christgen murder.

St. Joseph in August moved like the Missouri River, a crawling mass of steaming molasses. The heat and humidity forced everyone to move slower. But this August was different. There was plenty of movement. The general public might not have detected it, but local, state and federal authorities were moving quickly. Holtslag was turning over the old stones of the Eric Christgen murder case and was receiving information on the murders in other parts of the country that Hatcher had described. Some of the local police were still helping assemble evidence in St. Joe's most recent child murder. But others were trying to monitor Holtslag's movements as he retreaded the paths of an old one.

Lewis and Holtslag reviewed copies of police reports in the prosecutor's files. They went to the St. Charles Hotel and found that a man named Richard Grady had stayed there in May 1978. At the time of Eric Christgen's murder, police had checked the St. Charles Hotel for a man who matched the description of Eric's abductor. They had not found him.

The corporate headquarters of the Dugdale Packing Co. in Michigan confirmed that copies of payroll checks for the May 1978 period showed that a man by the same name had worked at its plant in St. Joseph. Holtslag reviewed copies of the two St. Joseph newspapers in the city library. He reread all the stories about the case, paying particularly close attention to the details the police released about witnesses who had seen the boy with an older man.

He was startled to see a likeness of Charles Hatcher staring at him from the front page of one edition. It was the composite drawing of the man who witnesses said they had seen with Eric Christgen. None of the accounts named the witnesses or described what the witnesses were doing when they had seen the man and the boy. Holtslag and Lewis realized that Hatcher had to have been the abductor in order to know that one of the people who saw him was loading something into a truck parked along MacArthur Drive.

Holtslag and Lewis re-interviewed two of the witnesses. Carl Simpson, the Wire Rope Co. employee, had said that he had seen the little boy and the older man on the other side of the fence that surrounded the company's parking lot. Holtslag and Lewis showed Simpson a copy of a picture of Reynolds.

"Could this have been the man?" Holtslag asked.

"Definitely not," Simpson said. "He was an older man."

"Were you subpoenaed to testify at Reynolds' trial?"

"Not that I know of. I was served with a subpoena to report to the courthouse, and I was interviewed by a woman who was working for the defense. I told her the same things I told the police."

"Were you out of town during the trial?"

"No, I was here the whole time."

The same day that they talked to Simpson, Holtslag interviewed Jeffrey Davey. His story was similar to Simpson's. He said that he had followed the Reynolds case in the papers but no one had asked him to testify for the defense at the trial. As he read the stories in the newspapers, Davey thought that perhaps the people he had seen must not have been Eric Christgen and his abductor because the man he saw with the boy was not Reynolds.

As he went over the case, Holtslag filed daily written reports with his supervisors in Kansas City, and they in turn passed them on to the U.S. Attorney's office. Reporting on the interviews with Simpson and Davey, Holtslag said: "It should be noted that neither of these witnesses positively identified the child they saw on the day the Christgen boy was murdered as being Christgen. These witnesses, however, are most like the individuals referred to by Clark in his confession as the people he saw while he was with the Christgen boy."

The biggest problem with Clark's confession was his description of Eric's cause of death. Clark said he had strangled the boy, while Bridgens, the man who had performed the autopsy, said the victim's windpipe had been blocked during an act of oral sodomy. Hatcher could never be convicted of killing the Christgen boy as long as Bridgens insisted that he was right.

But Holtslag was picking up data that indicated that Bridgens was not right. On August 8, the Contra Costa County sheriff's office reviewed the autopsy report on the death of William Freeman. A deputy advised Holtslag that the cause of death was asphyxia. The reason for the asphyxia had never been determined. As in the case of Eric Christgen, the murderer had left no marks on the throat of William Freeman.

Insco contacted Bridgens. The doctor said that he still believed his initial finding was accurate. He said that signs of strangulation were not apparent during the autopsy and, in his opinion, strangulation by choking had not occurred.

While Holtslag was reviewing the Eric Christgen case, Robb was still working to amass evidence against Hatcher for the murder of Michelle Steele. Robb doubted the accuracy of the initial report that had been written by Dr. York Silliman, the young Buchanan County medical examiner. Silliman, like previous pathologists who examined Hatcher's work, had difficulty in determining Michelle's cause of death. He concluded that she died from "positional asphixiation"; the positioning of her body had cut off the flow of oxygen to her lungs. Robb asked John Kreiser, a St. Joseph police detective, to ask Bridgens his opinion about the cause of death of Michelle Steele.

Kreiser found his session with Bridgens bizarre. To begin with, Chief Hayes had asked Kreiser to tape record the entire meeting and to save the tape for him. Secondly, Bridgens spent most of the time telling Kreiser how Eric Christgen had died, rather than discussing the Michelle Steele case. Kreiser could not understand why Bridgens was dwelling on a murder that had happened five years earlier. The strange aspects of Kreiser's session with Bridgens confirmed Robb's suspicions that Bridgens and Hayes were worried about the new twists in the Christgen case.

Holtslag contacted Dr. Angelo Lapi, a Kansas City physician with experience in reviewing child abuse, child deaths and homicides. Lapi told Holtslag that under certain circumstances, it would be possible for a child to be strangled or choked without any marks showing up on a pathology examination. He said that pressure from thumbs and fingers on a child's throat might not cause any apparent damage, since their bones and cartilage are softer and more supple than an adult's. He said microscopic examination of a disruption of fat cells located over the trachea might indicate strangulation. Lapi added, however, that it was difficult to determine, especially in children.

There were other signs that Hatcher was telling the truth. The agents in Illinois had examined the shirt found on the bones of James Churchill, and had concluded that the slits in the front were consistent with stab wounds.

Holtslag and Robb believed that they had assembled the evidence needed to convince Insco of Hatcher's guilt. The turning point came after Hatcher sent Holtslag a letter. In it, Hatcher discussed the existence of a house which he had seen on the day of the murder and which had caused him to leave by another route.

When Holtslag and Robb visited the murder scene, they found easily enough the steep bank that Hatcher said he climbed by grabbing onto saplings and pulled himself up. They struggled up the incline and there they discovered the house that Hatcher said he had seen after killing the boy.

Robb showed Insco the photographs of the scene, taken at the time of the murder. In one wide-angled shot, a house is visible at the top of a bluff.

"That house is there," Robb said. "Just like he said it was. It's behind the trees and you can't see it now unless you climb to the top of the hill east of where they found the body. But five years ago, you wouldn't have had to have climbed so high to see it."

For several minutes, Insco said nothing.

"Mike, you're going to have to prosecute this guy," Robb said finally.

"I can't do that," replied Insco.

"Why not? You've got more on this guy than you had in the Reynolds case."

"Do you know what a trial like that would do to this community?"

"You wouldn't have to do it," said Robb. "I could do it."

"Pat, you'll never be able to prosecute him with what we've got. We've already got one guy who has confessed to it."

"You could bring in a special prosecutor, someone from outside, to do it."

"Don't you see how this thing could blow up in our faces?" said Insco. "What if Hatcher said he'd plead guilty. We let Reynolds out. Then we put Hatcher on the stand and he laughs and says he made the whole thing up . . . that he read it all in the newspapers and that he thought he'd play a little joke on us. What if he's just maneuvering to set us up some way on the Steele case?" Robb had no answer, but he continued to raise the issue of Hatcher's guilt during daily staff meetings.

Before every working day, a gathering took place in the basement of the Buchanan County

Courthouse. Police officers, judges and lawyers mingled over coffee in a small restaurant there. They sat at a long table, and gossiped, talked politics and exchanged jokes. It was over one such breakfast that two police officers told Insco they were concerned about what Robb was doing with regard to the Christgen case.

"Why don't you do something about that Robb working for you?" one of them said.

"What do you mean?" Insco said. "What can I do?"

"You're his boss. You can do any God damn thing you want. You can get rid of him."

They were also angry and upset with Holtslag. Hayes considered Holtslag's inquiries into the Christgen case as an attempt to discredit his department. The chief had not forgotten a country club encounter with Holtslag two years earlier when he had overheard the agent say that he doubted that Reynolds had killed Eric Christgen.

The encounter had taken place in the summer of 1981 when Holtslag was investigating the vigilante killing of Ken Rex McElroy in Skidmore, a small town just north of St. Joseph. McElroy, the town bully, had been gunned down on the village's main street one morning as 60 people watched. Afterwards, no one would identify the killers.

A few weeks after the McElroy murder, Holtslag, Hayes and a group of people were mingling at the St. Joseph Country Club following a charity golf match. Holtslag was asked about his theory on the McElroy murder, and then about the Eric Christgen case. Holtslag said that he did not believe Melvin Reynolds had killed Eric Christgen. Hayes overheard the remark and reacted angrily. His face turned red and his eyes blazed. He slammed his hand down on the table.

"What kind of law enforcement officer are you here?" Hayes demanded. "That man was guilty. He was convicted by a jury. Who are you to second guess that?"

Hayes believed that Holtslag, by speaking with Hatcher and inquiring about the Christgen murder, was actively working to prove his theory that Reynolds was innocent. His re-questioning of witnesses seemed to openly challenge the police department, and Hayes moved to put a stop to it. He telephoned Robert Davenport, special agent in charge in Kansas City, and told him to keep Holtslag out of St. Joseph police business. He said Holtslag's activities were jeopardizing the cooperative relationship between the city and the FBI. And he threatened to take his complaints about Holtslag all the way to the FBI headquarters in Washington, D.C.

"If I have to, I'll get on an airplane and see the director," Hayes told Davenport. "He's meddling in business he shouldn't be."

Davenport considered taking Holtslag off the case to protect the FBI's relationship with the local police department. But he decided against it because he believed that no one else could establish a rapport with Hatcher. And Davenport was satisfied with Holtslag's performance on the case. Since Hatcher had first begun to talk, the FBI agent had informed Hayes' office of all major developments.

In late August, the FBI sent 13 separate documents to local authorities in an attempt to force them to reopen the Christgen case. In a letter accompanying the documents, Davenport wrote: "These interviews include all the information furnished by Clark to date, and are being furnished to you for whatever action you deem appropriate." Both U.S. Attorney Robert Ulrich and his first assis-

tant Thomas Larson believed that someone should
reopen the Christgen case. Reynolds' lawyer, Lee
Nation, was not aware of Hatcher's confession,
and Ulrich and Larson debated about whether to
inform him of the development. Larson was a former assistant public defender who had once supervised Nation. They decided to give Insco more
time.

The prosecutor was using the information extracted from Hatcher concerning his history of the
crimes he committed elsewhere to help develop the
Michelle Steele murder case. Detectives visited Lincoln and Omaha, Nebraska, and Des Moines and
Bettendorf, Iowa, to complete the portrait of Michelle's murderer. Insco wondered if he should
grant Hatcher's request and file capital murder
charges against him. He had received information
from Bridgens that he believed Michelle had been
strangled. Given Hatcher's lengthy record of ab-
ducting children, Insco thought a capital murder
charge could be supported in court and it carried
the death penalty that Hatcher said he wanted. In
late August, Insco asked a Buchanan County grand
jury to consider whether the weight of the evidence
would back up the charge in the Michelle Steele
murder case. But there was no movement from the
prosecutor regarding Melvin Reynolds.

The grand jury met behind closed doors on September 1 and 2, 1983, and heard enough to indict
Hatcher on capital charges. But the jurors also
heard some disturbing information on a murder
case they thought St. Joseph had solved years ago.
Insco had asked Holtslag to testify in general terms
about what Hatcher had told him. The testimony
was designed to establish that Hatcher was an admitted killer; that there was probable cause that he
had killed Michelle Steele. In the course of his tes-

timony and in response to questions from members of the grand jury, Holtslag testified that Hatcher had related to him intricate details regarding the murder of Eric Christgen—so intricate that Holtslag was convinced Hatcher had committed the murder.

"I have reviewed the Reynolds confession," Holtslag said. "If I was to make a guess, if you are asking my opinion, with the exception of the details involving what allegedly was done to the Christgen boy that he does not recall doing, his description of the crime scene, the witnesses that he saw, that he thought saw him that we did not know about immediately after the Christgen case, I would say Mr. Hatcher's description and confession is more believable, and this is my own opinion."

One juror asked Holtslag whether there was any relationship between Hatcher and Reynolds.

"There is none as far as I can tell. I hit on that for quite some time. I asked whether Reynolds may have been one of his victims at one time. He said no. He claimed he has not been in St. Joseph from I think he said 1968 till he came back in 1977. And then he left and came back again in May 1978, the month he said he killed Eric Christgen. And figuring out, you know, ages at that time, Mr. Reynolds would have to have been very young when he left. And I thought possibly Reynolds was maybe a victim of his that he was trying to make amends to in one way or another, but he says no.

"He is certain he does not know Reynolds. He said he did not know of Reynolds until he read about him in a police magazine about two years after the Christgen murder that he had been convicted of it. He was not aware they had convicted anybody of the Christgen case until about two years later. He said in about 1980."

On September 6, Hatcher was indicted by the Buchanan County grand jury on capital murder charges, and he was arraigned the next day. The new charge said the murder of Michelle Steele was premeditated and that she had been strangled. He pleaded not guilty on September 12, and still another trial date for the Steele murder case was set for January 9, 1984. If the trial jury would convict him, Hatcher's death wish might come true.

By mid-September, there was still no movement on the other "reason" for Hatcher's confession. Melvin Reynolds was still in prison, and the patience of the federal authorities was at its limit. On September 19, U.S. Attorney Robert Ulrich and Larson came to St. Joseph to meet with Insco. They wanted to know what he intended to do with with Hatcher's confession.

"Mike, you are either going to tell Nation what has come up here or we are," Ulrich said.

But Hatcher had beaten them all to it. He had written Nation and advised Holtslag of it later.

"The way I see it, if a person is innocent, he shouldn't have to wait for months just so some people won't have to admit that they were wrong," Hatcher wrote. "The time has come for the truth to be known. To wait any longer is a waste. Far more than what the damage can do to the people who made the mistake in the first place."

On September 20, Lee Nation asked for a meeting with Holtslag and the U.S. attorneys in Kansas City. Based on what had been collected, Nation could petition the court to free Reynolds, the U.S. Attorney's office could file a civil suit alleging that Reynolds' civil rights were being violated by his continued incarceration, or Insco could file murder charges against Hatcher, thereby leading to Reynolds' release.

Rumors about Hatcher's confession had begun to make the rounds in tiny circles in St. Joseph. Lawyers in Insco's own office were amazed that the story had not surfaced yet in the newspapers.

Insco tried to assess what the damage would be once the information became public. Four years earlier, he had worried about his political future, because he believed that he might lose the case against Melvin Reynolds. Instead, he had won it. Now, the case had come back to haunt him, and he believed he would not survive the repercussions of Reynolds' release.

Insco began to reverse his thought processes. For months, he had been trying to prove in his own mind that Hatcher was a liar. Now Insco had to convince himself that Hatcher had indeed committed the crime. He knew Hatcher was an expert manipulator, and he tried to determine Hatcher's motive for pleading guilty. Insco also mapped out his strategy regarding the logistics for Melvin's release. Hatcher would have to be safely behind bars before Melvin Reynolds would be released. Insco wanted Hatcher to plead guilty before any arrangements were made for Reynolds' release.

"This won't be a deal," Insco told Wilt Lewis, the county prosecutor's investigator. "We're going to have to goad him into it."

"He'll never do it," said Lewis. "I'll bet you twenty dollars he won't do it."

On October 6, Insco had Hatcher brought from the jail to his office. His public defender, Richard Dahms, was with him.

"You have been causing a lot of problems around here," Insco said. "I'm going to give you an opportunity to put your money where your mouth is. If you really did what you say you did, I'm going to give you the opportunity to plead guilty to that.

We'll just march you up to the judge and give you the opportunity to plead guilty. I don't believe you. If you can make the judge believe you, so be it. I'll give you the chance to convince the judge."

Hatcher looked at Insco for a long time.

"I'll think about it," he said at last. Insco thought Hatcher would want to talk to Holtslag. He called the agent and told him he had challenged Hatcher to plead guilty and that Hatcher said he would consider it.

"He is going to want to talk to you," Insco said. "What do you think he'll do?"

"Charlie will tell you to stick it in your ass because he doesn't like you and doesn't trust you," Holtslag replied. "He knows what you did on the Reynolds case."

When Hatcher was returned to his cell, he drafted a note and handed it to a jailer. It was a summons for Holtslag and it read a lot like the one that had dragged the FBI agent into the case: "Would you call Joe Holtslag and tell him when he has time, I would like to see him. Charlie Hatcher."

The morning of Friday, October 7, showed little promise. A thick fog rolled off the river and obscured a lead-colored sky. It stayed until noon, preventing the sun from warming the city. The chill seemed to stay all day, and Holtslag still felt it as he came to the jail for yet another meeting with Hatcher. It had been the middle of spring when Hatcher first indicated that he had killed the boy. It had been the height of summer when he wrote his detailed confession. Now, the tips of the leaves of the trees along the Missouri River had begun to turn crimson and still Melvin Reynolds was in prison. As he stood at the door of the county jail, Holtslag wondered if he was any closer to bringing Eric's murderer to justice than he had been that day more than five years ago when he stood at the front door of the Christgen home to get his first briefing on the case from Detective Skip Jones.

The steel bars of the jail doors kept the cold as surely as they kept their prisoners, and they numbed the agent's hands as he grasped them, waiting for his meeting with Hatcher. He felt another kind of cold. It was loneliness. Over the years, the agent had managed to avoid getting emotionally involved in his cases. But the Eric Christgen-Melvin Reynolds-Charles Hatcher dilemma was not the kind of case taught at the FBI Academy. He had grappled with the case until it had consumed him. Now, he looked around St. Joseph and found that he was alone in his desire to free Melvin Reynolds. He was angry that no one, with the exception of Pat Robb, had worked as he had to release Melvin from prison.

Up until the Hatcher case, Holtslag felt a deep trust in his fellow lawmen. He thought they would always work together.

"I was naive to think that everybody would work just as hard to get an innocent man out as they would to put a guilty one in," he thought. "But they could give a shit."

Holtslag shared all the feelings about his job with his wife, and during the lonely summer months of 1983, she was his only refuge.

Sometimes the telephone at their home would ring late at night. Sandy would answer it. On the other end would be a St. Joe cop.

"Sandy, tell Joe there are a lot of officers who believe in what he's doing. We know he is right. But we just can't say so publicly. We'll lose our jobs."

She was livid. The situation reminded her of their first few months in the FBI, when Joe worked in North Carolina and had investigated the Ku Klux Klan.

"Don't tell anybody you are in the FBI because you won't have any social life," Sandy had been told. "The police down there are either in the Klan or related to people in the Klan."

Holtslag felt now as he did then.

"I'm the Lone Ranger," he said to himself.

Holtslag had even gone to see the judge who had sentenced Melvin Reynolds, hoping to initiate some action. Holtslag knew Frank Connett. They sometimes played golf together. Holtslag felt he knew the judge well enough to talk to him "man to man."

In the judge's chambers on a September afternoon, Holtslag used three hours to describe the entire case for him. The judge listened and asked a few questions.

At the end of Holtslag's long narrative, all Connett said was: "It seems like Mike Insco has some problems on his hands."

But there was one person who encouraged Holtslag to dig deep for the truth, no matter whom it hurt. Considering the timing and the source of the statement, it was all the inducement Holtslag needed. It was late September and the case seemed to be at a dead end. Holtslag sat at the bedside of a police detective who had helped convict Melvin Reynolds. Charles "Skip" Jones, the man who had handed Reynolds the written questions that led to his confession and who had walked with him to the scene of the crime, was dying of cancer.

Holtslag was with his 37-year-old friend every night during that last week of his life. Up until then, the two men had never discussed the new developments in the Christgen murder case.

Holtslag told Jones' wife, Terry, that he hoped

the attention he was devoting to the Hatcher case was not adding to Jones' suffering. She replied that her husband was "very concerned" about it, but that he felt certain Reynolds was "the one."

The night before Jones died, Holtslag sat at his bedside at St. Joseph Hospital. Jones had come to realize he was not going to beat the cancer.

"Skip, is there anything I can do for you?" Holtslag asked.

For a long moment, the dying man said nothing. Then in a whisper, forced from air-starved lungs, Jones said: "If Reynolds is innocent, get him out of prison."

Holtslag reviewed the scene again as he waited in the familiar interview room as the jailers brought Hatcher from his cell. He reviewed everything he had done in the five and one-half months since he had first met Richard Clark. Holtslag knew that he had played Hatcher's game the best he could. What other turns the case would take, Holtslag did not know. He had grown tired of both the case and the city in which he worked. Two of his three children were close to going to college. He and Sandy talked about moving, and he placed his name on a reassignment list. Hawaii was his first choice. Perhaps Hatcher was calling him back now to say he was tired of it too. Holtslag expected him to say that if the justice system would not respond to his confession, he would forget the whole thing.

Hatcher padded quietly into the room in the soft-soled shoes the county had issued to him. A bushy mustache and long sideburns had altered his appearance, and Holtslag was surprised again by the man's ability to change his looks.

"Insco has asked me if I will plead guilty to a

capital murder charge in the killing of the Christ-gen boy," Hatcher began. "What do you think?"

"Let's together consider the implications of do-ing that," Holtslag replied. "If the judge accepted your plea of guilty, he would in essence be saying that Reynolds is innocent. If he accepts your plea of guilty, he's got to release Reynolds from prison."

"Yeah, that makes sense," said Hatcher. "I think I'll just do that then."

"The judge could accept it or not," said Holtslag. "I don't think he will. If he does, Insco could get Reynolds back in St. Joseph in about a week on a writ of habeus corpus. Then, he could get Reynolds released on personal recognizance until he can get clemency or pardon."

"I'll just go ahead and do it. I'll do it sometime after the weekend. I'll contact you when I'm ready."

The Indian Summer sun had scattered the clouds and Holtslag squinted as he emerged from the jail's darkness. One more weekend to wait, he thought. It will all happen next week, one way or another. Next week will be a week St. Joseph will never for-get.

CHAPTER EIGHTEEN

"I did take the boy and I did kill him as I stated in the statement by strangulation, and that's all I'm going to say about it."

—Charles Hatcher

ANTICIPATION WAS GROWING IN THE CITY. PIECES OF the truth had begun to seep out, pushed by a pressure that had been building for months. It happened first very far away, thousands of miles to the west, in Contra Costa County, California, where a newspaper reported that Charles Hatcher had confessed to the murder of a boy in Antioch in 1969. The report also stated that Hatcher had told an investigator that he had killed a four-year-old boy in St. Joseph in 1978. When the report was picked up in St. Joseph, everyone knew who the little boy was. The curiosity grew with the "no comments" Lee Nation fed to the hungry reporters who called him at all hours, and by the "wait and see" looks on the faces of Mike Insco and Joe Holtslag.

By Thursday, the atmosphere was hot and charged, as word had spread through the courthouse that a major development was about to take place in Judge Connett's courtroom. For 30 minutes before Hatcher's appearance, Dahms met with him and reluctantly helped him fill out his petition to plead guilty. Repeatedly, Dahms advised Hatcher he was making a mistake. But Hatcher insisted on completing the document, although he refused to sign under his real name, and instead signed the name Richard Clark.

Insco held a meeting too. It was with Ken Christgen, Sr., and his son, Ken Jr., the grandfather and uncle of Eric Christgen.

"We feel that Hatcher is the guy who killed Eric," Insco said.

"You told us four years ago that you were sure Reynolds was the guy," said the boy's grandfather.

Insco had not notified the press of the hearing. He thought that if Hatcher backed out at the last minute, he would be saved of embarrassment. But Connett thought the press should be told and he had his clerk inform the reporters that a hearing was scheduled for 9:00 A.M. The last time Hatcher had appeared before Connett was in 1959, when Hatcher faced charges for the attempted abduction of a newsboy. Only a handful of people had witnessed that trial. But this time, the courtroom was packed with curious clerks, lawyers and journalists, who traded guesses with one another about what would take place.

At first, it was like any other courtroom scene. Insco and Robb, the prosecutors, were sitting where they belonged. But joining Public Defender Dahms at the defense table was Joe Holtslag, the FBI man. All the spectators wondered whether Holtslag was going to help defend an accused murderer. Holtslag was there at Dahms' request because Hatcher was still giving him the silent treatment and the public defender needed Holtslag to communicate with his client. Holtslag was also the sole witness at the hearing.

Judge Connett and the lawyers were moving in uncharted waters. Somehow, the lawyers had to provide the court with sufficient evidence to support the man's guilty plea even though the man refused to discuss the murder in great detail. The only evidence would be the man's written statement and hearsay evidence which had been given to an FBI agent. Unwrapping the conviction of Melvin Reynolds would not be easy, since he too had confessed to the same murder.

When Judge Connett brought the courtroom to order, Dahms began by reading all the formal advice to Hatcher regarding the reasons why he should not enter the plea. Hatcher looked as though he was listening, but every once in a while, he would turn to Holtslag and wink.

"We told him early on it was not in his best interests to talk to the FBI," Dahms said. "He told us he knew what he was doing and he would do what he wants. He did all this on his own. I cannot take any credit for any of it."

Judge Connett looked at Hatcher.

"Are you the same man we are talking about?" the judge asked.

"I'm Richard Clark. Somebody put Charles Hatcher on me."

"Mr. Insco filed these charges on you and you signed the guilty plea?"

"That's correct," said Hatcher, staring up at the judge from his seat.

"You will have no preliminary hearing and no grand jury indictment. Do you understand I could dismiss his charges on a simple motion? All you have to do is say so."

"I understand all my rights. I want it to stand as is."

"You know, all you can get is life with 50 years. Do you understand that?"

"I understand that."

At the time Eric Christgen was murdered, Missouri law did not provide for the death penalty in capital murder cases. Its laws and those of several other states had been declared unconstitutional by the U.S. Supreme Court. The State Legislature had adopted a new law, but it had not yet gone into effect at the time the Christgen boy was murdered. Although Hatcher's guilty plea was being submitted at a time when the law was in effect, the crime to which he was confessing had taken place when the state could only punish first degree murderers with 50-year prison terms. Thus, Hatcher's desire for the death penalty would not be realized by confessing to the Christgen murder.

"How old are you?" Judge Connett asked.

"Fifty-four," replied Hatcher.

"So that means you would have to live to be 104 at least, so there's not much chance of that."

"I'm not worried about it."

"All right. How long have you had it in your mind to do this, Mr. Clark?"

"For some time."

"Well, I don't have to know exact time, but has it been an hour? Some time means several hours or several days or several weeks?"

"Months. Months."

"Several what?" the judge asked, raising his eyebrows.

"Months."

"Have you ever participated in a jury trial as a party? Have you ever had a jury trial anywhere?"

"I have."

"And where was that?" Judge Connett asked.

"Right here in this court. Whatever," Hatcher responded, looking around the room.

"And what was the charge?"

"I believe it was assault and intent to kill, I believe. I'm not sure."

"And did you have a lawyer with you during that trial?"

"I did."

"And what happened in that trial?"

"I was found guilty."

"Well, you understand that by pleading guilty you are giving up your right to trial by a jury, that you have a right to trial by a jury?"

"I understand that."

Dahms handed the judge a copy of Hatcher's petition for a guilty plea that Clark had signed earlier that morning. Attached to it was the confession letter he had written more than two months earlier.

"Mr. Clark, would you stand up please?" the judge said. "When did you write this letter?"

"I don't remember," answered Hatcher. "I put a date on the letter. It should be on there."

"Well, it says July 25, 1983, by Richard M. Clark."

"That's the date I wrote it."

"Well, I thought when they had this filled out, this petition, you got a lot of details there, but generally I just want a brief statement of the situation; and I understand from this two and a half pages that you did take the boy and so forth, but I want to hear from you, and I want to be sure. This is a letter that you didn't fill out at the time you filled out this petition, and I appreciate it, and I want to take the time to go through all this, but I'm not comfortable with the situation yet."

"I have a statement here," said Hatcher. "It's correct as I wrote it."

"You have a statement?" the judge asked, apparently confused.

"I have the statement right here. It is all correct as I wrote it."

Dahms broke in. "I gave him a copy of the petition which has the three pages attached to it the same as what the court has, and he is telling the court that he has read this and that the three pages are correct."

"All right," the judge replied. "Well, I understand you took the Christgen boy. I'd like you to tell me how you went about killing him and why you killed him."

"It's all in the statement as it happened."

"Well, I appreciate that, but I'd like to hear it from you."

"Well, if you believe part of it you have to believe it all because it's all right there in front of you."

"Well, I appreciate it's all right there, but why don't you want to tell me? Why don't you want to tell me?"

"It's easier to write it than it is to explain it before you. That's the reason."

"Well, I appreciate it may be easier. You got a little more time, but I didn't want to go through all of it and put words in your mouth. That's what I'm trying to avoid doing. And I realize it's not a matter that you'd like to discuss but it's an important matter, and I got to hear it from your mouth in open court in order for me to accept it."

"I did take the boy and I did kill him as I stated in the statement by strangulation, and that's all I'm going to say about it."

"Can you tell me any reason why you killed him?"

"I don't know the reason."

"There is nothing in the statement about why you did it."

"I don't know why I did it."

"You don't know why. You understand that by filing this petition to plead guilty that you are waiving your right to a formal arraignment? Is that what you intend to do?"

"I understand that all."

"You won't be able to come back later and say, 'Well, now I've changed my mind.' This is going to be a final act, and I want you to be sure you completely understand that fact, Mr. Hatcher, because I don't want to put somebody down there that didn't know what he was doing."

"I'm making the statement because it's true, and I killed him alone in this case and nobody else," answered Hatcher. "And it happened the way I said it did. Because some pathologist said it happened some other way, I can't help that. I know how it happened. That's the way it happened."

The judge turned to Hatcher's lawyer.

"And I take it, Mr. Dahms, on his behalf, that you are waiving formal arraignment?" Connett asked.

"It's my understanding that Mr. Clark does wish to waive formal arraignment, and I would at this time on behalf of the defendant waive formal arraignment on the capital murder charge," Dahms said.

The judge said that before he would decide whether Hatcher's plea was voluntary, he wanted to hear more from Dahms. The public defender told the judge that he knew very little concerning how Hatcher had confessed, and that it was only within the last few days that he had learned that Hatcher wanted to enter a guilty plea.

"My first conversation with Mr. Clark about the Christgen case was this morning at 8:00 in the court's jury room, and therefore, I cannot recommend Mr. Clark at this time, and I do not recommend to him that he enter a plea of guilty to this charge," said Dahms. "This was his doing. He wants to do it. He and Mr. Holtslag have made the arrangements, and I'm here at the request of the prosecutor and at the request of the court to assist him in filling out the petition to plead guilty, and I have done so."

"Do you have any reason to believe that it's not voluntary or not understandingly made?" the judge asked.

"No, I do not," responded Dahms.

The judge turned to Insco, seated at another table.

"Mr. Insco, you have anything to say?"

"Yes, your honor. About a week ago, we received communications from Mr. Hatcher, Mr. Clark, indicating that something should be done about this. In a meeting with Mr. Dahms and Mr. Clark, he said he would think about pleading guilty to this charge, and this was about a week ago. Mr. Clark informed our office through Mr. Holtslag Monday evening or Tuesday evening that he wished to plead guilty to the killing of Eric Christgen, and that he wished to do it this morning. These arrangements have been made."

Judge Connett then announced that the court believed Hatcher's plea was voluntary, but that before the plea would be accepted, a factual basis would have to be established that Hatcher was Eric Christgen's murderer.

Mike Insco faced the most important step so far in his legal career. He was on the brink of admitting that a massive judicial mistake had been made and that he was at the center of it. As big as the step was, Insco had no alternative. There was no doubt in his mind now, that it was Hatcher, not Reynolds, who killed Eric Christgen. The psychological profile, the precision of Hatcher's confession and Hatcher's criminal history had brought him step by step from doubt to conviction. Insco realized that Hatcher's manipulative ability had allowed him to carry out his murderous compulsions almost uninterrupted.

Insco stood up near the prosecutor's table.

"Your honor," Insco said, "I can tell you that the detail of Mr. Hatcher's or Mr. Clark's statement is accurate and accurate in very specific degrees about very important and significant parts of the crime."

Insco recounted for the judge all the evidence that had been gathered in previous weeks. He asked FBI agent Joe Holtslag to take the stand. For the next hour, Joe Holtslag related the series of events that had finally brought Clark to Connett's courtroom. He did not talk about Clark's other murders, but described all the details of the Christgen case—he said that Clark fit the description of the man Jeff Davey had seen and that Davey said Melvin Reynolds could not have been the man he had seen with the boy. He stated that Clark insisted that Dr. Bridgens was wrong about how the boy died. Clark's gleaming eyes never left Holtslag as he answered Insco's questions. Then, Dahms was given a chance to interrogate the agent.

"Do you have an opinion as to how long Mr. Clark has had it in his mind to enter a plea of guilty to some kind of a charge in connection with the death of Eric Christgen?" Dahms asked.

"I think Mr. Clark had in mind clearing up the situation that he felt was an injustice from the first day he contacted me," answered Holtslag.

Judge Connett asked Holtslag some questions about his investigation. Holtslag then stepped down from the stand and returned to the defense table where Dahms and Clark were seated. Clark looked at the agent, nodded his head and grinned.

For a long moment, the judge stared out the window behind his bench. Rust colored trees covered the Missouri River bluffs like thousands of explosions in orange, yellow and red. It had been in the same month four years earlier that Melvin Reynolds had sat before him at trial. It was in this same crowded courtroom that Connett had sentenced Reynolds to life imprisonment the following January. It had taken a week for a jury to decide that Melvin Reynolds was guilty. Now, Judge Connett was being asked to reverse that decision, based on a two-hour hearing and the testimony of two people. The judge's thoughts were not with Melvin Reynolds. He believed Reynolds had caused his own predicament. He was more concerned about the jurors and what they would think when they realized they had made a mistake.

The judge considered several legal questions. Did Clark need another mental exam to show he was competent to enter a guilty plea? Was it necessary for an independent fact finder to go over the Christgen murder case and determine whether Clark could really have done it? Should someone investigate whether the FBI man fed Clark the details that he had written down but would not discuss? The list of questions was long. But the real question, the judge knew, was one of justice, whether or not Clark was guilty. Judge Connett believed Clark, and he knew that every day's delay meant an innocent man would sit in prison.

"Mr. Clark, would you stand up please?" the judge said.

The courtroom became very still. Reporters, lawyers, and courthouse workers listened quietly, their eyes fixed on the judge.

"This court has listened very carefully and has considered your petition; and the court has been satisfied that it is voluntary on your part, and you understand up to this moment that you could withdraw your petition to plead guilty and stand trial on the matter, and I again offer you the opportunity to withdraw your plea if you wish to do so."

There was a long pause, and all eyes turned to Hatcher, who stood by his chair at the defense table. He did not move, but stared intently at Holtslag.

"You have heard the testimony of Mr. Holtslag and the statement of the attorneys which indicates there might be some defense. Certainly you are going to be waiving any chance to bring those defenses up later if you don't do so now. You still desire to persist in your plea of guilty?"

"I do," replied Hatcher, in a low voice.

"And you understand the court . . . there will be no alternative for the court to do anything but accept your plea and to sentence you to imprisonment in the state Department of Corrections for the remainder of your life and no parole for 50 years; you understand that?"

"I understand."

"And you still wish to proceed?"

"I do."

Insco held his breath. Holtslag and every other person in the courtroom, with the exception of Hatcher, watched Connett. Hatcher looked across the defense table at Holtslag.

"All right. The court finds the defendant is waiving his formal arraignment; waived his right to preliminary hearing, that he has filed a petition to plead guilty which the court finds to be voluntary on his part. The court further finds through the testimony presented that there is factual basis for acceptance of this plea and sentences you to imprisonment for the remainder of your life with no parole for 50 years. That's the order of the court."

As Hatcher was being led from the courtroom reporters asked him to make a statement. He gazed from reddened eyes and said, "He's innocent and they know it. That man down there is innocent. That's all I can say."

CHAPTER NINETEEN

"I told my lawyer I wasn't good for it. I said one of these days the right guy's going to confess."
—Melvin Reynolds

MELVIN REYNOLDS CRANED HIS NECK OVER THE PEO-
ple who had crowded the visiting room of the
Missouri State Penitentiary. Inmates, wives, girl-
friends and mothers kissed, petted and talked on
the stuffed naugahyde chairs, as their children ran
and played in the crowded aisles. Brown-uni-
formed guards, watching for the exchange of contraband, stood vigil with shiny chrome vending
machines along the walls. Melvin spotted the familiar figure of his mother, Wanda O'Meara, across
the busy room. He had been in the Missouri State
Penitentiary for nearly four years, and his mother
had been a regular visitor.

This visiting day—five days before Hatcher's
guilty plea was accepted by Judge Connett—would
be a special one. It would be the last. Wanda
O'Meara was beaming and waved to get his attention. Melvin threaded his way politely across the
brown tiled floor to get to her side. Together, they
found a spot on a sofa. The inmates and their visi-
tors were pressed close to one another, like one big
prison family, and their conversations mixed and
mingled like the thick smoke from their cigarettes.
As Melvin and his mother sat down, an inmate be-

hind them said hello and Melvin returned the greeting. He began to say something more to the inmate, but his mother raised her hand to get Melvin's attention. She looked straight at her son.

"Another man . . . a man named Charles Hatcher . . . has confessed to killing Eric Christgen."

Melvin said nothing. He stared blankly at her for a long moment. Finally, she snapped her fingers in front of his eyes.

"Melvin, wake up."

"What?"

"What did your mom just say?" asked the inmate sitting behind them. "Something about your going home?"

"Yeah, I think that's what she said," Melvin replied. Then he turned to his mother, blinking and wide-eyed. "Is that what you said?"

"Yes."

"You're kidding."

"Nope, I'm not."

After Hatcher's guilty plea on Thursday, October 13, reporters began arriving at the penitentiary with requests for interviews with Melvin. The interviews lasted from about noon, when news of Hatcher's confession had flashed across the state, until suppertime. Melvin wondered when the questions would end, and it reminded him of that marathon interrogation of Valentine's Day 1979, when the police had asked him over and over again if he had killed Eric Christgen.

"I told my lawyer I wasn't good for it." Melvin said. "I said one of these days the right guy's going to confess."

"Why did you confess?" a reporter asked.

"What would you do if you was questioned about 13 to 14 months straight, every day 12, 13, 14 hours a day? A person's got a breaking point. I just couldn't take it no more."

He described what he had had to do in prison to survive, and described how he had been bought and sold for homosexual acts.

"I had a lot of guys wanting to kill me. A lot of the inmates told me it could have been one of their own kids. I was lucky to survive."

Melvin said he held no grudges against authorities and did not plan to sue them for false imprisonment. He said that it was his own confession that led to his imprisonment. Melvin said he planned to stay with his mother, get a job and find new friends who would not get him into trouble. He believed that once he returned to St. Joseph, the people living there would believe in his innocence. "I figure them prosecutors were just doing their job. They just got the wrong person. I just figured there was no sense hoping. I was going to be here 12, 15 years, however long a life sentence was. Now, all I want is out. My freedom is more important than any lawsuit could ever be."

"I really think the people think I didn't do it. I didn't do it. I don't think I would have any trouble returning to St. Joseph. They got the guy in jail. If they got the guy in jail they can't hold me, can they?"

"Do you know Hatcher?" a reporter asked.

"No."

"Would you like to talk to him?"

"No. In a way, he's the one who put me in here. I'm glad they found the right guy."

Reynolds was unaware that Hatcher's actions had been responsible not only for his confinement but for his release. Reynolds, at that point, mistakenly believed that his release was due either to the diligent efforts of his lawyer, Lee Nation, or to

Mike Insco's willingness to admit he had made a mistake. The reality of the situation was that Hatcher had initiated Reynold's release. In the end, the fact that the police had convicted the wrong man had goaded Hatcher into confessing that he committed the crime. A twist of fate—the fact that Hatcher read in a detective magazine that another man had been convicted for his crime—motivated him to return to St. Joseph to confess to the crime. Without the wrongful conviction of Melvin Reynolds, the Christgen murder case may never have been solved.

The day after Hatcher's dramatic appearance in Judge Connett's courtroom, the man Michael Insco had once said "should never be allowed to walk the streets again" was released from prison.

God, this air smells good, Melvin thought.

The return trip to St. Joseph took more than three hours, and Melvin enjoyed every minute of it. The highway between Jefferson City and St. Joseph covers rolling countryside and small towns, a trip that would bore most people. But freedom made it all very beautiful. The car carried him between golden fields of soybeans, khaki-colored cornstalks and milo as brown as toast. In the distance, the little towns seemed to spring from the land and grow larger before his eyes. The skylines were all the same—church steeples, grain elevators and a solitary, silver water tower.

Once in St. Joseph, Melvin appeared at a five-minute hearing before Judge Connett, who released him on his own recognizance. A formal hearing on a writ of habeas corpus was scheduled for the following month. Things were moving very quickly.

"Do you understand what's happening?" Connett asked him.

Melvin, looking a little bewildered, said that he did.

The editors of the *St. Joseph Gazette* and *News-Press* were bewildered too, and in a front page editorial—the first since the day after Eric Christgen's body was found—they expressed the community's feelings.

"St. Joseph is stunned. Residents are shocked by an apparent miscarriage of justice that unfolded Thursday. Doubt has been aroused about the capability of our law enforcement officials. Their credibility has been wounded. Insco said the Hatcher sentencing completed the last chapter in the Christgen murder. Rather, it wrote the preface of a new book about what is wrong with the criminal justice system in Buchanan County."

The newspaper asked questions: "Did police use proper tactics to get a confession from Reynolds? The fact that another man, Harry Fox, died of fright while being interrogated adds to the suspicion. Why did the prosecutor use such flimsy evidence in the Reynolds trial? Why didn't the judge grill officials more closely about the Reynolds confession? Is there a lack of cooperation among lawmen?"

In separate news conferences and interviews in the days that followed, the actors in the legal drama provided their versions of the answers. Insco masterfully explained how he had worked to get Reynolds out of prison. He did not mention that at first he had disbelieved Hatcher's story that he was the real killer. He did not say that federal authorities had had to prompt his action on the case. The fact that Melvin might have been released months earlier was not disclosed.

Insco was irritated that the press seemed to blame the criminal justice system for Melvin's problems, while Nation, with the use of two key witnesses—the people who had seen the boy with an older, heavier man—probably could have prevented Reynolds' conviction.

"Ultimately, Reynolds put himself there because he confessed," Insco said. "Everything was done properly. In the trial, he argued his confession was forced, involuntary, but the jury didn't agree with him and neither did the judge or the Supreme Court. We're confident that we have written the final chapter in the Eric Christgen slaying. There is no question that Hatcher was guilty and that he acted alone. I'm not so sure a mistake was made. The system operated as it had to operate. I'm very disturbed that this happened. But I'm pleased that we've done the right thing now, and I'm also very disturbed that at one time we did the wrong thing. Not only did an innocent man go to prison, but a guilty man walked free."

Nation said he never thought Melvin was guilty:

"Melvin is not a pillar of strength," Nation said. "Melvin was questioned about what he did and didn't do on the details of the crime. Hatcher didn't get fed a lot of lines. I have always thought Melvin was innocent. There is something you see in people who are innocent. They have this oblivious stare in their eyes, like they have cancer and they don't know what's going on. Life isn't supposed to be fair, and it hasn't been for Melvin since the day he was born. He accepts it very well."

As Melvin was released, Insco and his investigators headed for Omaha to begin retracing Hatcher's ugly odyssey. In Insco's absence, Chief Hayes acted as a lightning rod for reporters who pursued the story. Hayes, who had directed the actions which led to the charges filed against Reynolds, had not been involved in the new developments on the Hatcher case. He had been surprised by the judge's quick acceptance of Hatcher's guilty plea and Reynolds' release. In the days that followed, Hayes helped Hatcher divide and embarrass the St. Joseph legal system. The chief sowed seeds of doubt that would plague the city for years. The law enforcement system began feeding on itself, as Hayes, Bridgens and Anderson argued publicly with Holtslag, Insco and Robb over the veracity of Hatcher's confession.

Hayes said Hatcher was "still beating the system" and was "smarter than anyone we've ever dealt with." He suggested the possibility that Reynolds and Hatcher had acted together. The chief said Reynolds had told a relative that he had killed the boy, although that information had never been brought out at his trial. Hayes said Reynolds had led investigators to the exact spot where the body had been found. He said the evidence connecting Reynolds with the crime was much stronger than Hatcher's confession. The chief also said that Holtslag had fed Hatcher the information he used in his confession.

"This case may be over for some people, but the case of Reynolds and Hatcher is not over as far as I'm concerned," Hayes said. "For four and a half years, the Eric Christgen case has been my outside reading. I think we're just re-opening the case. I think it's probably just as active now as it was on May 27, 1978, in my opinion. We're just not content with what has happened, and we will continue the investigation. We will continue what we've been doing every time there is a confession in this case —open an investigation."

Hayes continued to voice his opinion until St. Joseph officials, concerned about the city's legal liability for Hayes' remarks, issued an order forbidding him from discussing the case. The chief began to refer all calls about the confession to Dr. Bridgens.

Bridgens continued to believe that Eric died from suffocation rather than strangulation. He said that Hatcher's confession was not consistent with the facts. He also said he believed the confession was part of Hatcher's plan to manipulate the legal system so that he could be freed in both the Christgen and Steele cases.

"I've heard about his confession and there are a number of significant holes," Bridgens said. "There are too many errors in Hatcher's written statement."

St. Joseph Police Lieutenant John Muehlenbacher refused to discuss the case with anyone. Sergeant Bob Anderson of the Missouri Highway Patrol said he had used no undue influence, threats, intimidation or coercion to get Reynolds to confess.

"I am convinced that Melvin Reynolds did it," Anderson said at one point. "I always have been convinced. Until I am shown something else, I always will be." But at another time, he said, "I must admit I am not convinced one way or the other of the guilt or innocence of either individual."

Judge Connett would not discuss the case in great detail.

"The system works sometimes and sometimes it doesn't," he said. "Justice Holmes said, 'Justice is a fair trial.' The ones I'm worried about are the members of the jury. They should know they didn't do anything wrong. They had the confession. They just did what anyone else would have done."

Tom Larson was the assistant U.S. attorney in Kansas City. He reviewed Reynolds' conviction for possible civil rights violations.

"Jurors are members of the community and the atmosphere in the community was right for a conviction," Larson said. "The disturbing part is not so much that a mistake was made, but that so many mistakes were made. You could get Melvin to confess to anything."

When reporters asked him about the case, Holtslag said he did not believe that St. Joseph police or the Missouri Highway Patrol had done anything illegal to Melvin:

"They didn't railroad him. They were just smarter than he was. They got tunnel vision. If there is anybody to blame, Melvin's to blame. It's a shame his character was so weak that he did confess. Everybody got wrapped up in the heat of the thing. Melvin was telling them that he did it. It's hard to turn your back on that."

Hatcher's confession had disclosed the horrors of Eric's last moments to the Christgen family. They were forced to relive the crime. They were deeply troubled by Reynolds' release. Hayes had told the family members repeatedly that there was "no way" Eric could have died the way Hatcher described it.

"The pathologist told me that, and I have it on a taped interview that the pathologist's findings do not match the way Charles Hatcher said he took the boy's life," Hayes said.

Ken Christgen, one of Eric's uncles, asked Holtslag to meet with the Christgens at the Walnut Products Co. to explain how Hatcher could be Eric's murderer. Eric's grandparents and uncles were there, but his father and mother were not. The Christgens told Holtslag that Hayes had assured them that Reynolds was guilty and would never be let out of prison.

"They couldn't understand how they were told one thing by such a reputable individual as the police chief and it turned out to be wrong," Holtslag said. The FBI agent tried to assure them that justice had finally been accomplished in Eric's death.

Ed and Vicky Christgen had attempted to put the whole case behind them, but the new developments reopened old wounds.

"We've been through five years of hell," Ed Christgen said. "We hope and pray that they have the right fellow. If the courts would ever take a serious stand, that's what's wrong with this country. If the courts would just crack down."

The mother of another of Hatcher's murder victims felt the same way, but expressed it differently. William Freeman's mother Josie had been told by sheriff's deputies in California that a man in Missouri had said that he had killed her son in 1969. She read about Hatcher's various crimes in the newspaper:

"Some people call it revenge, I call it avenge," she said. "The guilty ones should be punished. After doing what he did and going scot free is pitiful. Children are punished when they do wrong."

For Annette Steele, Hatcher's confession to the Christgen murder and the fact that he had been set free repeatedly in Iowa and Nebraska added to the bitter irony of her daughter's death and prolonged her agony. For more than a year, she had been waiting for Hatcher's trial. Each week, she would place a tearful telephone call to Debbie Burich, the victim-witness advocate in Insco's office. She would complain about the delays in the trial, criticize Insco and Hayes, and cry.

"I would want him to go to the gas chamber if there was a possibility that he could ever kill again," she said. "Can you imagine what Michelle went through? I don't want him to do it again. The system is not right. For me to go on, it's got to be over. The system let Hatcher go how many times? This town is where the problem happened. What if four years from now another child is killed?

"You cannot live in fear. Most kids have to go to school further than Michelle did to get to the dentist. If Michelle were alive today and had a dental appointment, I don't think I would have told her anything different. You can't lock your kids up. It's not healthy if they don't talk to anybody. I don't feel guilty. I'd do the same thing tomorrow. Just because the police let insane perverts downtown it's not my fault.

"She knew not to go with people who were bad. I don't know. We'll never know. I have to believe she thought he was a policeman or something. You trust policemen. Maybe he had a fake ID. If downtown was that bad, they should have done something about it."

During his first days at home, Melvin woke up wondering why he did not hear the shouts of other inmates and the slamming of prison doors. Then he would realize that he was not in the penitentiary anymore. Other than that, he had no trouble readjusting to his familiar surroundings. He called Holtslag and thanked him for what he had done. Holtslag told him to keep his nose clean. Reynolds and his family had considered but decided against filing a lawsuit against the state seeking restitution for false arrest or imprisonment.

Harriet Frazier, the criminology professor who had doubted Reynolds' guilt four years earlier, believed that Melvin deserved some sort of restitution. She wrote her state senator in Kansas City suggesting that the Missouri Legislature pass a bill to compensate Reynolds for the five years he had spent in jails and in prison. The senator replied that such a bill would have to be sponsored by Roy Humphreys, Reynolds' state representative. Humphreys, Holtslag's former partner, had been an FBI agent for 25 years and had run as a Democrat for the state House of Representatives in 1978. He had been re-elected to two more terms. Humphreys was against the bill, and did not introduce it.

"You have to remember, he confessed," Humphreys said. "He got a fair trial. The fact is, he's put the state to a lot of expense."

But Reynolds received plenty of publicity. He appeared on several television shows, including ABC's "Good Morning America." The producer said he would need Reynolds on the show for about two minutes.

"That's going to be a long two minutes," said Nation, who accompanied Melvin to New York.

Hatcher had also become famous. Detailed stories about Hatcher's hideous life and Melvin's wrongful conviction appeared in newspapers as far away as Los Angeles. *US* magazine and *Reader's Digest* featured Hatcher's crimes in detailed stories about serial murders and crimes against children. The notoriety of the case brought many letters to Holtslag. Most of the letters contained queries for information. Police in areas where Hatcher had resided began combing their files, attempting to determine whether Hatcher might have committed the murders that remained unsolved.

Dozens of telephone calls were exchanged between detectives in Omaha and Rock Island. During the discussions, the officers discovered that two nearly identical murders had occurred in separate cities. In both Omaha and Rock Island, boys were found with their hands tied behind their backs.

Each had died from a blow to the head. Hatcher was ruled out as a suspect because he was in a mental hospital at the time. However, the officers believed the same man, perhaps a transient like Hatcher, was responsible for both crimes. Dr. Bridgens wanted Holtslag's help too. He wrote to Insco suggesting that Hatcher be asked about the disappearance and death of a young man from a Topeka bowling alley on May 20, 1979.

Police in West Des Moines, Iowa, wondered whether Hatcher knew what happened to John Gosch, a 12-year-old newspaper boy, who vanished September 5, 1982, while delivering newspapers. Hatcher had attacked a newsboy before and he had been in Iowa that year. But St. Joseph police found that Hatcher had been in their custody at that time.

Someone else must have abducted Johnny Gosch, whose photograph was on television, in post offices and on milk cartons. He had become the best known victim of the national nightmare of missing children. There were enough victims to support the creation of a nationwide network of parents of missing and murdered children. They formed groups like Child Find and the Coalition for Children's Justice. The groups lobbied Congress for a law that would bring the FBI more quickly into missing children cases.

There were other Charles Hatchers out there. They were almost impossible to identify and apprehend, because they were strangers to their victims and often moved on after committing one or two murders. Hatcher's picture joined the FBI gallery that included Ted Bundy, who had murdered at least 25 women, and Henry Lee Lucas, who said he used "everything but poison" to kill people.

Hatcher's arrest and confession occurred just as Congress was considering whether to fund a national program to find and apprehend serial killers. The Violent Criminal Apprehension Program, if funded, would be used by police departments across the country to funnel information concerning vicious, motiveless murders to the Justice Department. The department could then match the crimes according to type of victim, method used and evidence gathered, and then facilitate interaction among police departments when it appeared that they were looking for the same killer. Advocates of the program circulated copies of newspaper stories about Hatcher to the lawmakers. Congress appropriated the money for the program.

Detectives in other cities filed requests for interviews with Hatcher, but he would only speak to Holtslag. The FBI agent had become the conduit between the psychopath and society. The agent still hoped to pry more information from Hatcher about killings in other parts of the country. Holtslag was anxious to exploit Hatcher's cooperative mood. He wondered if there were other cases in which the wrong man had been imprisoned. And he wondered how many relatives of Hatcher's victims spent sleepless nights wondering what had happened to their loved ones.

Holtslag did not doubt that Hatcher had killed 16 people. The consistent record of violent encounters in Omaha and Lincoln, Des Moines and Bettendorf —cases in which unsuspecting victims almost miraculously survived contacts with a phantom of death—convinced him that there were others who were not so lucky. He believed Hatcher's murderous impulses had first emerged in 1959 when he tried to grab a newsboy off the streets of St. Joseph. He knew Hatcher was capable of multiple murder in a very small window of time. From his interviews with Hatcher, Holtslag was aware that more than one murder was sometimes necessary to satisfy his violent urges. He knew how Gilbert Martinez nearly became a murder victim the day after William Freeman. There were disturbing gaps in the record of Hatcher's life. He had been in Minnesota for nearly a year. But Hatcher had referred to trips he made to Texas and New Mexico. What had he done in those states? Had he left bodies in his wake?

The agent tried to prod Hatcher with questions like "Did you kill any other children?" and "When was your first murder?" At one point, Hatcher admitted killing another child, but provided no specifics.

"That happened a long time ago," Hatcher said. "I don't think anybody would remember."

Holtslag thought it might have been in the early Sixties. He also concluded that from the discussions with Hatcher, the 1969 murder of William Freeman was probably the fourth or fifth murder he had committed.

Hatcher would not provide any more details on the 16 killings, and Holtslag began to wonder whether he ever would. He thought perhaps that Hatcher could not remember enough details of other killings to appear credible. Perhaps he was saving those stories for bargaining sessions after the trial on Michelle's murder. Hatcher studied requests for information on each of the killings Holtslag asked about and then denied involvement. The agent began to detect that the distance was growing between himself and Hatcher. Holtslag could feel him retreat and wondered if Hatcher was finished with him because he had accomplished only part of what he had wanted. Was Hatcher resentful because he had not been given a death sentence?

Their conversations often revolved around

Hatcher's desire for death. Hatcher still wanted to be known as Richard Clark to the outside world. But a familiarity had grown between the two men, and they called each other Joe and Charlie. Hatcher had trusted Holtslag from that first day in the county jail when he dispatched the note on a "very important case." Holtslag did not know why. Perhaps it was because the FBI man was the antithesis of Hatcher. Holtslag was everything that Hatcher was not. Tall, handsome, successful, churchgoing, honest—Holtslag could be trusted with the truth. There were other lawmen with similar credentials. But Holtslag, as a federal agent, had the power to probe the activities of local authorities. And Hatcher seemed to recognize from the beginning that Holtslag was the kind of man willing to tackle the job; he was willing to be an instrument for truth.

In addition to Hatcher's stated reasons for confessing, Holtslag believed that Hatcher was tormented by a strong sense of guilt. Holtslag thought Hatcher had a deep seated need for something that neither his parents nor society had ever given him —punishment. The scheming side of Charles Hatcher had always denied society its right to punish him for his crimes. From the time of the murder of Jerry Tharrington in the state prison 22 years earlier, Hatcher had managed to avoid paying any penalty for his 16 murders. But another side of Charles Hatcher seemed to want to pay the price for his crimes.

Holtslag believed that Hatcher had a deep-seated need to be caught. That part of him was in control the day he loitered by the scene of the murder of Michelle Steele. Hatcher had hovered around the area until he was identified and questioned by a number of people, including the police.

"The only way society will be safe from people like me is when it starts using the death penalty," Hatcher told the FBI agent.

When Holtslag asked him if he wanted to plead guilty to the murder of James Churchill, whose body had been found in Rock Island, Illinois, Hatcher said, "Will it bring me the death penalty?"

"Charlie, I doubt that this crime carries the death penalty in the federal system."

"Then I don't want to mess around with it."

The FBI's behavioral science unit at Quantico, Virginia, fed information about Charles Hatcher into its computer to compile a psychological profile which would help identify murder suspects like Hatcher in the future. The computer contained questions and answers about Hatcher:

How is he described by people who know him? Manipulative, calculating, logical, illiterate, intelligent, strong willed, con man, angry, depressed, neat and drunkard. He rarely displays emotion. He hates the establishment, authority and blacks. He admires no one.

What are his hobbies or pastimes? Writing poetry, reading, writes and devises methods to beat the system. What does he read? Detective magazines.

What about his family? He hates his family and does not discuss it. He hates his brother and does not even wish to be known as Charles Hatcher. He had no close relationships with either men or women. He was never married. He had one common law relationship for six months. It was very stormy. He was always a drifter.

What are his weaknesses? Unknown.

Ambitions or dreams in life? Few if any.

What are his spending habits? Frugal, except for booze.

Is he a homosexual? Yes, but he denies it. He is possibly bisexual.

Does he have a history of mental health care? Yes, frequently. Earliest known attempt to avoid prosecution by deliberate feigning of mental defect occurred in San Francisco on August 29, 1969. He dresses neatly and cleanly, unless feigning mental illness. He has a poor concept of self.

How does he travel? He gets around by public transportation, although he has frequently stolen cars. He would get employed if he needs the money.

Is he intelligent? Yes, street sense and institutional knowledge. Hatcher could be very decisive. And he has a wry sense of humor. He sleeps little and is not excessively profane. He is not sloppy and he is organized. He is an introvert, takes risks and lies.

Law enforcement officials and others wondered whether there was anything to be learned from Hatcher's technique of luring children, and whether parents could be given advice regarding how to warn children about men like him. With Hatcher, it seemed that a single unguarded moment could be fatal.

Insco visited the places where Hatcher had committed his crimes and found that he had assumed whatever role necessary to entrap his victim. Perhaps more than anyone else, Insco wanted to learn everything he could about Charles Hatcher.

"We need to know as much about this kind of person as we can," Insco said.

Six drawers in two filing cabinets in Insco's office began to fill up with records on Hatcher's movements. Thousands of dollars were spent in copying fees alone as Insco petitioned courts for duplicates of Hatcher's mental health reports. Insco found that every time Hatcher was involved in a crime he ended up in a hospital. Insco was shocked to read that police in five cities had never properly identified Hatcher. On two occasions—in California and Nebraska—police had taken him to the same hospitals under different names, and nurses had recognized him under a previous identity. Insco burned with anger as he learned that two children murdered in his hometown had died because various government systems—the police, the courts, the hospitals, the prisons—had repeatedly given an obviously dangerous man his freedom. Insco admitted that his own system had made a mistake. A man had paid for it with almost five years of his life. But other communities had failed as well, and many victims had paid with their lives.

Insco saw that Hatcher had cunningly turned the mental health system into his own sanctuary to avoid criminal prosecution and then had used the hospitals as the path of least resistance back to freedom. He read dozens of psychiatric exams and saw that Hatcher first fooled the doctors into believing he was crazy and then had turned the mental health systems into a revolving door by convincing them that he was "cured."

"Psychiatry is not really a discipline," Insco concluded. "The system is looking for an excuse to kick people out so they don't have to do the work." He called it the "secret system"; psychiatrists who repeatedly freed Hatcher were not accountable to the public because patient records were confidential.

The prosecutor found that despite all of law enforcement's sophisticated identification techniques and an FBI bank of 22 million fingerprints, police in Willmar, Minnesota; Lincoln and Omaha, Nebraska; and Des Moines and Bettendorf, Iowa, could not connect Hatcher with his criminal past. Hatcher repeatedly slipped through the fingers of distracted police and indifferent prosecutors even though he was in custody, often for sex-related crimes. None of them had ever pierced his aliases to identify him as a fugitive from California.

Insco interviewed Roger Galatoire, the man who interrupted Hatcher during a sexual attack on the boy in San Francisco. Insco went to the scene of the crime, the spot atop Bernal Heights. He stood there a long time and wondered why there had been no Galatoires to interrupt the crimes that had taken place at two lonely sites near downtown St. Joseph. And he could not understand how this menace had ever been released by the corrections systems in California.

"What he did in San Francisco was blood curdling," Insco said. "The brazenness of it. You can see downtown from there. The system fucked up in Missouri, but Hatcher would never have committed crimes in Missouri if he had been punished for the rest of his life in California. He was caught sodomizing a child. The point is, he should have been punished for the rest of his life. It's almost like we're afraid to use our institutions or we don't believe in what we are doing. We don't believe in punishment.

"There are too many cracks for people like him to slip through. What we see here is law enforcement, for 15 years, felt that if the case against him wasn't perfect, the decision was made to let him go. I really feel although there's a lot of laziness involved, there's an attitude thing too. There was a major breakdown in the resolution and goal of the criminal justice system."

William Freeman, Eric Christgen, James Churchill, Michelle Steele and the others were sacrificial victims to a give-everyone-the-benefit-of-the-doubt system; the everyone-deserves-a-second-chance system; the innocent-until-proven-guilty system. Melvin Reynolds and Harry Fox were also victims—victims of the system's excesses.

Insco knew it was a good system, the best in the world. But as good as the system was, it could not stop a man like Charles Hatcher. Insco also saw that when it came time to punish Hatcher, society was still unwilling to give him the ultimate punishment.

CHAPTER TWENTY

"If you think I did this, you have one job."
—Charles Hatcher speaking to the jurors who
convicted him of capital murder, telling
them to give him the death penalty.

BY THE BEGINNING OF 1984, THE MISSOURI CRIMI-
nal justice system was preparing to deal with
Hatcher once again. His trial for Michelle Steele's
murder was set for January 9 a year and a half
after the killing. But there were more delays.
Dahms had had enough of his client. Hatcher not
only refused to cooperate with his defense lawyer,
but he wrote him ugly letters addressed to "Mr.
Richard W. Duroc."

Hatcher had found a new game. Instead of toy-
ing with the mental health system, he played with
the legal system and its officers. Outmaneuvering
the lawyers and the courts was almost as exciting
to him as checkmating the psychiatrists.

Describing Hatcher's letters, Dahms told Terry
Brummer, supervisor of state public defenders:
"They get worse every time he writes me, I don't
get paid enough to take this kind of crap off any
client, especially this guy."

At one point, Dahms was afraid of what Hatcher
might do to him physically, and Dahms concluded
that he could not adequately defend Hatcher.
Brummer granted his request to be removed from
the case. Dahms was succeeded by James Fletcher,

an energetic public defender from Kansas City. Brummer chose Fletcher because he was adept at handling very difficult cases. Dahms gave Fletcher his lengthy files on the case. The new lawyer asked for an extension to become familiar with the case, and another delay was granted.

The trial was moved to Warrensburg, about 45 miles west of Kansas City, and set for September 17, 1984—two years, 50 days and 25 court motions after Michelle was murdered. Judge Robert Russell presided over the five-day trial from 9:00 A.M. to 9:00 P.M. each day. A jury of eight men and four women was picked the first day, followed by opening arguments. The second day, four witnesses testified about how they had seen Hatcher, using the name Richard Harris, near the scene where Michelle's body was found. Several police officers testified concerning the investigation of the crime. During a break in the trial, Judge Russell remarked to his bailiff that if he had to commit a murder, he'd do it in St. Joseph.

On the third day, dental experts disagreed about whether Hatcher's teeth made the bite on the girl's arm. Hatcher's cellmate testified that Hatcher had told him that he killed the girl and had taken earrings from her pierced ears. On Thursday, the case was turned over to the jury. The jurors deliberated for an hour Thursday night, slept on it, and considered the case again beginning at 9:00 A.M. Friday. At 2:44 P.M., the verdict was ready. Guy Griggs, the jury foreman, told the court that the jury had found Hatcher guilty of capital murder.

After the verdict was read, Leonard and Annette Steele broke down in tears and ran from the courtroom.

"Thank God," Annette said. "They returned the

right decision. It's the only decision they could make. I can't say I'm happy, but my little girl was given justice. I'm glad he won't be out walking our streets again."

"The system maybe took two years, but the system worked," Leonard said.

Capital murder trials in Missouri consist of two parts. In the first, a jury considers a defendant's guilt or innocence. In the second part of the trial, the punishment phase, the jury considers aggravating circumstances, such as other convictions, in determining which punishment to mete out to the defendant. Having been convicted of capital murder for Michelle's murder, Hatcher could receive either the death penalty or life imprisonment without parole for 50 years.

All during the trial, Hatcher sat stiffly at the defense table, listening to the testimony and conferring at times with his lawyers. After the guilty verdict, Hatcher seemed to relax. The judge called a brief recess and Hatcher leaned back in his chair and placed his feet on the chair next to him. He seemed the picture of contentment. He would occasionally gaze at the courtroom crowd, smile and wink.

The punishment phase of the trial began after the recess. The prosecutor wanted to tell the jurors everything Hatcher had done in his life, but they were handcuffed by legal restrictions. Robb and Insco could not tell them about the deaths of Jerry Lee Tharrington, William James Freeman or James Lewis Churchill, because Hatcher had never been convicted of those murders. Hatcher's conviction on the Eric Christgen case had taken place after Michelle's murder, and thus was not admissible. They were able to read to the jurors the list of all of Hatcher's property crimes, and his attempted abduction in 1959 of the St. Joseph newsboy, but they could not introduce Hatcher's molestation of a boy in San Francisco because they had not brought to court the necessary evidence to prove that he was Albert Price.

Hatcher did what he could to help Insco. Defendant and prosecutor did agree on one thing: that Hatcher should be put to death. In a surprise move and against the wishes of his lawyers, Hatcher took the stand. He would not look at the jurors but stared at the floor with his hands folded in front of him.

In a low, almost mumbling voice, he told the jurors his name was Charles Hatcher. He said he was born on July 16, 1929. He said he was now 55 years old.

"If you believe the prosecutor's allegations are true, you have only one job. If you think I did this, you have one job. You have to make sure it doesn't happen again. I have a record of escapes. I may try it. You must prevent it from happening again."

With his cryptic message delivered, Hatcher returned to the defense table. Insco and Robb thought this had been just another gesture by the manipulative psychopath—an expression of contempt for authority by daring the state to execute him. The defense attorneys thought that Hatcher was asking for state-conducted suicide. Judge Russell quickly ordered the jury to disregard the remark.

Charlie Rogers, an attorney assisting Fletcher in the defense, and Insco then began a debate before the jury over whether Hatcher deserved to live. Rogers paced back and forth in front of the jury box, using the standard argument defense attorneys wage everywhere to oppose capital punishment. He pointed out that if the jury sentenced the defendant to 50 years in the Missouri State Penitentiary, Hatcher would be 105 years old when released. Hatcher already had 50 years to serve for the murder of Eric Christgen, but Rogers did not mention that fact.

"This is a serious case. And the death penalty is serious punishment," Rogers said. "If the life of Mr. Hatcher would bring back Michelle Steele, let's do it. But the prosecutor does not want a life for a life. He wants a death for a death. The evidence in this case is not the kind of evidence to put a man to death. I'm going to ask for mercy for the sake of Mr. Hatcher, whether he wants it or not."

For Insco, the argument was more personal. The year before, he had taken a long march along the violent trail of Charles Hatcher. He had personal knowledge of the pain Hatcher had inflicted on his victims. He had seen the bodies of two of them.

Insco stood up and took a position at the corner of the prosecutors' table.

"What value do we as a society, as a community, as a family, place on the lives of our children, who are the only link that you and I have to the future?" Insco asked. "The most important thing in the lives of all of us has got to be our family; has got to be our children. If this is not the case that asks for the death penalty, then what is?"

With Insco's question ringing in their ears, the jury resumed its deliberations. Less than an hour later, it returned and announced that it recommended Hatcher be sentenced to life without the possibility of probation or parole for 50 years.

Hatcher had come full circle. When he was 18 years old, society had decided to punish him for car theft with time in the state penitentiary. For the next 37 years, hundreds of thousands of dollars were spent to incarcerate him in prisons and mental hospitals. More than three dozen psychiatrists in six states had attempted to delve into his mind, and they had always come up empty handed. They could not determine what he was, or what was to be done with him. And in the end, at the age of 55, society again decided that a prison sentence was the best answer.

When they learned of the jury's decision, many people in St. Joseph were angry. They thought that pure justice would dictate Hatcher's execution. He had done irreparable and horrible damage and could never be rehabilitated. His continued existence would be a constant reminder of a terrible sorrow. But there was a minority view. Hatcher, himself, had wanted to die. Perhaps sitting in a prison cell for the rest of his life, brooding over his evil past, might be the greatest punishment of all.

Prosecutors were still drawing up murder charges against him. Bob Hole, the prosecutor in Contra Costa County, California, planned to visit Hatcher to speak with him about the death of William Freeman. Police in Contra Costa had concluded that Hatcher had either murdered the boy or had watched someone else do it, because he knew things about the murder that were never reported in the newspapers. But there was no prospect for capital punishment for Hatcher in that case, since California did not have the death penalty at the time the boy was murdered.

On October 14, 1984, Melvin Lee Reynolds and his family threw a party to celebrate his first anniversary of freedom. He had gained a few pounds from his mother's cooking since his release, but he was trying to lose it jogging. He had plans to be married.

"I'm doing real good. Everybody's been real good

to me. For the first four or five months I was home,
I was having nightmares. I would hear guards and
keys."

Melvin harbored no ill feelings toward the community that put him in jail.

"I have a lot of time to think. I really put myself
in there for confessing to it."

He said he was having trouble finding a job. He
attended classes at a vocational center in Kansas
City, but quit after he had trouble getting along
with other students. He said his problems at the
school were unrelated to his prison experience.

Hatcher had sprung Reynolds from the penitentiary and now had replaced him there. It had been
20 years since Hatcher had been behind the walls.
There had been some changes. Federal court orders had made the cells less crowded and now the
races were mixed. But on the whole, the place was
still the same. To his horror, he found that some
faces were as familiar as the bars and the walls.
There were plenty of inmates willing to grant
Hatcher's request for the death penalty. They
would be willing to duplicate his knifing of Tharrington 23 years earlier. Hatcher was a child killer
and he occupied the bottom rung of prison society.
His crime was the most despicable of all, and several inmates would gladly make him their target.

But there was one man in particular that
Hatcher feared in a special way: Carl Pierce.
Hatcher had betrayed Pierce by revealing Pierce's
escape plot in the Kansas State Penitentiary in
Lansing in 1969.

For years, the memory of what he had done
haunted Hatcher. When he was in California, he
begged to stay out of Folsom Prison and San Quentin because he thought Pierce had friends there
who would kill him. Pierce was now serving a sen-

tence in Missouri for planning a bank robbery. Hatcher had last seen Pierce in Kansas, and now Hatcher thought that Pierce had purposely engineered his transfer from Kansas to Missouri so that he could be in a position to hurt him. Even before he arrived at the penitentiary, Hatcher tried to make peace. From his cell in the Buchanan County Jail, he sent Pierce a poem on August 31, 1984:

> Time goes by, I can't forget
> The code was broken and haunts me yet,
> I can run but not escape
> The memory of our faith.
> There are things we cannot amend.
> We just make certain that not again.
> —PROBABLY APPROPRIATE

Once in prison, Hatcher wrote Holtslag to say he feared for his life because he thought Pierce or someone else would seek revenge. He asked the FBI agent to use his influence to have prison officials keep him in protective custody. Holtslag contacted Warden William Armontrout and asked him if Hatcher could be separated from the rest of the prison population. Hatcher said that in return for protection, he would "clear up" the other killings in which he was involved.

Prison officials took elaborate precautions to ensure Hatcher's safety. He was housed in the protective custody unit, the suffocating type of confinement that Reynolds had refused. Hatcher took all his meals in his cell and he never left it without a guard to escort him. He lived in fear behind the thick iron doors of the protective custody unit, where he was insulated from the rest of the prison population. There, he would keep company with the memories of his murders for the rest of his life.

Holtslag met with Hatcher for the last time in November 1984 in a penitentiary interview room. The agent had come to Jefferson City hoping to get answers to the questions that plagued his mind about remaining murder cases. The two men saw each other in the same cubicle where Reynolds had answered reporters' questions the year before.

The case of Charles Hatcher had become the high point of Holtslag's career. Shortly after the Steele trial, Insco had written to FBI Director William H. Webster. Insco, the man who had become big enough to admit a mistake, singled out for praise the man who had reversed an injustice.

"He is largely responsible for the release of an innocent man from prison. Mr. Holtslag did his job meticulously and professionally in the face of serious pressure to leave the case alone. It was only by his dogged determination to discover the truth that the right man was convicted and the innocent man freed. He represents what is best in good law enforcement. That is a total commitment to the truth and a willingness to work for it."

Webster commended Holtslag on October 16 for being "instrumental in proving the innocence of an individual already incarcerated for the crimes later attributed to Hatcher, Missouri's first convicted serial murderer."

Hatcher's feelings toward Holtslag had changed. He was brooding and surly and contempt was written on his face when the two men confronted each other for the last time. He doesn't want anything more to do with me, the agent thought. He's angry with me because he didn't get what he wanted, as if I can pave his way to the gas chamber.

"Charlie, we made a deal to talk about the other murders," Holtslag said.

"I got nothing more to say to you," Hatcher replied. He turned around and walked out of the interview room.

On Tuesday, December 3, Hatcher appeared before Judge Russell in Warrensburg on his motion for a new trial. During the hearing, Hatcher stared at Insco and attempted to spit on him.

"Come close enough, and I'll kill you," Hatcher said.

Hatcher told the judge he thought he hadn't received a fair trial.

"They haven't proved I killed anyone as far as I'm concerned. Of course, the system has more power than I do."

Russell turned down the motion, and Hatcher was sent back to prison to serve his two life terms.

Four days later, on the clear and cold morning of December 7, 1984, Corrections Officer William Scott made his routine 4:00 A.M. count in housing unit 5-C. He shined his flashlight through the window of the metal door to cell 213 on the west wing, and in the harsh light he saw the dangling body of a man, his feet just off the floor. The man was hanging by a piece of electrical wire that had been tied to the brace of a heavy metal ventilation grate on his cell wall. The knot in the wire was located just beneath his right ear, leaving a two and one-half foot length that reached up to the brace and suspended his body four inches from the floor. The man's hands had been tied behind his back with a piece of shoelace. Scott called for help, entered the man's cell and tried to revive him. But it was too late; Charles R. Hatcher's wish for death had come true.

The days when penitentiary deaths (like Jerry Tharrington's) were investigated by prison guards were over. Within minutes of the discovery of Hatcher's body, Warden Armontrout had been notified, and he called in Cole County Sheriff's Deputy John Hemeyer to investigate the death. Hatcher was wearing no shirt and his pants hung loosely around his hips. The sheriff noticed that there were some small abrasions on Hatcher's left eyebrow and right shoulder which appeared to have bled. But there was no sign of struggle within the cell area.

The wire used to hang Hatcher was part of a call light system installed in each cell. The wire had been stripped out of the metal sheathing that housed it. His own shoelaces had been used to tie his hands behind his back. No suicide note was found, but Hemeyer concluded that Hatcher had hanged himself. To do so, Hatcher would have had to stand on the commode to tie the metal wire attached to his neck to the brace. Then, he would have had to tie his own hands together. Finally, while balancing himself on the commode, he would have had to "step through" his hands to get them behind his back. Hemeyer believed that that was how it had happened. He thought Charles Hatcher had strangled his last victim.

George Brooks, a prison investigator, said two Currier and Ives prints of children were found near his body.

"This case does not appear to be of a suspicious nature from the preliminary examination of the scene and victim," Hemeyer said. "Reportedly, he had told someone 'they're going to be sorry they didn't give me the death penalty.' Whether or not his suicide was the termination of that veiled threat is not known to me."

At 7:00 A.M., after the investigators completed their work, Armontrout contacted Hatcher's older brother, Floyd.

"We didn't find any sort of a suicide note," Armontrout said. "I don't know if he was despondent, or whether this last sentence was enough to drive him to it or what. I talked with him Monday night, when he came in from Warrensburg. We don't know if he mailed any letters out in the last few days."

Armontrout wanted to know where to send Hatcher's body and his personal effects, a radio, his clothes and legal papers. But Floyd Hatcher said, "I don't want anything to do with him."

After the news of Charles Hatcher's death reached Insco that morning, he said he never believed Hatcher had the courage to kill himself.

"One thing for sure, he didn't do it out of remorse, but rather out of frustration because he was no longer in control," Insco said. "He didn't feel anything for his victims. He told the FBI once that he had no remorse. My belief is that Charles Hatcher never did think much of himself. He attempted to prove he was something else. He tried to manipulate everyone around him. I think he looked at his sentence and was frustrated by the fact that he would no longer get attention, and the prospect of that and the world knowing what he really was, was too much for him to take.

"I believe there are 11 other victims, whose names we'll probably never know," said Insco. "That, I regret. People say that is a lot of killing, but look at the California cases. He committed a murder and an attempted murder all within a day of each other. Charles Hatcher didn't require much time to do any damage. This man probably repre-

sents the epitome of an evil person. He is as close
to evil as a human being can become."

"Evil" is not a psychiatric term, but the word
does seem to fit at least those true psychopaths
characterized by irresponsible, callous brutality.
Psychiatrists might say that social, psychological,
biological and environmental influences inter-
twined to cause Hatcher's hideous actions. Perhaps
it was improper brain development, poor nutri-
tional habits, insufficient prenatal care, brain injury, chemical imbalance or emotional
disturbance. Surely alcohol or some illicit drugs
stimulated his impulsive and aggressive acts. But
Insco's answer was much simpler: Charles Hatcher
was the devil's emissary to earth.

At 9:00 A.M. on Tuesday, December 11, 1984, a
detail of volunteers from L-hall, the honor dorm of
the Missouri State Penitentiary, carried a fiber-
board box containing Charlie's body to a slit of
ground in Longview Cemetery, the city-owned
graveyard on the outskirts of Jefferson City. Since
no one from Charlie's family had claimed him, taxpayers paid for the plot and the plain coffin. It was
the last installment in a criminal career which had
cost hundreds of thousands of dollars for police
investigations, court fees, mental examinations
and food and lodging in prisons and hospitals
across the country. With a guard watching, eight
inmates dug the trench, lowered the box into the
ground and covered it. The men then stood in a
semi-circle around the fresh grave. Reverend Clyde
Garriott, the Protestant prison chaplain, read from
the 103rd Psalm. Garriott raised his voice and a
chilly pre-winter wind carried his remarks over the
fields and the nearby Missouri River.

"As far as the east is from the west, so far has He
put our transgressions from us. As a father has

compassion on his children, so the Lord has compassion on those who fear Him, for He knows how we are formed; He remembers that we are dust. Man's days are like those of grass; like a flower of the field he blooms; the wind sweeps over him and he is gone, and his place knows him no more."

Then he read briefly from the 10th chapter of Matthew's gospel.

"Are not two sparrows sold for next to nothing? Yet not a single sparrow falls to the ground without your Father's consent. As for you, every hair of your head has been counted; so do not be afraid of anything. You are worth more than an entire flock of sparrows."

Garriott then briefly recounted what he knew of Hatcher's life.

"He killed a number of children, and this is an end one could expect from that kind of life. I could not change or bless the person in life. He was created in the image of God, and it was a tragedy that any human being would come to such an end. It is a reminder that we all stand before God as a final Judge." The entire ceremony took five minutes.

There is no headstone to show where Charles Hatcher is buried, and there are no physical reminders of his evil life. There was an attempt to include the electrical cord that Hatcher was hanged with and the shoelaces that bound his hands in a display at the Jesse James Museum in St. Joseph. The display was to be called "A Century of Crime in St. Joseph." Citizen protests prevented the exhibition.

All that's left of Charles Hatcher is his epitaph. It is contained in a note that Hatcher sent to St. Joseph Police Chief James Robert Hayes at the time Hayes was insisting that Melvin Reynolds—not Hatcher—had murdered Eric Christgen. Hayes stores the note with the tape recordings of Melvin Reynolds' confessions.

Chief James R. Hayes.

You're right about the Christgen case. I didn't do that one.

Good Luck
Charlie Hatcher.

EPILOGUE—1989

JAMES ROBERT HAYES RESIGNED AS THE POLICE chief of St. Joseph in October, 1989. He will not discuss the Christgen murder case publicly. The chief said that one day he will write a book about the entire incident. Hayes said it would be entitled *You Be the Judge.*

Edwin B. Christgen believes that Melvin Reynolds, not Charles Hatcher, murdered his son. He said that every time he reads about a particularly brutal murder anywhere in the country, he is reminded of the death of his son.

"There is not a morning that Vicki and I don't wake up thinking about Eric," he said. "You can't forget something like that."

But the Christgens have rebuilt their lives around a new son, who Ed Christgen said God had miraculously sent them.

He said, "Vicki thought she could never have another child. But the good Lord sent us a son. He hasn't replaced Eric, but he looks exactly like Eric. He has blue eyes and talks just like Eric. Sometimes I forget and call him Eric.

"It's a miracle," Christgen said. "The Big Boy upstairs took care of us. It's changed my life completely."

Judge Frank Connett Jr., who sentenced both Reynolds and Hatcher to prison for the same crime, has retired. Before the judge left the bench, Melvin Reynolds asked him if he would marry Melvin and his fiance. Connett refused, and another circuit judge performed the ceremony.

Reynolds and his wife have two children, a boy and a girl. They have remained in the St. Joseph area, but Melvin lives at the home of Bill and Wanda O'Meara, his stepfather and mother. Melvin's wife and children live at another residence and he visits them every day. By living apart, his wife and family qualify for $285 per month in Aid to Families with Dependent Children payments.

Melvin Reynolds has not been in trouble with the law since his release from prison, but has not been able to hold a job. He said that employers either refuse to hire him, or end up dismissing him, because of his connection to the Christgen murder case. His last job was delivering pizzas in the summer of 1988.

"I was fired after two weeks," Reynolds said.

"Do you think it was because of the Christgen case?" a reporter asked him.

"I know it is. Chief Hayes still thinks it was me. They fired me when they found out who I was."

Reynolds said he did not have enough money to move out of the area and start a new life.

Michael Insco is still the Buchanan County prosecutor. He ran for a vacancy on the circuit court and lost. He has begun to circulate a newsletter to Democrats in the congressional district. This has led some people to believe he plans to run for the United States House of Representatives.

Patrick Robb, who had been the assistant Buchanan County prosecutor, ran for the judicial vacancy created by Connett's retirement and won. He now presides over the courtroom where Hatcher received his final sentence. Robb was reminded recently of the devastation Hatcher wrought.

He was asked to speak about the legal profession to the senior class at St. Joseph Central High School. During a question-and-answer session, one of the students mentioned the Charles Hatcher case. The student said Michelle Steele had been a classmate—had she not encountered Charles Hatcher, she would have been in that senior class.

"That really hit me," Robb said.

Annette Steele, Michelle's mother, has remarried. After Michelle died, she thought about adopting a little girl, but her friends talked her out of it. She now understands the wisdom of that advice. But she has, through an overseas relief agency, sponsored a nine-year-old Ethiopian girl. She pays $20 a month to help feed, clothe and educate the girl in her home country.

Annette feels the nightmare of her daughter's murder will never really be over.

"Michelle was special and God chose her to stop this man," she said. "That's how I deal with it. If I didn't look at it that way, I couldn't deal with it."

Thousands of miles away, in Antioch, California, Josie Freeman still remembers the day in 1969 when her son William disappeared. She believes his abduction and murder changed some things in Antioch.

"Before it happened, there were no education programs for youngsters," she said. "It made us more aware. Now they have courses to tell children to avoid strangers."

Josie Freeman is a soft spoken woman whose

phrases often seem to echo Scripture passages. She said her grief for her long dead son was like an object on a shelf.

"Sometimes I take it down and look at it occasionally," she said.

Joseph F. Holtslag Jr., the FBI agent whose work finally solved the Eric Christgen murder case, transferred from St. Joseph to the FBI office in Honolulu, Hawaii. Those who know him well say Joe Holtslag is absorbed in his new assignment.

Just before he left St. Joseph, Holtslag said in a newspaper interview that he would always remember the Hatcher case because it helped get an innocent man out of prison. After the story appeared, Melvin Reynolds' wife called Holtslag to say thanks.

Since Charles Hatcher's death, there have been no child murders in St. Joseph.

THE VIOLENT ODYSSEY OF CHARLES HATCHER

July 16, 1929: Charles R. Hatcher born in Mound City, Missouri.

October 9, 1947: Convicted of auto theft in St. Joseph, Missouri, and received a two-year suspended sentence.

February 5, 1948: Convicted of auto theft in St. Joseph and sentenced to two years in the Missouri State Penitentiary.

October 10, 1949: Convicted of forgery in Maryville, Missouri, and sentenced to three years in the penitentiary.

March 18, 1951: Escaped from prison, recaptured and sentenced to an additional two years.

August 25, 1955: Sentenced to four years imprisonment for car theft in Orrick, Missouri, and sentenced to additional two years for attempted escape from the Ray County Jail in Richmond, Missouri.

November 20, 1959: Convicted of attempting to abduct a St. Joseph newsboy using a knife. Sentenced to five years in the Missouri State Penitentiary. Failed in an escape from the Buchanan County Jail in St. Joseph.

July 2, 1961: Jerry Tharrington stabbed to death in the penitentiary. Hatcher, the prime suspect, lived in solitary confinement from August 21, 1961 to October 27, 1962. The crime was never solved.

August 30, 1963: Arrested for burglarizing store in Maitland, Missouri. While free on bond and using the name of Dwayne Wilfong, arrested for burglarizing a business in Iola, Kansas. Escaped from the Allen County Jail in Iola on March 7, 1964.

May 28, 1964: Sentenced to 18 months in the Oklahoma State Penitentiary for car theft in Oklahoma City. Made unsuccessful attempt to escape.

September 20, 1965: Sentenced to five years in the Missouri State Penitentiary for the burglary in Maitland. The burglary and escape charges based on crimes in Iola, Kansas, dropped.

December 7, 1967: Sentenced to the Kansas State Penitentiary for one to five years for car theft in Kansas City, Kansas. Escaped from prison farm August 21, 1969.

August 28, 1969: William Freeman, 12 years old, abducted and murdered in Antioch, California.

August 29, 1969: Arrested under the name of Albert Price for sodomizing a five-year-old boy in San Francisco, California.

September 25, 1969: Sent to the California State Hospital in Atascadero for mental evaluation. Four times Hatcher was found competent, returned for trial and recommitted for more mental tests. Escaped for one week and arrested under the name of Richard Grady on car theft in Sacramento.

December 17, 1972: Convicted under the name of Albert Price for attack on the boy in San Francisco. Sent to California State Hospital for presentence mental examination. Attempted to escape.

April 25, 1973: Sentenced to one year to life imprisonment in the California State Prison. Paroled to halfway house May 20, 1977, and violated parole five days later.

July 27, 1977: Arrested after a 13-year-old boy was abducted from a Minneapolis bus station, molested and strangled. Committed to a mental hospital at St. Paul, Minn. Escaped April 20, 1978.

May 27, 1978: Eric Christgen, four years old, abducted and murdered in St. Joseph, Missouri.

June 5, 1978: Harry A. Fox, 64 years old, died of a heart attack while being questioned by St. Joseph police investigating the Eric Christgen murder.

September 5, 1978: Hatcher arrested under the name of Richard Clark for sodomizing a 16-year-old boy in Omaha, Nebraska. Determined to be mentally ill, taken to Douglas County Hospital and then the Norfolk Regional Center. Released January 31, 1979.

February 14, 1979: Melvin Reynolds confessed to St. Joseph police that he abducted and murdered Eric Christgen. Later convicted and sentenced to life imprisonment in the Missouri State Penitentiary.

May 3, 1979: Hatcher arrested under the name of Ron Springer for assault and attempt to kill seven-year-old Thomas J. Morton in Omaha. Felonious assault charges were dropped and Hatcher was committed to the Regional Mental Health Center in Lincoln, Nebraska. Discharged May 21, 1980, and arrested in Omaha two months later for assault. Judged to be mentally ill on July 21 and returned to Norfolk Regional Center. Escaped September 16, 1980.

October 9, 1980: Arrested under the name of Richard Clark for attempting to assault and sodomize a 17-year-old male in Lincoln. Discharged by Regional Mental Health Center on October 30, 1980.

January 13, 1981: Arrested under the name of Richard Clark in Des Moines, Iowa following a knife fight. Committed to Broadlawns Medical Center, the University of Iowa Medical Center and the Iowa Mental Health Institute at Mount Pleasant. Discharged to Salvation Army shelter in Davenport, Iowa, on April 10, 1981.

June 20, 1981: James L. Churchill, 38 years old, stabbed to death at a remote spot on the banks of the Mississippi River near Rock Island, Illinois.

July 16, 1981: Arrested under the name of Richard Clark for attempting to abduct Todd Peers, 11 years old, from a shopping mall in Bettendorf, Iowa. Criminal charges dropped, and Hatcher committed on March 18, 1982, to the Mental Health Institute in Mount Pleasant, Iowa. Discharged May 7, 1982.

July 27, 1982: Attempted to abduct Stephanie Richie, 19, from the downtown mall in St. Joseph.

July 28, 1982: Attempted to abduct Kerry Heiss, 10, from the East Hills Shopping Center in St. Joseph.

July 29, 1982: Michelle Steele, 11 years old, abducted and murdered in St. Joseph.

July 30, 1982: Checked into the St. Joseph State Hospital using the name Richard Clark. Charged with first degree murder in the death of Michelle Steele on August 3.

April 19, 1983: Ruled competent to stand trial. Met with FBI Agent Joseph Holtslag for the first time on May 3 and gave written confession to Eric Christgen's murder on July 25.

August 3, 1983: Confessed to murdering James Churchill in 1981 and William Freeman in 1969.

October 13, 1983: Judge Frank Connett accepted Hatcher's guilty plea to murder of Eric Christgen and sentenced Hatcher to life imprisonment in the Missouri State Penitentiary. Melvin Reynolds released from prison a day later.

September 22, 1984: Convicted of murdering Michelle Steele and sentenced to life imprisonment without parole for 50 years.

December 7, 1984: Found hanged in his cell in the Missouri State Penitentiary.